LABOUR MARKET
FLEXIBILITY

Mark Beatson

6

The views expressed in the report are the authors' and do not
necessarily reflect those of the Department.

ED Research Series

The Employment Department is committed to promoting a competitive, efficient and flexible labour market so that Britain can compete effectively within the European Community and in wider world markets.

The Department has policies and programmes in place to help to achieve this goal. For example, to ensure that unemployed and other disadvantaged people have the skills and motivation they need to compete actively for jobs; to help improve the skills of the workforce and entrants to it; to maintain a framework which provides a fair balance between the interests of people at work and their employers; to protect people at work from industrial risks; to encourage employment patterns, practices and attitudes which promote individual choice and enterprise; and to promote the interests of women in the workplace and beyond.

To ensure that public money is well spent we must continue to monitor the extent to which the Department is achieving its aim and objectives. To do this we need systematic and impartial information on the operation of the labour market and the Department therefore funds a comprehensive range of research and evaluation work to complement regular labour market statistics.

The Department's Research Series makes the findings of these studies publicly available as a contribution to discussion and debate on improving the workings of the British labour market.

Richard Bartholomew
Chief Research Officer

CONTENTS

LIST OF TABLES

LIST OF FIGURES

Acknowledgements

This paper had its genesis in work undertaken for a Government Economic Service seminar in September 1991. The analysis has been extended considerably since then, principally while I was an Economic Adviser in the Employment Department's Employment Market Research Unit.

I have received much helpful assistance along the way. Shaun Butcher collected much of the data on labour mobility, employment and hours worked, and pay determination; Louise Corcoran and Andrew Wareing provided a number of unpublished WIRS analyses; and Michael Chaplin supplied unpublished data on pay and skills. Useful comments have been received from, among others, Zmira Hornstein, Bill Wells, Duncan Melville, Stephen McClelland, Paul Lanser, Michael Chaplin, Gary Watson, and Frances Sly. Responsibility for any remaining errors is nevertheless mine alone.

It also goes without saying that the views presented in this paper do not necessarily represent those of the Employment Department or of my current employer, HM Treasury.

Executive summary

This study's aim is to assess whether the British labour market has become more flexible. Flexibility is not an easy concept to define and measure. It is, however, concerned with the market's ability to adapt and respond to changing conditions.

The paper considers relevant indicators, and whether trends are consistent with greater flexibility. A particular emphasis is placed on developments since the end of the 1970s. This is for two reasons. First, many indicators vary systematically over the economic cycle, so at least one complete cycle needs to be examined. Second, 1979 saw a change of emphasis in economic policy, with the election of a government committed to strengthening the role of market forces. Indeed, a competitive, efficient and *flexible* labour market is the overarching aim of the government's labour market policies.

Labour markets can adjust to changing conditions through quantities (employment or hours worked) or prices (wages). Relevant indicators of each are covered at both the microeconomic and the macroeconomic level. It is important to note that some types of flexibility may be substitutes rather than complements, and that there is more than one means of achieving a flexible labour market.

Microeconomic indicators: quantity (employment) flexibility

Firms operate in an uncertain and changing environment. They can secure flexibility in two ways. **Flexibility on the extensive margin** is the ability of employers to vary the amount of labour they use by changing the number of people they employ. **Flexibility on the intensive margin** can be achieved through changes in the number of hours worked, or in the range of tasks that employees perform.

Part-time, temporary and self-employment (Chapter 2)

These types of work may enhance flexibility on the extensive margin. Part-time and temporary work may enable an employer to match labour supply and demand more efficiently (e.g. part-time work to cater for extended shop opening hours). There have also been some differences in the regulatory treatment

afforded to these types of work. In the case of self-employment and sub-contracting, the potential for flexibility exists because the firm enters into a contract for services rather than a contract of employment.

Part-time work has grown steadily over (at least) the past twenty years. Self-employment also increased very rapidly between 1979 and 1990 - by 1.2 million - after remaining broadly flat throughout the 1970s. In contrast, the increase in temporary work over the past decade has been relatively modest.

These types of work have increased in significance for a number of reasons. The most important appears to be the better 'fit' between these types of work and specific business needs. Other changes, including pressures from workers themselves, have also been significant.

Engagements and dismissals (Chapter 3)

More generally, costs and other constraints incurred in changing employment levels will add to the (expected) fixed costs of employment. This reduces flexibility on the extensive margin.

The trend in recruitment and training costs is uncertain. However, joint regulation (between management and employees) of recruitment and staffing levels declined considerably between 1980 and 1990.

British employers face relatively few constraints on their ability to make redundancies. The coverage of unfair dismissal legislation was also narrowed during the first half of the 1980s. The (limited) evidence suggests that the impact of this legislation has been relatively small, compared with other factors. The relatively light regulatory burden placed on British employers in this area, however, makes it difficult to assess the effect of changes in the regulatory regime.

The evidence therefore suggests that British employers face relatively few constraints on their ability to exploit external flexibility, and these constraints appear to have eased during the 1980s. However, there are gaps in the data, especially on hiring costs, so conclusions about change over time must remain provisional.

Working time (Chapter 4)

Turning to flexibility on the intensive margin, a distinction can be made between flexibility in the average number of hours worked (achieved through practices such as overtime or short-time working) and flexibility in working patterns given a specific number of hours worked.

Average hours worked were on a downwards trend for most of the post-War period. This trend, however, levelled off in the 1980s. Average hours also fluctuate over the business cycle, mainly due to variations in overtime.

Recent survey evidence suggests there is considerable diversity in working time patterns. Flexibility in working arrangements comes from a number of sources. These range from 'traditional' sources of flexibility, such as part-time work and shiftworking, to more modern arrangements contingent on demand (e.g. annual hours contracts, reservism). Many employers and employees also had less formal means of flexibility available, such as flexitime. The information on trends is limited, although it seems likely that working time arrangements have become more diverse in recent years.

Functional flexibility (Chapter 5)

This is the ability of a firm to deploy labour on a number of tasks within the production process according to demand and supply conditions.

'Full-blown' functional flexibility appears to be something of a rarity in Britain. From the employer's perspective, it can involve costs as well as benefits. There is evidence, however, that manufacturing firms took steps during the 1980s to increase flexibility, principally through the removal of barriers such as job demarcation.

More generally, in 1990, managers in more than two thirds of workplaces felt there were no constraints on their ability to organise work as they saw fit.

Labour mobility (Chapter 6)

Another essential element of flexibility. The information available means less can be said here about developments before the mid 1980s.

Each year, between 12 and 15 per cent of people of working age change their economic status. Among people in work, significant numbers of job moves (changes of employer) take place each year. Nearly half of all job moves involved a change of industry. Many also involved a change of occupation, although occupational mobility can occur without a change of employer.

The proportion of the population moving between regions over a year varies between 1.4 and 1.8 per cent. Migration tends to be higher when the labour market is buoyant.

Net flows (immigrants minus emigrants) tend to be more modest. Certain regions - the South West, East Anglia, and the East Midlands - have tended to be net 'importers' of population. Other regions - the West Midlands, the North West, the North, Yorkshire and Humberside, and Scotland - have tended to be net 'exporters'. These patterns may have changed a little in recent years.

Microeconomic indicators: price (wage) flexibility

Wage determination (Chapter 7)

The institutions of wage determination themselves influence the degree of wage flexibility. Wage determination in Britain has become increasingly decentralised. Indeed, by 1990, it is likely that less than half of employees were covered by collective bargaining arrangements. Where collective bargaining remained, there was substantial decentralisation, most clearly seen in the decline of industry-wide national agreements. While these trends are not new, they received a substantial boost during the 1980s.

The available evidence also suggests that co-ordination between unions and/or employers is very limited. The proportion of larger workplaces affiliated to employers' associations halved between 1980 and 1990.

Performance related pay (PRP) appears to have grown in importance during the 1980s. The evidence suggests that three quarters or more of medium/large organisations use some form of PRP. A third or more of employees may be covered by these arrangements.

Relative wage flexibility (Chapters 8-10)

If relative wages respond to imbalances in demand and supply, this provides incentives for firms and individuals to put capital and labour to their most productive use. Relative wage flexibility is considered along three dimensions: region; industry; and 'human capital'.

Regions (Chapter 8)

Outside the South East, average earnings vary little between regions. Although the trend towards convergence has been halted, the regional earnings distribution has only widened since 1979 because wage growth in the South East has been higher than elsewhere.

Nevertheless, the regional distribution of earnings has changed since 1979. Some regions - the West Midlands and Wales in particular - have seen relative earnings decline. Other regions - such as East Anglia and the South West - have seen their position improve. These changes may have helped narrow regional unemployment disparities.

Even after controlling for other factors, there appear to be significant wage differentials between regions. These may be due to differences in the cost of living and/or other compensating factors. But they could also represent residual barriers to adjustment.

Econometric studies suggest that earnings do respond to supply and demand conditions in regional labour markets. However, it is too soon to say if earnings have become more responsive in recent years.

Industries (Chapter 9)

Inter-industry wage differentials narrowed during the second half of the 1970s. The 1980s and 1990s have seen differentials widen again.

Wage differentials between industries remain after allowances are made for personal characteristics and human capital, although their dispersion is substantially reduced. The evidence suggests that these differentials have also widened during the 1980s.

Industry-specific and aggregate labour market factors have relatively little effect on wage increases at the industry level. There is some evidence that short term wage flexibility has increased since the early 1980s.

Human capital (Chapter 10)

Relative wage flexibility is important if wages are to provide incentives for individuals and firms to invest in human capital (i.e. the skills and experience that people bring to their work). Human capital cannot be observed directly, so indirect measures are used: education; skill levels; and occupations.

The evidence suggests that education differentials (controlling for other factors) narrowed during the second half of the 1970s, before widening again during the 1980s.

The picture is similar for skill differentials. These narrowed between 1973 and 1979, before increasing quite strongly between 1979 and 1990.

And this is also the case for occupations. Both highly aggregated measures (the ratio of non-manual to manual earnings) and more disaggregated measures support this view.

Hence, across all three measures, the evidence consistently points to a reduction in the returns to human capital during the second half of the 1970s. This was (more than) reversed during the 1980s.

The evidence suggests that, throughout this period, there was a shift in labour demand, in favour of better educated and more highly skilled workers. The most convincing explanation of the facts is that the narrowing of wage differentials during the 1970s was a distortion, possibly due to the effects of incomes policies and union bargaining strategies. As these distortions have been removed or eased during the 1980s, differentials have reflected market forces.

Macroeconomic indicators: quantity (employment) flexibility

Aggregate employment and hours worked (Chapter 11)

UK data for the last three cycles suggests there has been a change in the way the labour market has behaved during recessions. During the early 1990s recession, the downturn in productivity was much less pronounced than in previous recessions. One possible explanation is less labour hoarding (i.e. firms keeping on excess labour when demand is weak).

The evidence also suggests, more generally, that the labour market tends to adjust through changes in employment levels, rather than average hours worked. Hence the balance of adjustment is primarily on the extensive rather than intensive margin. The balance may also have changed during the 1980s and 1990s, with employment levels becoming more sensitive to demand conditions.

Macroeconomic indicators: price (wage) flexibility

Aggregate real wage flexibility (Chapter 12)

Nominal earnings growth and inflation have varied considerably over the past 25 years. Real earnings growth, however, has been more stable. Apart from 1976 and 1977, real earnings have increased every year - usually by between 1 and 4 per cent.

Aggregate real earnings growth appears to have been little affected by unemployment. There is some correlation between the growth of real earnings and labour productivity, but the precise linkage is fairly weak.

Nominal earnings growth has declined quite sharply since 1992, reaching a low point of 3 per cent in November 1993. Since then, earnings growth has remained at or below 4 per cent. These are very low figures compared to recent history, and may be encouraging signs of greater flexibility.

Econometric studies tend to agree that real wages in the UK are relatively rigid, ie. not very responsive to unemployment. Some studies find statistical evidence which suggests that wage-setting behaviour has become more flexible post-1979, but others find no such evidence.

Assessment (Chapter 13)

The key question is whether the British labour market has become more flexible since the end of the 1970s. The evidence is summarised in the table below.

It can reasonably be concluded that the British labour market has indeed become more flexible. A number of indicators point quite strongly towards this conclusion - such as measures of wage determination, or relative wage flexibility. Due to gaps in the data, the evidence is less clear on some of the others. None of these indicators suggest the labour market has become less flexible.

In general, the evidence is stronger at the micro level than the macro level. This may be because it takes time for changes at the micro level to become clearly visible at the macro level.

There is a gender dimension to labour market flexibility. Women are more likely to work in part-time or temporary jobs than men (and more often through choice). They also appear more likely to move between jobs.

Has the labour market become more flexible? A summary

Indicator	Evidence of greater flexibility?
Microeconomic indicators: quantity (employment) flexibility	
Part-time, temporary and self-employment	Yes
Engagements and dismissals	*Probably* yes
Working time	*Probably* yes
Functional flexibility	Yes
Labour mobility	*Uncertain*
Microeconomic indicators: price (wage) flexibility	
Wage determination	Yes
Relative wage flexibility: regions	Yes
Relative wage flexibility: industries	Yes
Relative wage flexibility: human capital	Yes
Macroeconomic indicators: quantity (employment) flexibility	
Aggregate employment and hours worked	Yes
Macroeconomic indicators: price (wage) flexibility	
Aggregate real wage flexibility	*Uncertain*

International comparisons (Chapter 13)

Wherever possible, an attempt is made to draw comparisons between the UK and other OECD countries. To a large extent, different means of securing flexibility have evolved in different countries:

- In the USA, the lack of regulation means there is great scope for adjustment on the extensive margin, through varying employment levels. Labour is also highly mobile. This has meant that working time has needed to adjust less than elsewhere. Wages tend to be more flexible than elsewhere at the micro level, although this may not be the case at the macro level.

- Japan and Germany are similar in a number of respects. There is considerable flexibility on the intensive margin (working time, functional flexibility). Together with aggregate wage flexibility, this means that employment tends to be relatively stable over the cycle.

- The Nordic economies (Denmark, Finland, Norway, Sweden) appear to exhibit little relative wage flexibility, but they have traditionally compensated for this by aggregate real wage flexibility and high rates of mobility out of unemployment.

- In a number of EU member states, flexibility tends to be limited at the micro level, possibly because of labour market regulation. The available evidence suggests, however, that this is not compensated for at the macro level.

The UK would appear to be in an intermediate position, with some features of its labour market resembling the USA and some resembling its EU partners. However, the UK has probably moved closer to a US-style labour market since the end of the 1970s.

Causes (Chapter 13)

The evidence available suggests there have been four broad factors behind the move towards greater flexibility:

- **Changes in product markets**
  More competitive product markets have sharpened the incentives for firms to seek greater flexibility.

- **Changes in the production process**
  Changes in technology - defined in its widest sense - have created pressures for new working arrangements.

- **Changes in demand and supply**
  Changes in the structure of labour demand have

emphasised the importance of relative wages and mobility. Similarly, long-term changes in the composition of labour supply, especially increased participation by women, have implications for the range of working patterns offered by employers.

- **Government policies**
  A whole range of policies are likely to have encouraged greater flexibility (see Appendix 5). As well as labour market policies, macroeconomic and other supply-side policies are important.

Consequences (Chapter 13)

The impact of greater flexibility on the overall performance of the labour market is difficult to judge. In general, effects are difficult to detect.

Hence a small number of 'top level' indicators of labour market performance were considered (Appendix 6). For each of these, recent trends were assessed, as well as international comparisons. The flexibility of the labour market will be only one of the factors influencing these indicators, although it is probably one of the most significant.

The overall picture is mixed, but there are some encouraging signs. In terms of participation and employment opportunities, the UK does especially well when compared to most other EU member states, and reasonably well by worldwide standards. Unemployment is still high, but there are signs that the labour market may have become more responsive to economic conditions: unemployment began to fall at a much earlier stage in the current recovery than it did in the early to mid 1980s.

Productivity increased faster in the 1980s than it did in the 1970s. Given the worldwide productivity slowdown, the UK's relative performance has almost certainly improved.

Whether these indications of improved labour efficiency are translated into higher output and employment depends on a number of factors. The growth of aggregate earnings is clearly a key variable. If job opportunities are to be created on a sustainable basis, aggregate real earnings growth needs to remain restrained. The next few years will be a critical test of whether signs of greater flexibility at the micro level feed through into greater real wage flexibility at the macro level.

Chapter 1

Introduction

Labour market flexibility is an issue that has received considerable and growing attention in recent years. Indeed, greater flexibility has increasingly become an objective of economic and labour market policy. This is based on the view that rigidities in the labour market have been one of the main causes of the high unemployment seen in most European Union (EU) countries over the past twenty years.

UK policy objectives reflect this view. Thus the over-arching aim of the Employment Department is 'To support economic growth by promoting a competitive, efficient and *flexible* labour market' (Employment Department (1994)).

At an international level, the Organisation for Economic Co-operation and Development (OECD)'s framework for labour market policies, agreed by its Manpower and Social Affairs Committee, lists 'improving labour market flexibility' as one of its three policy priorities for the labour market (OECD (1990a)). The others are improving the quality of labour supply and facilitating access to jobs and adjustment to structural change.

Focusing on Britain, two propositions appear to underpin much of the analysis and discussion of policy options. One is that the British labour market has become more flexible in recent years (since the end of the 1970s, say). The other is that the labour market *ought* to be more flexible. The aim of this study is to present a thorough analysis of the first proposition, namely whether the British labour market has become more flexible.

The study provides an overview of relevant labour market trends. At times, depth has been sacrificed for breadth. However, a broad view is necessary to place labour market changes in context.

From the existing literature, perhaps the nearest in spirit to this study is Klau and Mittelstädt (1986). They focused on a number of different indicators of flexibility at both micro and macro levels, and assessed trends in a number of OECD countries. This study does not use the same indicators but follows a similar approach, albeit concentrating on just one country.

Defining labour market flexibility

There is a large and expanding literature on labour market flexibility, spanning both labour economics and other social sciences (see Wood (1989) for an overview of the debate). However, labour market flexibility is difficult to define in precise terms.

No attempt is made here to provide an exclusive definition. However, in essence, 'flexibility' would seem to be about the *ability* of markets (and the agents that operate in them) to *respond* to *changing* economic conditions. Ability is highlighted because flexibility is concerned with the potential to respond to market conditions, as well as with cases where an observed response has taken place (see Jones and Ostroy (1984)). Change is highlighted because flexibility is a dynamic concept.

In terms of identifying and measuring flexibility, there would seem to be two broad approaches.

The first is to focus on flexibility at the **microeconomic** level. The emphasis is on the behaviour of economic agents - individuals, firms and institutions.

From the firm's perspective, there would appear to be three principal means of securing flexibility. The first two were suggested by Hart (1987), and refer to the different ways in which firms can alter the way they use labour as economic conditions change:

- **Flexibility on the extensive margin** is the ability of firms to change the number of people they employ. Although the imperative here is normally seen as coming from the firm (the demand-side), this heading can also encompass the ability of individuals to participate in the labour market and undertake various forms of paid work (i.e. a supply-side flexibility). This form of labour market adjustment is often called *numerical flexibility*.

- **Flexibility on the intensive margin** is the ability of firms to vary the amount of labour they use without resorting to the external labour market. One means of achieving this is through variations in working time. This form of flexibility is sometimes referred to as *temporal flexibility* (although some consider it part of numerical flexibility). The other means of optimising the effectiveness with which labour is used is *functional flexibility*, i.e. having a labour force that is able to carry out a wide range of tasks.

In addition, firms can change their pay and reward systems. **Wage or reward flexibility** is the ability of pay and payment systems to respond to labour market conditions and to reward and encourage improved performance.

The degree to which individual firms will use any of these forms of flexibility will vary, depending upon the technological and organisational nature of the production process, the degree of product market competition, and the presence of external constraints (such as government regulation).

At a more aggregated level, **relative wage flexibility** becomes an important mechanism for correcting imbalances between demand and supply conditions in different parts of the labour market (e.g. between regions, industries, occupations).

The overall scale and speed of market adjustment is also influenced in part by the ability and willingness of individuals to change their labour market status. Hence **labour mobility** is also important.

Boyer (1987) notes that some types of flexibility may be substitutes rather than complements. For example, one means of achieving flexibility on the intensive margin is through internal labour markets. These offer a high degree of job security to employees, in return for functional flexibility. This sort of labour market structure, however, is unlikely to be compatible with pay flexibility (in terms of pay being responsive to external labour market conditions) or adjustment on the extensive margin (as turnover is likely to be discouraged, especially

among skilled employees). Hence there is more than one route to a flexible labour market, and more than one destination. It is especially important to remember this when analysing the behaviour and characteristics of labour markets over time and across countries.

The second approach to the identification and measurement of labour market flexibility is through the analysis of **macroeconomic** variables. To illustrate the issues involved, consider the competitive, spot market model of the aggregate labour market set out by Kniesner and Goldsmith (1987), shown in Figure 1.1.

Suppose the labour market is in equilibrium at point E_0 with real wage w_0 and employment n_0. Labour demand then falls (e.g. because relative factor prices change) and the demand curve shifts inwards from D_0 to D_1. In the competitive labour market, prices and quantities are flexible, and the market moves relatively quickly to a new equilibrium at E_1 with a lower real wage, w_1. In such a model, involuntary unemployment would be temporary at worst. If real wages were sufficiently flexible, unemployment need not increase at all.

However, Kniesner and Goldsmith suggest that, for the USA at least, movements in aggregate labour

Figure 1.1   A competitive labour market

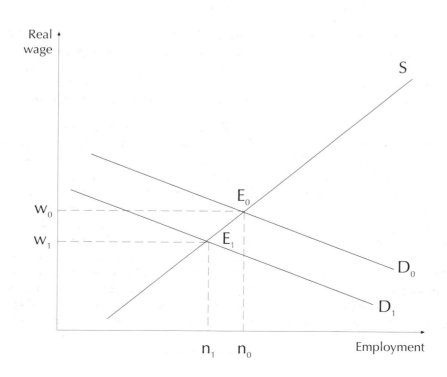

2

Figure 1.2   A labour market with rigidities

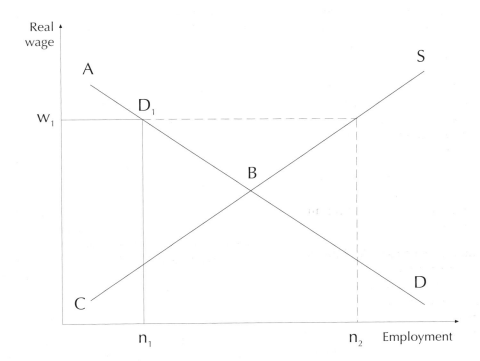

market variables over the post-war period are not consistent with a fully competitive labour market. They suggest a disequilibrium model would be more appropriate; the market often fails to clear and labour market outcomes are determined by the short side of the market[1].

A model along these lines is illustrated in Figure 1.2. Observed wages and employment lie along the segment ABC. For example, suppose there is rationing on the demand side of the market so that effective labour demand (as distinct from notional demand) is fixed in the short term at point D_1. Firms employ n_1 at wage w_1. However, at wage w_1 effective labour supply is n_2, so the result is involuntary unemployment equal to $(n_2 - n_1)$.

In a competitive labour market, this unemployment would exert downward pressure on real wages. The unemployed have an incentive to bid down wages while employers have an incentive to offer them jobs at wage rates below those currently offered. The market would converge towards point B. However, if real wages are rigid for any reason, this process could take time, or even fail to occur at all. The cost of real wage rigidity in this case is involuntary unemployment. Indeed, a commonly used measure of aggregate wage rigidity is the amount of unemployment necessary to produce a given change in real wages.

Policy discussion, as well as theoretical and empirical work, has tended to concentrate on *wage* flexibility. This is entirely consistent with a neoclassical research programme that stresses the role of the price mechanism. In addition, the specific nature of the labour market, where excess supply is involuntary unemployment with its attendant economic and social costs, has helped to focus attention on the behaviour of real wages[2].

Markets, though, can adjust through quantities as well as prices (Marshallian as against Walrasian adjustment). The responsiveness of effective labour demand and supply is also relevant to any discussion of labour market flexibility as a whole.

The discussion above also provides a useful metric. In this framework, a flexible labour market is one that behaves, at the aggregate level, like a competitive labour market. In other words, it behaves more like Figure 1.1 than Figure 1.2. Some important conclusions can be drawn from this observation. One is that a highly competitive labour market *is* a flexible labour market, so policies designed to make the labour market (and other markets) more competitive should secure greater flexibility. However, this does not imply that a flexible labour market has to be highly competitive. Other configurations of market structures and institutions may be capable of delivering the aggregate real wage flexibility illustrated in Figure 1.1.

Structure of the paper

The aim of this study is to assess whether the British labour market has become more flexible. Given this objective, the following points about its parameters need to be made:

- The emphasis is on whether the labour market has become more flexible since the end of the 1970s. This is for two reasons. First, many labour market indicators vary systematically over the economic cycle, so comparisons need to cover at least one full cycle. Second, 1979 saw the election of the present government. Economic policies since then have placed a much greater emphasis on the role of market forces, and hence represent a distinct break with the past. They include policies designed to make the labour market more flexible. Where possible, the paper therefore reviews trends since the beginning of the 1970s or thereabouts. In some areas, though, a lack of reliable data on long-term trends means that a shorter time period has to be considered.

- It is often useful to judge British experience in an international context, so cross-country comparisons are made where possible.

- The emphasis is on whether the labour market has become more flexible. If the answer is yes, two further questions follow. Why has the labour market become more flexible? And what are the consequences for overall economic performance? Some thought is given to each of these questions, especially in the concluding chapter, but they are not given the same degree of attention.

Both the micro and the macro aspects of labour market flexibility are covered. Figure 1.3 illustrates the way in which the material is structured.

The available evidence is presented within a two-dimensional framework. One dimension is the nature of the market adjustment - prices (wages) as against quantities (employment or hours worked). The other is the distinction between microeconomic and macroeconomic indicators.

The remainder of the paper is structured as follows:

- **Chapters 2 to 6** review the microeconomic evidence on quantity adjustment. **Chapters 2 and 3** cover flexibility on the extensive margin, and the ways in which this is achieved. **Chapter 2** reviews trends in the prevalence of part-time,

Figure 1.3   Indicators of labour market flexibility

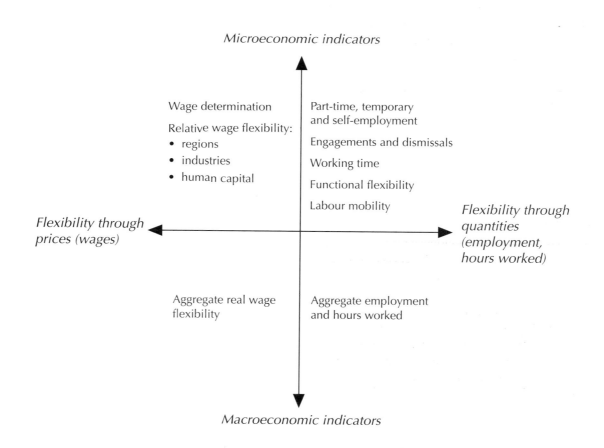

temporary and self-employment, and considers the demand and supply-side pressures behind them. **Chapter 3** treats adjustment on the extensive margin in more general terms, focusing on the ability of firms to vary the size of their workforce. **Chapters 4 and 5** cover flexibility on the intensive margin. **Chapter 4** summarises the evidence on trends in working time, while **Chapter 5** discusses functional flexibility. **Chapter 6** deals with labour mobility.

- **Chapters 7 to 10** review the microeconomic evidence on wage flexibility. **Chapter 7** looks at whether changes in wage determination point to greater flexibility. The next three chapters focus on relative wage flexibility. Trends are reviewed along three dimensions: **Chapter 8** covers regions and **Chapter 9** industries, while human capital (proxied by education level, skill group and occupation) is dealt with in **Chapter 10**.

- **Chapter 11** considers the macroeconomic evidence on quantity adjustment in the labour market, through an analysis of the behaviour of aggregate employment and hours worked.

- **Chapter 12** looks at the macroeconomic evidence on real wage flexibility.

- **Chapter 13** concludes. It summarises the evidence presented in chapters 2 to 12, and compares the UK with other OECD economies. The conclusion is that the British labour market has indeed become more flexible. The Chapter also includes a brief discussion of the factors likely to have generated greater flexibility as well as some of the consequences.

- More detailed information on a number of specific topics is presented in **Appendices**.

Footnotes to Chapter 1

1. There is also empirical evidence for Britain which lends support to this view (Makepeace and Lewis (1982), Hall, Henry, Markandya and Pemberton (1989)).

2. Large changes in wages can also have destabilising effects. Hahn and Solow (1986), while noting the general desirability of real wage flexibility, stress the uncertain and potentially damaging effects of large reductions in *nominal* wages, a central concern of Keynes's *General Theory*.

Chapter 2
Part-time, temporary and self-employment

This chapter begins the summary of evidence on quantity (employment) flexibility at the microeconomic level. It is useful, as an introduction, to set out some of the relevant considerations.

Firms in competitive markets need to minimise costs and maximise the effectiveness of all factors of production. Firms also tend to operate in one or both of two environments:

- product market uncertainty, where future demand conditions cannot be predicted with great accuracy;

- product market variability, where demand varies over time but in a reasonably predictable manner (e.g. where demand for a product is seasonal, or where sales patterns vary over the week).

There may be similar uncertainty and variability in factor prices.

Employers therefore look for some flexibility in the amount of labour they use at any time, i.e. making labour a variable rather than fixed factor of production. The extent to which this happens is likely to vary between firms, depending upon the extent of demand uncertainty, the nature of the production process[1], and the degree of product market competition.

Hart (1987) formalises much of this within a model of a cost-minimising firm. He suggests that employers will seek flexibility through two channels:

- **flexibility on the extensive margin**, by varying the number of people they employ;

- **flexibility on the intensive margin**, by varying the number of hours people work, the times at which those hours are worked, and the range of tasks that employees are able to carry out.

The degree of flexibility achieved in practice, and the balance struck between flexibility on the intensive and extensive margins, is likely to depend upon the relative costs of the various options. A number of factors will lie behind these relative cost calculations:

- the (quasi-fixed) costs of recruiting and training new employees;

- the costs and constraints associated with reducing the workforce (e.g. redundancy payments, employment protection legislation);

- the availability of suitable labour;

- the wage and non-wage costs of changing the hours of existing employees;

- the willingness of current and potential employees to accept any specific working arrangement;

- the nature of the production process and the degree to which different types of labour can substitute for each other.

This suggests that firms' real-life behaviour may be difficult to interpret. Furthermore, it may vary considerably between industries, occupations and individual firms.

The evidence on flexibility on the extensive margin is reviewed in two parts. This chapter charts recent trends in specific working patterns - part-time, temporary and self-employment - which may give employers greater flexibility in setting employment levels. The demand and supply-side factors behind their use are also considered, as these show that flexibility is not just a demand-side or employer-led phenomenon. Chapter 3 considers the extent to which employers adjust the size of their workforce more generally, through engagements and dismissals, and the constraints they face in doing so.

a) Trends in part-time, temporary and self-employment

One commonly cited means of acquiring greater flexibility on the extensive margin is the use of certain, specific forms of employment, namely part-time and temporary employees, and the self-employed. (These are the types of work often referred to as 'atypical' or 'non-standard' work). Sub-contracting is also covered here, as it is closely related.

These types of work are associated with greater flexibility because it is arguably easier, in principle and in practice, for employers to vary their use of these types of worker than it is to vary numbers of full-time, permanent employees. Abraham (1987) suggests that lower quasi-fixed labour costs may be a key reason why firms employ workers on terms that differ from those they would normally offer. If product demand or labour supply are variable enough[2], it can be worthwhile for firms to employ such workers, even if they are not as productive as full-time, permanent employees.

A model embodying many of these considerations is the 'flexible firm' model (see Atkinson (1984)). This model suggests that firms make distinctions between different types of labour, either in reaction to specific circumstances or as part of a conscious strategy. The firm has a 'core' group of full-time, permanent employees performing key tasks, who may be well-paid and enjoy considerable job security in return for functional flexibility on the employees' part. This 'core' is insulated from product market variability and uncertainty by the employment of a 'periphery' of workers brought in and out of the firm as economic conditions change. The 'periphery' is often involved in the provision of 'non-core' business activities. These 'peripheral' workers may well have different working arrangements, such as temporary status. Indeed, the direct employment relationship with the 'periphery' can be broken altogether through the use of sub-contracted labour.

This model has been criticised as an over-simplification and because it appears to have little empirical relevance. Its real value lies in its ability to clarify some of the conceptual issues surrounding the use of different working patterns. It is, however, very much a demand-driven view of the labour market. As a result, it may downplay the role of labour supply and people's preferences.

Part-time employment

The main reason why part-time work offers greater flexibility to employers is likely to be the ability to match part-time hours to specific business requirements, e.g. extended shop opening hours. However, there are also differences in employment legislation. Part-time employees who work for less than 16 hours a week had to have 5 years' continuous service with their employer before they were covered by employment protection legislation or entitled to statutory redundancy payments. In contrast, employees working over 16 hours a week are entitled to these rights after 2 years' service. Those employees who work less than 8 hours each week were not covered at all by employment protection legislation. The government has announced its intention to amend these regulations.

In addition, the system of National Insurance (NI) contributions provides an incentive for employers to use certain forms of part-time work. This is because employers do not have to pay NI contributions for employees with weekly earnings below the lower earnings limit (currently £57 per week).

Hence part-time employment would appear to have offered employers some non-wage cost advantages over full-time employment. In fact, though, only a minority of part-time employees (those working under 16 hours a week and earning less than £57 a week) fell into this category. The majority of part-time employees are, in effect, treated the same as full-time employees.

The arguments above focus on statutory entitlements. A further cost advantage favouring the employment of part-time workers may arise if there is differential access to non-wage benefits such as occupational pensions or sick pay.

Finally, Hakim (1987) argues that part-time work is often *perceived* as having a different status to full-time work, and these perceptions may matter as much as any objective differences between the two forms of work.

For statistical purposes, a part-time job is defined as one involving 30 or less hours work each week. On this definition, the number of part-time jobs[3] has grown strongly over the past twenty years. Figure 2.1 shows that the number of part-time jobs in Britain held by employees increased from 3.3 million in 1971 to 5.9 million by 1994.

Across the workforce in employment as a whole, the proportion of jobs that are part-time increased from 19 per cent in 1978 to 28 per cent by 1994.

Part-time workers are predominantly women. In 1994, 78 per cent of part-time jobs were held by women. However, the corresponding percentage in 1978 was 82 per cent, so male part-time employment has increased faster.

Figure 2.1 suggests that growth in the number of part-time jobs has occurred throughout the last twenty years. Growth was actually higher over the period 1971-1981 (averaging 3 per cent a year) than it was for the period 1981-1994 (2.6 per cent a year). This was mainly due to a rapid increase in part-time work between 1971 and 1974.

Changes in the industrial composition of employment account for a good deal of the growth in part-time work. Shift-share analyses using Census of Employment data showed that less than half (44 per cent) of the growth in part-time employees between 1971 and 1981 was due to changes in industrial composition. Between 1981 and 1991, however, nearly three quarters (72 per cent) of the growth in part-time employment could be accounted for by shifts in industrial structure. Thus, while still significant, the extent of the shift towards part-time work within individual industries may not be as substantial as the overall growth in the number of part-time jobs suggests.

Temporary employment

Temporary employment is a means of adapting to both demand uncertainty (through the use of casual

Figure 2.1   Part-time employment, 1971-1994

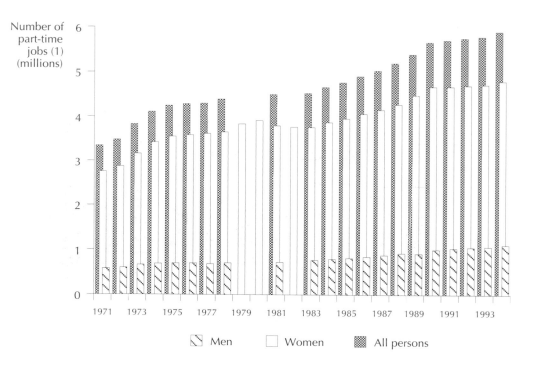

Notes

1   Number of part-time jobs held by employees, Great Britain, June, seasonally adjusted.

Source: Employment Department.

or fixed-term appointments) and demand variability (through the use of seasonal workers).

In terms of regulation, however, there is little difference between a 'temporary' and a 'permanent' employee with less than 2 years' continuous service. A permanent employee does not become entitled to protection from unfair dismissal or to a statutory redundancy payment until the end of this period. Hence there are likely to be other reasons why employers and employees enter into explicitly temporary contracts of employment. These may include differential access to various non-wage benefits, budgetary constraints, or a desire to establish clear expectations on both sides about the time-limited nature of the work.

Data on temporary work is available from the Labour Force Survey (LFS). More information on the design and coverage of the LFS can be found in Appendix 1. This data is based on respondents' own assessment of whether their job was permanent or temporary. There are considerable difficulties involved in measuring temporary work. One particular problem with the LFS definition is that it is impossible to be sure that, when talking about 'permanent' and 'temporary' jobs, respondents are

not referring to their own attachment to the job, rather than the job's innate characteristics (see Casey (1988a) for a more detailed discussion of the issues). Nevertheless, there is no reason to suppose that the LFS is not a good barometer of trends.

A consistent time series is available from 1984 onwards, although the self-employed are only covered for the period 1984-1991. Figure 2.2 shows that the number of temporary workers changed little between 1984 and 1991. Table 2.1 shows that the proportion of employees in temporary work during this period was a little over 5 per cent. From 1992 onwards, the data indicates an increase in the incidence of temporary work.

Women are more likely to hold temporary jobs than men. Table 2.1 also shows that, for the period 1984-1991, people on fixed-term contracts were a minority of temporary workers. There was a marked change after 1991, with a large increase in the number of fixed-contract workers. A change in questionnaire design in 1992 affects comparisons over time, but all the growth in temporary work since 1992 has come from more widespread use of fixed-term contracts.

8

Figure 2.2   Temporary employment, 1984-1994

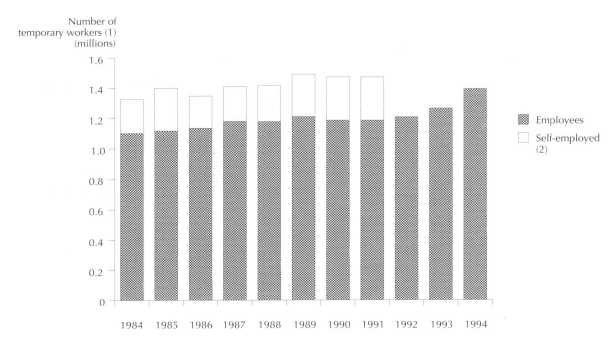

From the employers' perspective, data from the Workplace Industrial Relations Survey (WIRS) series confirms there was little change in the incidence of temporary work during the 1980s. WIRS is a nationally representative sample survey of establishments (workplaces) with 25 or more employees[4], based on interviews with managers (see Appendix 1 for further details). The proportion of establishments that employed people on short, fixed-term contracts increased only marginally between the 1984 and 1990 surveys, from 19 per cent to 22 per cent. Casey (1988b) records an increase of only 1 percentage point during the earlier period, 1980-1984.

Self-employment

Self-employed workers can also enhance flexibility on the extensive margin. In these cases, the firm enters into a contract for services, rather than a contract of employment. The presumption is that this arrangement may be easier to tailor to the needs of the firm than direct employment.

Measuring self-employment is particularly difficult. People's own perceptions of whether or not they are self-employed may not always match their taxation status, or their status in law. The official estimates of self-employment reported below are based on respondents' own view of their status. These do not correspond exactly with data collected from taxation records, but they are probably the best indicator of trends. As Hakim (1988) concludes, 'As a general rule, statistics of self-employment are best used as a rough measure of change at the macro level'.

Figure 2.3 shows that self-employment fell during the 1970s before growing rapidly (by 88 per cent) between 1979 and 1990. As a percentage of the workforce in employment, self-employment increased from 7 per cent to 13 per cent.

Self-employment is more common among men than women. In 1994, 18 per cent of the male workforce in employment was self-employed, the comparable proportion for women being 7 per cent. The proportion of the self-employed who are women had risen, however, from 20 per cent in 1971 to 25 per cent by 1994.

Not all the self-employed are engaged in activities which, from the firm's perspective, involve or represent flexibility on the extensive margin. For example, retail traders working in their own shop are unlikely to form part of any other firm's labour

Table 2.1   Incidence of temporary work in Britain, 1984-1994

Nature of temporary work[1]	Percentages of employees and self-employed, United Kingdom										
	1984	1985	1986	1987	1988	1989	1990	1991	1992	1993	1994
Employees and self-employed											
Men											
Seasonal, temporary and casual jobs	2.4	2.4	2.3	2.5	2.7	2.6	2.6	2.9			
Contract, fixed period	1.8	1.7	1.6	1.7	1.6	1.7	1.7	1.7			
All temporary jobs	4.2	4.1	3.9	4.3	4.3	4.3	4.3	4.5			
Women											
Seasonal, temporary and casual jobs	6.3	6.5	6.4	6.5	6.1	6.1	5.7	5.8			
Contract, fixed period	1.5	1.4	1.6	1.5	1.4	1.5	1.7	1.4			
All temporary jobs	7.8	7.9	8.1	7.9	7.5	7.7	7.3	7.3			
All persons											
Seasonal, temporary and casual jobs	4.0	4.1	4.1	4.2	4.1	4.1	3.9	4.2			
Contract, fixed period	1.7	1.6	1.6	1.6	1.6	1.6	1.7	1.6			
All temporary jobs	5.7	5.7	5.7	5.8	5.7	5.7	5.6	5.7			
Employees only											
Men											
Seasonal, temporary and casual jobs[2]	2.3	2.3	2.3	2.5	2.7	2.6	2.6	2.8	2.2	2.4	2.5
Contract, fixed period[3]	1.5	1.4	1.3	1.4	1.2	1.1	1.1	1.0	2.3	2.5	3.0
All temporary jobs	3.8	3.7	3.6	3.9	3.9	3.7	3.7	3.9	4.5	4.9	5.5
Women											
Seasonal, temporary and casual jobs[2]	5.8	6.0	6.1	6.2	5.8	5.9	5.5	5.6	3.6	3.5	3.6
Contract, fixed period[3]	1.4	1.4	1.5	1.4	1.4	1.4	1.5	1.3	3.1	3.3	3.9
All temporary jobs	7.2	7.4	7.6	7.6	7.2	7.4	7.0	7.0	6.7	6.8	7.5
All persons											
Seasonal, temporary and casual jobs[2]	3.8	3.9	4.0	4.2	4.1	4.1	3.9	4.1	2.9	3.0	3.0
Contract, fixed period[3]	1.5	1.4	1.4	1.4	1.3	1.3	1.3	1.2	2.6	2.9	3.5
All temporary jobs	5.3	5.3	5.4	5.6	5.4	5.4	5.2	5.3	5.5	5.8	6.5

Notes

1   *Permanent/temporary status is self-defined.*

2   *For the 1992 survey onwards, includes all seasonal work, casual work, agency temping and work that is 'not permanent in some other way'.*

3   *For the 1992 survey onwards, 'contract for a fixed period, fixed task'.*

Source: Labour Force Surveys, Spring.

Figure 2.3   Self-employment, 1971-1994

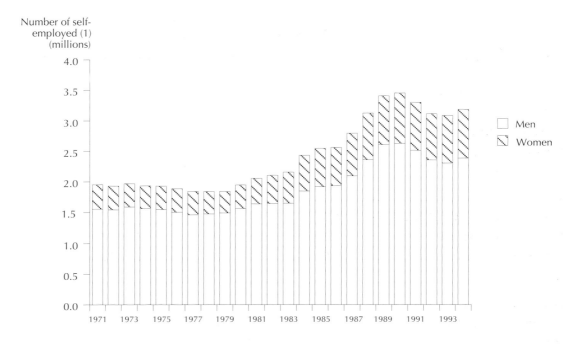

Notes

1   Great Britain, June, seasonally adjusted.

Source: Employment Department.

adjustment strategy unless they are part of a franchising operation. In contrast, self-employed caterers used by companies on a contract basis would presumably be a source of labour flexibility to the firms using their services.

It is extremely difficult to assess the quantitative significance of these arguments. One proxy measure may be the proportion of the self-employed who have no employees: these appear more likely to be freelance workers. Campbell and Daley (1992) found that the proportion of the self-employed with employees fell from 39 per cent in 1981 to 31 per cent by 1991. In addition, WIRS data shows that the proportion of workplaces employing people on a freelance basis increased from 14 per cent in 1984 to 16 per cent by 1990.

While this evidence suggests that the rapid growth of self-employment during the 1980s increased flexibility on the extensive margin, it cannot be regarded as conclusive. All that can be said is that, compared with employee status, self-employment offers some important flexibilities to the self-employed and their customers. To that extent, the growth in self-employment during the 1980s may have been conducive to greater labour market flexibility.

Sub-contracting

The arguments above hold for sub-contracting more generally. From the firm's perspective, contracting offers one possible route to greater flexibility. Sub-contracting certainly forms part of the 'flexible firm' paradigm.

Abraham and Taylor (1993) discuss reasons why firms may choose to sub-contract certain activities. One reason may be to realise wage and/or fringe benefit savings. Another is that, especially in specialised areas of work, sub-contractors may be able to reap economies of scale and perform the task more cheaply. Sub-contracting may also enable the firm to manage variations in its work load more efficiently.

However, there are also costs involved in monitoring sub-contractors' performance and ensuring that agreed standards are met, and these can exceed the costs of direct employment. Furthermore, once a contract is entered into, it may be difficult to change (and hence be inflexible).

Whether an extension of sub-contracting represents greater flexibility across the labour market as a whole depends upon whether sub-contractors are able to adopt more flexible and efficient labour practices than the directly-managed alternative. Where work is sub-contracted to self-employed individuals, this seems quite feasible. Where work is sub-contracted to other firms, this is not so obvious - firms may be transferring the 'problem' of flexibility onto other employers.

Evidence on the extent of sub-contracting in Britain is limited. One reason is measurement difficulties: it may be hard to identify the dividing line between sub-contracting of 'non-core' activities and 'normal' vertical disintegration.

There are two sources of information on sub-contracting. The first is the 1987 Employers' Labour Use Strategies (ELUS) survey. ELUS was an establishment-based survey, drawing its sample from those interviewed in the (nationally representative) 1984 WIRS. However, the results are unlikely to be representative of workplaces as a whole (see Appendix 1).

ELUS asked respondents if they used sub-contractors (defined as firms or self-employed individuals with two or more employees) for any of a number of specified activities. They were asked about their use of sub-contractors in 1983 and 1987, and whether this had increased.

Table 2.2 reveals that a quarter of establishments surveyed did not use any sub-contractors. Of the remainder, the services most frequently contracted out were maintenance, cleaning and transportation. Comparing 1983 with 1987, there was an increase in the percentage of employers using sub-contractors

for each of the types of work specified. With the exception of cleaning and security services, the increase was relatively modest. However, where work was sub-contracted, employers were often making greater use of sub-contracted labour, especially for transportation, manufacturing and 'other' types of work.

The 1990 WIRS also collected some information on sub-contracting. Unlike ELUS, its findings can be taken as generally representative of larger workplaces.

Figure 2.4 shows that 72 per cent of establishments reported sub-contracting at least one of the specified list of services, a similar proportion to the ELUS survey. The three services most likely to be sub-contracted were the same in both surveys: maintenance, cleaning, and transportation.

In addition, financial managers interviewed as part of the survey were asked if the *value* of sub-contracted work had changed in the three years preceding the survey (i.e. 1987-1990). Nearly two fifths (38 per cent) of respondents said the value of sub-contracted services had increased, while only 8 per cent reported a decrease.

On the basis of the ELUS and WIRS results, sub-contracting seems to have increased during the 1980s. Indeed, the widespread adoption of competitive tendering in the public sector makes any other conclusion difficult to support. However, the precise scale of change is more difficult to estimate.

Table 2.2   Estimates of employers' use of sub-contractors, 1987

Percentages of establishments with 25 or more employees using sub-contractors, Great Britain

Type of work sub-contracted	Establishment used sub-contractors		Change in use of sub-contractors between 1983 and 1987		
	1983	1987	More	Same	Less
None		26			
Cleaning	32	42	12	82	5
Maintenance	49	52	22	72	6
Catering	9	12	24	66	11
Security	12	21	16	75	9
Transportation	32	34	36	53	11
Manufacturing	14	15	36	45	19
Other	11	14	50	45	5

Source: ELUS survey, McGregor and Sproull (1991), Table 2.19.

Figure 2.4   Estimates of employers' use of subcontracting, 1990

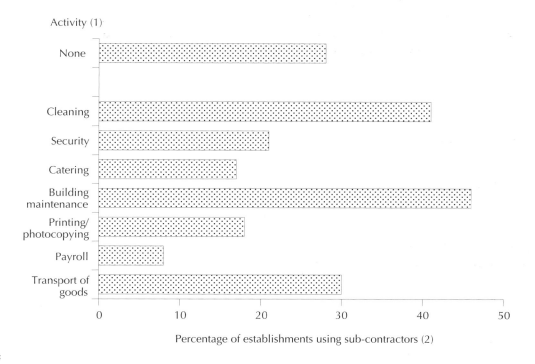

Percentage of establishments using sub-contractors (2)

Notes

1   *The definition adopted here is 'complete sub-contracting', where the activity in question is undertaken by a different firm.*

2   *Establishments with 25 or more employees, Great Britain.*

Source: Millward, Stevens, Smart and Hawes (1992), Table 9.5.

b)   The demand-side explanation

This section examines the extent to which the observed increase in part-time, temporary, and self-employment reflects a desire by employers for greater flexibility on the extensive margin.

ELUS asked employers why they employed part-time workers, temporary workers, agency temporary workers, and the self-employed. These are set out in Table 2.3. Employers were asked to state their reasons for using particular forms of labour as well as identifying which of these reasons they regarded as most important.

McGregor and Sproull (1991) divided employers' motives into three categories: 'traditional' reasons arising from the nature of the production process, demand conditions and the firm's organisation; 'new' rationales which did reflect cost and flexibility concerns; and 'supply-side' reasons which, essentially, were reactions to external labour market conditions.

The data suggest that 'traditional' reasons predominated. Even so, there were some differences across the various forms of work. 'New' rationales had more of a part to play in explaining employers'

use of the self-employed and temporary employees. 'Supply-side' reasons also had some influence in explaining employers' use of part-time employees and the self-employed. 'New' rationales were also mentioned more often by employers who had increased their use of these forms of work in the years preceding the survey[5].

The relative insignificance of the 'new' cost-centred rationales may be because few employers had a clear, strategic approach to the use of different types of worker. Hakim (1990) found that 35 per cent of the establishments surveyed in ELUS said that decisions about the types of worker they used were guided by some form of strategy or plan. Of these, less than a third (11 per cent of the entire sample) said this strategy included the division of the workforce into a 'core' and a 'periphery'. Hakim concluded that 'strategists' may have accounted for between 5 and 15 per cent of the establishments surveyed.

However, even this estimate probably over-states the position. Hunter and McInnes (1991) undertook case studies following up the main ELUS survey, and found that notions of what constituted a 'strategy' and what employers meant by a 'core-periphery'

Table 2.3   Employers' reasons for using part-time, temporary and self-employed workers

Percentages of establishments with 25 or more employees citing specific reasons for their
use of various types of work, Great Britain, 1987

Reported reason	Category of worker							
	Cited as most important reason for using them				Cited as one reason for using them			
	PT	T	AT	SE	PT	T	AT	SE
'Traditional' reasons								
Task requiring a limited time	59				76			
Match manning levels to demand patterns/ peaks in demand	17	19	16	17	30	35	35	29
Extend opening/production hours	3				10			
To give short-term cover for absent staff		40	62			55	71	
To deal with one-off tasks		7	5			29	35	
To provide specialist skills		11	6	51		22	16	60
'New' rationales								
To reduce wage costs	2	-	-	7	9	1	1	9
To reduce non-wage costs/avoid administering PAYE and NICs	1	-	-	-	4	1	1	6
Less likely to be in unions	-	-	-	-	1	-	-	1
Fewer rights under employment protection legislation	-	-	-	-	1	-	-	2
Reduce overheads				1				4
Reduce training costs				-				-
Gives greater flexibility in manning levels	1	12	2		4	26	18	
To provide cover while manning levels are changed		7				19		
To screen for permanent jobs		-	-			4	11	
More productive	-			6	3			8
More committed				-				1
'Supply-side' reasons								
Easier to recruit	1	1	6		9	4	15	
Applicants want part-time/ temporary/ self-employment	7	-		14	33	8		28
Retain valued staff	7				21			
Other reasons	2	3	3	4	3	6	3	4
All 'traditional' reasons	**81**	**78**	**89**	**73**				
All 'new' rationales	**3**	**21**	**5**	**13**				
All 'supply-side' reasons	**16**	**1**	**6**	**14**				

Key PT = permanent part-time employees; T = temporary employees; AT = agency temps; SE = self-employed.
  - indicates zero.

Source: ELUS survey, McGregor and Sproull (1991), Tables 3.1 to 3.8.

distinction varied widely. They found that very few of the employers in their case studies - selected because they were 'heavy users' of part-time, temporary or freelance workers - thought about their labour force in the terms demanded by the 'flexible firm' model. Hence the 'flexible firm' model does not appear to be an empirically valid description of how employers in Britain make decisions about the structure of their workforce.

Findings from the 1985 Company Level Industrial Relations Survey tend to support this conclusion. Marginson (1989) suggests that, although employers' use of different working patterns increased during the first half of the 1980s, this was very much a localised and piecemeal response to events. Practice at the workplace often did not match stated company policy.

These findings suggest that employers' decisions about the type of employment to offer tend to be made in an *ad hoc* manner, driven by product market conditions, technology and labour supply pressures. This is not too surprising. A truly flexible approach implies a degree of pragmatism, and may *appear ad hoc* even if grounded in an overall strategic principle, such as the need to minimise costs and stay competitive.

c)   The supply-side perspective

To explain adequately the increase in part-time and self-employment, it is necessary to look beyond employers' demand for these forms of work, and consider how they meet individuals' needs. These types of work may also contribute to labour market flexibility by increasing the responsiveness of labour supply, drawing people into the labour force who are unable or unwilling to consider full-time, permanent work.

In general, the evidence supports the view that at least some of these types of work meet the needs of employees as well as employers.

Table 2.4 presents LFS data on reasons given for working part-time. The data in the table is based on a broad-brush question, asking part-time employees to summarise all their reasons for working part-time in one of a fixed set of responses. It nevertheless points to some of the key factors explaining why people work part-time.

Most people who work part-time do not do so simply because they could not find a full-time job. The percentage of all part-time workers giving this reason is never more than 20 per cent: the figure may

vary over the cycle, although changes in questionnaire design in 1992 mean that results may not be precisely comparable over time. The remainder can be said to be working part-time through choice - even if, for some people, that choice may be constrained by factors such as domestic commitments.

There are clear differences between men and women. Men form a small and growing minority of part-time workers, but they are more likely to say they could not find a full-time job. However, even for male part-timers, the proportion who say they could not find a full-time job is less than the proportion who do not want a full-time job. Women are more likely to say they do not want a full-time job. The particularly high proportion of married women in this group points to domestic commitments as a key influence on the choice of whether to work full or part-time.

Watson and Fothergill (1993) examined these issues in greater depth using both quantitative and qualitative data. They found that peoples' reasons for working part-time were numerous. They also varied across the labour force. However, it was the ability to combine paid work with other activities that led to part-time work being valued highly. The authors suggest that part-time workers tended to fall into one of three groups: 'voluntary' part-timers; 'involuntary' part-timers who wanted to work full-time but could not do so because of domestic responsibilities or because of a perceived lack of full-time job opportunities; and 'involuntary' part-timers who did not want to work at all, but needed the income. Watson and Fothergill concluded that the first of these groups - the 'voluntary' part-timers - was very much the largest.

The LFS also collects data on the reasons why people take temporary jobs. This is reported in Table 2.5.

The data suggest a greater degree of dissatisfaction with temporary work. A larger proportion of temporary workers say they are in a temporary job because they could not find a permanent one. The proportion of temporary workers who could not find a permanent job varies substantially across the workforce (Casey (1988a), King (1988)). Older people and students are much more likely to say they do not want a permanent job than full-time, prime age workers. Compared to part-time work, temporary work may be a 'preferred' form of employment for a smaller proportion of the workforce.

There is less systematic evidence on peoples' motives for becoming self-employed. Smeaton (1992) presents results from the 1986 Social Change and

Table 2.4   Reasons why people work part-time, 1984-1994

Reason for taking part-time work	Percentages of employees and self-employed working part-time[1], United Kingdom						
	1984	1987	1990	1991	1992	1993	1994
All persons (thousands)	4,913	5,316	5,716	5,730	5,811	5,931	6,121
Student	7	8	10	10	11	10	11
Ill/disabled	1	1	2	2	2	1	1
Could not find a full-time job	10	9	6	8	11	17	13
Did not want a full-time job	68	65	66	63	77	73	74
Other reasons[2]	14	17	16	18	*	2	1
Married[3] men (thousands)	290	313	399	392	419	437	449
Student	1	1	2	2	3	3	3
Ill/disabled	5	4	6	5	5	4	4
Could not find a full-time job	19	23	17	19	27	33	33
Did not want a full-time job	52	45	53	48	64	57	59
Other reasons[2]	23	28	23	26	1	2	*
Non-married[3] men (thousands)	280	346	389	406	425	449	547
Student	53	53	63	61	63	55	57
Ill/disabled	3	3	2	2	1	2	2
Could not find a full-time job	18	20	12	13	17	25	25
Did not want a full-time job	17	14	14	14	18	16	16
Other reasons[2]	10	11	9	10	*	2	*
Married[3] women (thousands)	3,591	3,850	3,976	3,965	4,016	4,078	4,144
Student	*	*	*	*	1	1	1
Ill/disabled	1	1	1	1	1	1	1
Could not find a full-time job	6	6	4	5	7	8	9
Did not want a full-time job	79	77	79	75	91	88	89
Other reasons[2]	13	16	18	18	*	2	1
Non-married[3] women (thousands)	752	807	951	966	951	967	1,179
Student	26	30	32	32	35	33	30
Ill/disabled	2	2	2	2	2	1	2
Could not find a full-time job	17	14	11	12	17	18	20
Did not want a full-time job	42	37	41	37	47	45	48
Other reasons[2]	14	18	15	16	*	2	*

Notes

1   Part-time status is self-defined.

2   'Other reasons' includes cases where no reasons for working part-time were given. For 1984-1991, 'other reasons' was one of the valid responses to the question. From 1992 onwards, this category was dropped. Responses in those years only include people who did not give a reason for working part-time. Hence direct comparisons before and after 1992 cannot be made.

3   From 1989 onwards, 'married' includes people living as married.

*   indicates cases where the absolute numbers involved are less than 10,000, and are therefore unreliable.

Source: Labour Force Surveys, Spring.

Economic Life Initiative (SCELI) dataset showing that the most popular reasons for becoming self-employed were 'independence' (mentioned by 33 per cent of self-employed respondents), 'to make money' (23 per cent), and 'always wanted to' (22 per cent). In contrast, only 13 per cent mentioned unemployment as a motive for starting their own business, while 'employers request' and 'goes with the job' were even less common (6 per cent and 9 per cent respectively).

Similarly, Hakim (1989), reporting the results of interviews with a sample of people who had recently become self-employed, found that what she termed 'pull' factors - independence and the possibility of financial rewards - were more important than 'push' factors such as unemployment or family circumstances.

Involuntary push factors appear insufficient on their own to explain the rapid growth in self-employment during the 1980s. A growing readiness on the part of individuals to become self-employed also appears to have been a contributory factor.

The employer-based ELUS data in Table 2.3 provides some corroboration for these findings. Supply-side factors were influential in a majority of cases, especially for part-time employees and the self-employed. Hunter and McInnes (1991) found that, in some cases (e.g. draughtsmen), the use of highly skilled self-employed workers was actually thought to be undesirable by the firm. However, these professionals' market power was sufficient for them to effectively impose these conditions, and the freedom of contract they implied, on the firm.

This perhaps helps to illustrate the combinations of supply and demand factors that explain why particular forms of employment relationship occur, and why certain types of work have grown in importance. It is significant that those types of work that have grown most rapidly - part-time and self-employment - are those where there appears to be considerable demand from employees. In contrast, the growth of temporary employment has been more muted. The evidence does not suggest that these changes have arisen purely because employers want greater flexibility

Table 2.5   Reasons for taking temporary work, 1984-1994

Reason for taking temporary work	Percentages[1] of temporary employees[2], United Kingdom						
	1984	1987	1990	1991	1992	1993	1994
All persons (thousands)	**1,236**	**1,181**	**1,188**	**1,188**	**1,210**	**1,266**	**1,396**
Job included contract of training	6	4	4	3	5	6	7
Could not find a permanent job	35	30	24	28	37	43	43
Did not want a permanent job	32	31	38	38	28	26	27
Other reasons	28	34	35	31	31	25	24
Men (thousands)	**517**	**453**	**450**	**460**	**513**	**558**	**616**
Job included contract of training	8	7	5	4	6	7	7
Could not find a permanent job	44	43	30	35	44	50	50
Did not want a permanent job	19	17	30	27	18	17	19
Other reasons	29	33	36	34	32	26	25
Women (thousands)	**719**	**728**	**739**	**728**	**696**	**708**	**780**
Job included contract of training	4	3	3	3	5	5	6
Could not find a permanent job	28	23	21	24	31	37	37
Did not want a permanent job	41	40	43	45	35	34	33
Other reasons	27	35	34	29	29	24	23

Notes

1   People giving no answer are excluded from the percentage calculations. There was a surprisingly high proportion of temporary employees in this group in 1984 (about 15 per cent of the total).

2   Temporary status is self-defined.

Source: Labour Force Surveys, Spring.

on the extensive margin. Changes in the business environment, production methods and the composition of the workforce may have been equally, if not more, important.

d)   International comparisons

Figure 2.5 charts estimates of the share of part-time work for most OECD countries. While data for EU member states in later years will have been collected on a consistent basis, other data is based on national sources. This means the data is only a broad indicator of trends.

The UK's part-time share is relatively high: only the Netherlands, Denmark, Norway and Sweden have higher shares. The UK ratio also increased significantly between 1983 and 1992, with only the Netherlands, New Zealand, Australia and Belgium experiencing faster growth.

Data on the incidence of temporary work is available for a smaller number of countries. In part, this reflects differences in contractual regulation across the OECD area. In the USA, for example, temporary workers do not exist as a distinct statistical entity (Hakim (1987)). Figure 2.6 presents data for the EU member states (minus Italy) plus Japan.

The incidence of temporary work in the UK is relatively low[6]. Furthermore, it remained fairly constant over the period 1983-1991. In contrast, temporary work increased very substantially in some European countries, especially France and Spain.

Data on self-employment is set out in Figure 2.7. Since self-employment is much more common in the agricultural sector, the graph plots non-agricultural self-employment.

The UK's relative position changed considerably between 1979 and 1990, due to the substantial growth of self-employment. This increase was exceptional among the countries covered by the OECD (1992) study. Indeed, the report concluded that '... the rapid growth of self-employment in the UK in the 1980s is somewhat puzzling'.

Proportions of part-time, temporary and self-employed workers vary considerably between

Figure 2.5   International comparisons of part-time employment, 1983-1992

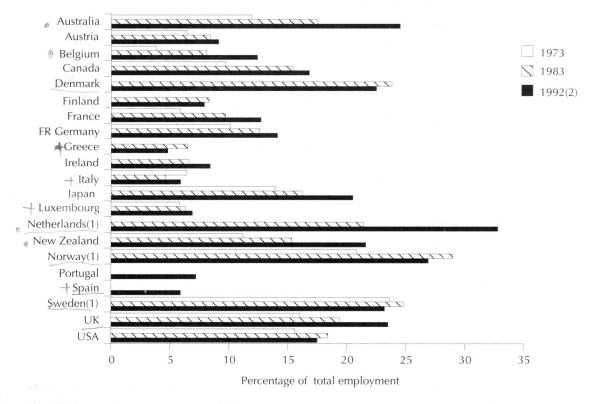

Notes

1   Discontinuity in the series between 1983 and 1992.

2   Except for Ireland (1991).

Source: OECD (1994c), Table D.

18

Figure 2.6   International comparisons of temporary employment, 1983-1991

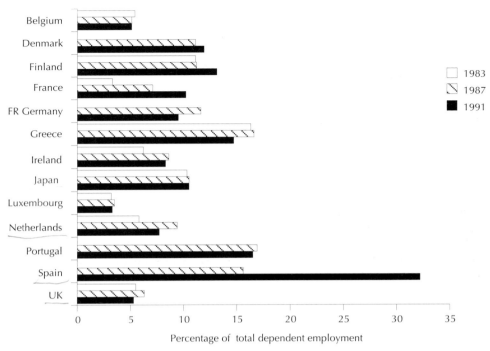

Percentage of total dependent employment

Source: OECD (1993).

Figure 2.7   International comparisons of non-agricultural self-employment, 1979-1990

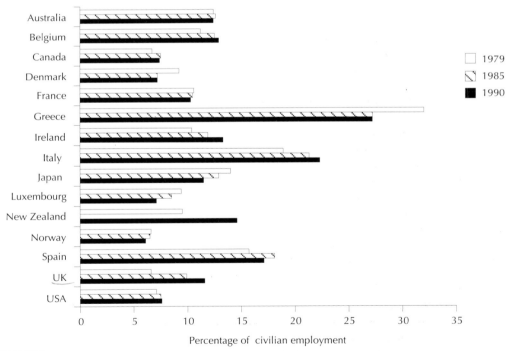

Percentage of civilian employment

Source: OECD (1992).

countries. Table 2.6 provides a summary of trends for a number of EU member states, plus Canada and Japan.

Many of the countries included in Table 2.6 have relatively high concentrations of some of these types of work and relatively low concentrations of others. Trends can also diverge, especially self-employment, which rose (as a share of employment) in some countries and fell in others.

Table 2.6   Summary comparisons of part-time, temporary and self-employment for selected OECD countries

Form of work	Belgium	Canada	Denmark	France	Greece	Ireland	Japan	Luxembourg	Spain	UK
Assessment of level (late 1980s/early 1990s)										
Part-time	*	**	***	**	*	*	**	*	*	***
Temporary	**	**	**	**	***	*	**	*	***	*
Self-employment	**	*	*	**	***	**	**	*	***	**
Assessment of change (early 1980s-early 1990s)										
Part-time	+	+	0	+	0	+	+	+	?	++
Temporary	0	?	++	+	0	0	0	0	++	0
Self-employment	+	+	-	0	-	+	-	-	+	++

Key

*In the top panel of the table, *** denotes a relatively high level; ** a medium level; * a relatively low level.*

In the bottom panel, ++ indicates a strong increase; + a noticeable increase; 0 no evidence of substantive change; and - indicates a noticeable decrease.

Table 2.7   Reasons for working part-time across EU member states, 1983-1990

Percentages of men and women in part-time[1] employment

Reason for working part-time	Belgium	Denmark	France	FR Germany	Greece	Ireland	Italy	Luxembourg	Netherlands	Portugal	Spain	UK
Student												
1983	4	16	..	..	4	9	4	8	3	..	..	6
1987	3	26	..	6	1	9	4	19	12	4	4	8
1990	2	31	..	7	5	9	6	18	14	6	4	10
Ill/disabled												
1983	2	3	..	..	8	3	*	2	2	..	..	1
1987	2	2	..	2	4	2	6	2	3	16	4	1
1990	2	2	..	2	7	2	6	2	3	21	4	1
Could not find a full-time job												
1983	22	11	..	..	25	27	30	4	3	..	..	9
1987	32	9	..	7	25	32	38	9	20	30	32	10
1990	29	12	..	5	29	29	37	8	19	23	26	6
Did not want a full-time job												
1983	37	59	..	..	35	59	32	27	25	..	..	71
1987	15	63	..	63	36	51	32	53	23	26	7	60
1990	12	55	..	64	36	53	35	56	27	29	9	65
Other reasons[2]												
1983	35	11	..	..	29	3	35	59	67	..	..	13
1987	49	*	..	23	33	6	20	18	42	24	54	21
1990	55	*	..	23	23	7	16	16	38	21	57	18

Notes

1   *Part-time status was self-defined.*
2   *Includes cases where no response was given.*
*   *indicates less than 0.5 per cent.*
.. *indicates that data was not available.*

Source: EU Spring Labour Force Surveys, reported in Wells (1992).

Table 2.8   Reasons for taking temporary work across EU member states, 1983-1990

Percentages of men and women in temporary[1] employment

Reason for taking temporary employment	Belgium	Denmark[2]	France[2]	FR Germany[2]	Greece	Ireland	Italy	Luxembourg	Netherlands	Portugal	Spain	UK
Period of training[3]												
1983	38	..	31	..	5	25	16	65	12	..	..	7
1987	41	45	32	51	4	20	14	66	10	10	5	4
1990	26	39	30	44	5	20	23	69	6	16	2	4
Could not find permanent job												
1983	32	..	-	..	78	54	65	19	64	..	..	36
1987	36	29	-	-	85	61	61	19	55	70	83	37
1990	63	36	-	-	85	61	55	15	68	69	88	24
Did not want permanent job												
1983	5	..	-	..	6	21	19	17	18	..	..	33
1987	29	27	-	-	5	16	11	15	12	2	1	27
1990	4	25	-	-	4	18	11	16	13	2	*	37
Other reasons[4]												
1983	26	..	69	..	11	-	-	-	7	..	..	24
1987	2	-	69	49	6	3	14	-	23	17	11	32
1990	7	-	71	56	7	2	11	-	13	13	10	36

Notes

1   *Temporary status is self-defined.*

2   *In these countries, respondents were presented with a more limited set of options.*

3   *Includes category of 'probationary period' in Belgium (1987), Luxembourg (all years), and Portugal (1987, 1990).*

4   *Includes cases where no reason given.*

-   *indicates zero.;   *   indicates less than 0.5 per cent;   ...   indicates no data available.*

Source: EU Spring Labour Force Surveys, reported in Wells (1992).

These differences suggest there is no simple explanation for the patterns observed. One relevant factor, however, may be the structure of labour market regulation (both legislation and generally applicable collective agreements). Of particular significance may be the regulations governing the 'standard' employment contract and the *differential* between part-time, temporary and self-employed work and the 'standard' employment contract.

Take Spain as an example. Regulation of employment is generally considered to be particularly stringent. There are very substantial constraints on employers' ability to reduce their workforce for economic or other reasons. Dismissals have to be sanctioned by the national labour authority (INEM). However, as unemployment rose during the 1980s, the government allowed the creation of new temporary employment contracts that were not subject to the same constraints. The result was a rapid growth in temporary work, with the vast majority of new contracts registered on this basis[7]. Contrast this with Britain, where the regulations covering all forms of employment are less onerous, and where the number of temporary workers has increased by much less.

Grubb and Wells (1993) examined the link between regulation and employment outcomes systematically for the EU member states (minus Luxembourg). They found statistically significant correlations between the *overall* stringency of employment regulation and the structure of employment. Countries with the most stringent employment regulation tended to have a relatively low incidence of part-time work, whereas they had relatively high proportions of employees on fixed-term contracts (although, in the latter case, this relationship was mediated in countries where there were also tight restrictions on the use of fixed-term contracts).

Grubb and Wells also found that countries with strict employment regulation tended to have high proportions of self-employed, possibly because the self-employed fall outside the scope of the regulation. However, wider institutional factors such as the tax system and the ways in which business is regulated may also affect the possibilities and incentives for self-employment. Government programmes designed to encourage self-employment may also be a factor in the UK and other countries (Staber and Bögenhold (1993)).

Supply-side factors are also important. Data is available from the European LFS on the reasons why people take part-time and temporary work. Table 2.7 presents data for part-time workers.

The UK is unusual in having a relatively low proportion of part-time workers who said they worked part-time because they could not find a full-time job. Only Denmark, Germany and Luxembourg reported similar levels. In fact, although the correlation is far from perfect, there tends to be a negative relationship between the proportion of employment that is part-time and the proportion of part-time workers who said they would rather have a full-time job. In other words, part-time workers tend to be most dissatisfied with their status in countries where part-time work is the exception.

Similar data for temporary workers is presented in Table 2.8. Temporary work in the UK appears to be more closely aligned with employee preferences than in most other EU member states. Temporary workers in those members states where this kind of work is most common - Greece, Portugal and Spain - registered high levels of dissatisfaction.

Grubb and Wells (1993) found that the degree of dissatisfaction with part-time and temporary work may be related to the stringency of employment regulation. Where the standards set by regulation are highest, the 'loss' from taking a part-time or temporary job may be greatest.

e)   Summary and conclusions

- Flexibility on the extensive margin is the ability of employers to vary the amount of labour they use by changing the number of people they employ.

- Certain types of work - part-time work, temporary work, self-employment and sub-contracting - may enhance flexibility on the extensive margin. It may be easier to 'fit' these types of work to specific business needs. In the case of part-time and temporary work, there are some differences in employment protection and statutory redundancy provision. In the case of self-employment and sub-contracting, the potential for flexibility exists because the firm enters into a contract for services rather than a contract of employment.

- Part-time work has grown steadily over (at least) the past twenty years. The majority of part-time workers are women, although the percentage who are men is increasing.

- In contrast, temporary work did not increase greatly in significance between 1984 and 1991, forming about 5 per cent of employment. Since 1992, there has been some growth in the incidence of temporary work.

- Self-employment grew very rapidly between 1979 and 1990, after remaining broadly stable throughout the 1970s.

- There is evidence to suggest that employers contracted out more of their activities during the mid to late 1980s than previously.

- The nature of the production process, demand conditions, and the environment in which employers operate seem to be the main reasons why part-time and self-employment were increasingly used by employers.

- There also appears to have been some supply-side pressure, with an increased demand from workers for part-time and self-employment.

- Like the Nordic countries and the Netherlands, the UK has a high proportion of part-time workers. In contrast, the incidence of temporary work in the UK is among the lowest in the EU, and the self-employment rate is higher in a number of other EU countries. The growth of self-employment in the UK during the 1980s was, however, exceptional.

- The UK is unusual in having a relatively low proportion of 'involuntary' part-time and temporary workers i.e. they would have preferred a full-time/permanent job, but could not find one.

- Labour market regulation appears to be an important factor in explaining differences between countries.

Footnotes to Chapter 2

1. The need for flexibility in labour input will be affected by the time lags involved in production, the costs of maintaining inventories, and the capital intensity of production.

2. Variability in labour supply arises from sickness absences, holidays, absenteeism and the like.

3. Unless otherwise stated, figures for part-time jobs in Britain also include participants in government training programmes.

4. Excluding agriculture, forestry and fishing, and deep coal mining.

5. Broadly similar conclusions can be drawn from Meager's (1986) study of temporary work.

6. Comparisons can also be made between the UK and Canada. Green, Krahn and Sung (1993), using broadly comparable LFS data for 1989, found that 8 per cent of Canadians in work had temporary jobs. The comparable figure for the UK was 7 per cent. (This UK estimate is some 2 percentage points higher than those presented elsewhere in this chapter. It appears to count all participants on government employment and training programmes as temporary workers).

7. See Bentolila and Dolado (1994) for further details.

Chapter 3
Engagements and dismissals

This chapter considers employers' ability to adjust on the extensive margin more generally, through the engagement and dismissal of employees. This appears to be a comparatively under-researched area. There are no reliable sources of data on flows into and out of employment that cover the whole economy over a long time period. Nor is there a great deal of quantitative information on the costs of hiring and firing, or the constraints that employers face in adjusting the size of their workforce. The discussion below therefore uses the information available.

a) Costs and constraints facing employers

The costs of hiring an employee are the costs of recruitment and training. Firing costs consist of redundancy payments (where applicable) plus the costs of being taken to an Industrial Tribunal if a dismissed employee is able to (and chooses to) pursue such a course. Since there is some probability that an employer will at some time have to dismiss any single recruit, both hiring and firing costs amount to a single (expected) fixed cost of employment.

These fixed costs have, in recent years, been identified as a potential source of labour market rigidity. If these costs are relatively high, employers are likely to take on less people, and employment ought to be relatively stable over the cycle. Hamermesh (1987) suggests that high fixed costs will also reduce the average level of employment over the cycle. This is because high fixed costs should lead to capital-labour substitution and/or longer working hours. In contrast, Bentolila and Bertola (1990) and Bertola (1992) suggest that, for quite complex reasons, the effect of high firing costs on long-run employment is neutral or even mildly positive[1].

Additional, indirect efficiency costs may be imposed if there are externally-imposed constraints on recruitment decisions, employment levels, redundancy criteria, or individual dismissals.

Data on flows into and out of employment is limited. The most comprehensive time series available is of engagements and separations in manufacturing. This data was collected by the Employment Department on a quarterly basis from employers. Problems with the data led to the series being discontinued in 1989[2].

Figure 3.1   Engagement and separation rates in manufacturing, 1975-1989

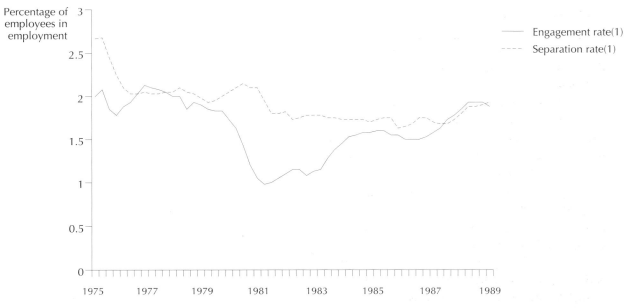

Notes

1   *Calculated as four-quarter moving averages, Great Britain. The measured engagement and separation rates systematically under-estimate the true level of turnover, as people who become employees and leave the firm within a single quarter are not recorded.*

Source: Employment Department.

A time series from 1975 onwards is plotted in Figure 3.1. It shows that both engagement and separation rates fell during the 1970s. Data presented by McCormick (1988) and Burgess and Nickell (1990) suggest this is a continuation of a longer-term trend. However, turnover rates stabilised during the 1980s.

Figure 3.1 measures turnover in terms of flows of *people*. However, turnover can also be measured in terms of *jobs*. Decisions about whether or not to create a new job, or terminate an existing one, also depend upon expected hiring and firing costs. Again, data in this area is not very good. Konings (1993), however, reports data for the manufacturing sector, graphed in Figure 3.2.

Two measures are provided, gross turnover and excess turnover. The latter measures the job turnover that takes place over and above that required to change the overall size of the employment stock, and hence nets out the impact of changes in aggregate employment levels. Data is available from company accounts and WIRS.

Gross turnover peaked in 1981/82, when employment was falling sharply. The excess turnover rate is more stable (although it may still be pro-cyclical). There is no conclusive evidence of a trend in this series, although the observation from the 1990 WIRS is much higher than previous years.

Given the lack of comprehensive and entirely reliable data on outcomes, have the fixed costs themselves increased or decreased over time?

Hiring costs and constraints

There is little quantitative time series data on the costs of recruiting or training an employee. However, it is reasonable to suppose that, relative to other labour costs, the *average* cost of training a new employee has increased in recent years. Changes in the occupational structure of employment have increased the demand for higher level skills. In addition, the LFS suggests that job-related training has been on an upwards trend since 1984.

Figure 3.2   Job turnover in manufacturing, 1973-1990

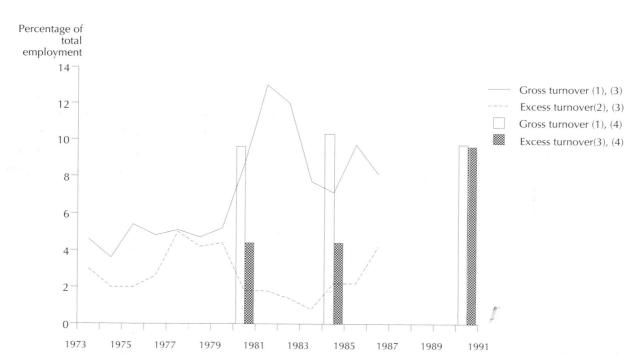

Notes

1   *Gross turnover is the sum total of job creation and destruction.*

2   *Excess turnover is gross turnover minus net employment growth (OECD (1994c)).*

3   *EXSTAT data based on company accounts. The companies in this dataset are primarily large companies in the manufacturing sector.*

4   *Establishment-based data from the WIRS series, private manufacturing industry, Great Britain.*

Source: Konings (1993).

There are few statutory constraints on employers' recruitment practices, beyond the (economically efficient) requirement that employers do not discriminate on grounds of sex or race.

Voluntary regulation must also be considered. Constraints on employers' freedom of action are not necessarily inefficient: they may be the result of mutually satisfactory trade-offs between flexibility and other objectives. Restrictions which represent the exercise of monopoly power by trade unions, however, may be more burdensome.

Table 3.1 shows that the incidence of joint regulation fell substantially between 1980 and 1990. What this data cannot provide, however, is any indication of the *effects* of joint regulation of recruitment.

A particular form of joint regulation likely to impose inefficient and costly constraints on employers' recruitment behaviour is the pre-entry closed shop; examples have included the printing industry and the docks[3]. The WIRS series shows that closed shops have declined dramatically in importance since 1980. The number of employees in establishments with 25 or more employees that were covered by a closed shop of any kind (both pre- and post-entry) was estimated to be nearly 5 million in 1980. By 1990, the number had fallen to only half a million.

Regulation of employment levels

Where employment levels are jointly regulated - either directly or through bargaining over manning levels or work rules - employers are likely to have less freedom to vary employment in line with business needs.

Table 3.2 provides some evidence on trends in the 1980s. Joint regulation of staffing levels tended to be slightly more prevalent than regulation of recruitment, but a similar trend is evident.

An alternative measure of union influence on employment levels was calculated by Sanfey (1993). Derived from a theoretical bargaining model, his estimates also suggest that union influence declined considerably between the mid-1970s and mid-1980s.

Firing costs and constraints

Firing costs are better researched than either hiring costs or the regulation of employment levels. It is important to distinguish between reductions in the size of the workforce for economic reasons, and the dismissal of individual employees because of poor employer-employee matches. In practice, the distinction between these two categories may become blurred, but there are qualitative differences in the costs and constraints associated with each.

Table 3.1   Joint regulation of recruitment, 1980-1990

Percentages of establishments with 25 or more employees where recruitment was the subject of joint regulation between management and the largest manual/non-manual bargaining unit, Great Britain

	Manual employees			Non-manual employees		
	1980	1984	1990	1980	1984	1990
Negotiated at some level:						
Private manufacturing	39	17	11	15	7	2
Private services	21	8	5	14	3	3
Public sector	53	43	31	71	46	39
All establishments	**38**	**23**	**14**	**32**	**21**	**15**
Negotiated at establishment level:						
Private manufacturing	35	15	9	14	5	2
Private services	16	6	3	9	3	3
Public sector	20	10	6	24	11	9
All establishments	**23**	**10**	**6**	**15**	**6**	**5**

Source: WIRS series. Own calculations, derived from Millward and Stevens (1986), Tables 3.1, 9.19 and 9.20; and Millward, Stevens, Smart and Hawes (1992), Tables 3.17, 7.16 and 7.17.

Table 3.2   Joint regulation of staffing levels, 1980-1990

Percentages of establishments with 25 or more employees where staffing levels were the subject of joint regulation between management and the largest manual/non-manual bargaining unit, Great Britain

	Manual employees			Non-manual employees		
	1980	1984	1990	1980	1984	1990
Negotiated at some level:						
Private manufacturing	47	26	15	17	11	5
Private services	23	15	9	15	9	8
Public sector	63	59	48	74	63	53
All establishments	**42**	**34**	**22**	**35**	**30**	**20**
Negotiated at establishment level:						
Private manufacturing	41	23	12	15	8	3
Private services	17	8	6	9	3	4
Public sector	19	16	16	22	17	16
All establishments	**25**	**15**	**10**	**15**	**9**	**7**

Source: WIRS series. Own calculations, derived from Millward and Stevens (1986), Tables 3.1, 9.19 and 9.20; and Millward, Stevens, Smart and Hawes (1992), Tables 3.17, 7.16 and 7.17.

The main financial cost associated with a reduction in the workforce for economic reasons is the redundancy payment. Since 1965, employers have been required by law to make a severance payment to all redundant employees with more than a specified length of service. The size of the payment is related to age, length of service and earnings. Few changes have been made to the scheme since its introduction, save for the abolition in 1986 of a partial state-funded rebate.

Burgess (1988) reported a sharp increase in the number of redundancy payments made during the recession of the early 1980s. Average amounts paid out (as a proportion of wages) remained relatively constant from the early 1970s onwards. Unfortunately, no information on this basis is available after 1982.

From 1975 onwards, information on the cost of redundancies is available from EU Labour Cost Surveys. Time series for a number of industries are presented in Figure 3.3.

The total cost of redundancy payments will depend upon the number of redundancies made and the average size of the payment. Hence total redundancy payments will vary over the cycle. Periods of structural change will also produce surges in the amounts of redundancy payments made. Nevertheless, redundancy payments appear to have increased as a share of total hourly labour costs.

A survey of establishments with five or more employees conducted in 1992, reported in Spilsbury, McIntosh and Banerji (1993), collected information on the impact of the legislation. In the main, employers did not think the requirement to make redundancy payments had a major impact on business decisions. Not a single employer thought the legislation had affected employment levels in their business. Employers also saw some benefits: many thought the existence of mandated payments made it easier to reduce the size of the workforce, or increased the harmony of industrial relations. In total, 88 per cent of respondents thought that redundancy payments had a broadly neutral impact on their business.

Nevertheless, there was some evidence that the requirement to make redundancy payments may have effects at the margin. A minority of employers felt the payments required of them were excessive, and 21 per cent said they probably/definitely would not make redundancy payments if there was no statutory requirement. The survey, however, took place during a recession, and perceptions of the legislation may vary over the cycle.

There is also a small amount of econometric evidence on the impact of redundancy payments. Burgess (1988) found that redundancy payments (measured by the average amount paid out per

Figure 3.3   Redundancy payments as a share of total labour costs, 1975-1992

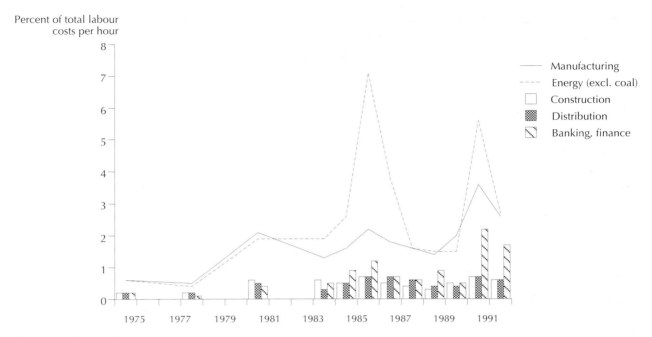

Source: *Employment Department.*

redundancy) reduced the *speed* with which employment adjusted to its long-run equilibrium level.

Burgess and Nickell (1990) used data on turnover between 1967 and 1980 (the ED engagements and separations data graphed in Figure 3.1). They found that redundancy payments had a small but positive impact on the separation rate. If redundancy payments made any contribution to reducing layoffs, this appears to have been more than offset by an increase in the propensity for employees to quit their jobs. The study also found that redundancy payments were associated with a dampening of fluctuations in employment, although the quantitative impact was small.

Burgess (1993) came to different conclusions. The study used much the same data but a different model specification. Burgess found that redundancy payments had no significant impact on the speed with which employment adjusted to its long-term level.

All of these studies, however only considered the manufacturing sector for periods from the mid-1960s to the mid-1980s, so they are now quite dated. The available evidence therefore suggests the impact of redundancy payments on employers' behaviour is relatively small[4].

While there is a statutory requirement to make redundancy payments, there are few legislative constraints on employers' ability to make redundancies. Employers making ten or more redundancies have to provide advance notification and consult trade unions (if any are recognised). However, while this may delay the process, it does not limit the employer's right to make the redundancies eventually. Individual firms, however, may face voluntary restraints on their freedom to make people redundant, presumably included in Table 3.2. Similarly, there is little regulation governing employers' choice of who to make redundant, beyond a requirement that selection criteria are 'fair' and non-discriminatory.

Some dismissals will inevitably arise because of poor employer-employee matches. If there are constraints on employers' ability to dismiss unsuitable workers, then a resource cost is imposed.

Employment protection legislation was first introduced in the 1960s and strengthened considerably in the mid-1970s. Between 1980 and 1985, however, the coverage of the legislation was progressively relaxed (see Appendix 5).

The legislation does not prevent employers from dismissing unsuitable employees. It requires the employer to demonstrate that the dismissal was 'fair' or based on objective criteria. Hence, in any particular case, there is some uncertainty about whether or not the Industrial Tribunal will find for the employer. Unfair dismissal applications are costly to employers: the average cost to employers of an application to a Tribunal increased from £900 in 1985/86 to £1,845 in 1990/91 (Tremlett and Banerji (1994)). Even where employers are successful in establishing that dismissal was justified, costs are still incurred and often not recovered[5].

Despite the reduction in the proportion of employees covered by employment protection legislation, the use of the system appears to have increased in recent years.

Figure 3.4 shows that applications for unfair dismissal registered with Industrial Tribunals fell between the end of the 1970s and the middle of the 1980s, mirroring the extensions to the qualification period. However, the number of applications has increased sharply in recent years. There may be a number of reasons for the recent increase:

- higher unemployment;

- increased familiarity with the legislation on the part of employees;

- an increased emphasis on using the legislation to enforce individual employment rights, as employees' ability and willingness to use collective action has declined;

- a more aggressive dismissals policy on the part of employers.

Empirical evidence on the effects of unfair dismissal legislation is limited. In addition, it either pre-dates the extensions to the qualification period during the first half of the 1980s, or does not fully reflect its effects. Results are also mixed. Daniel and Stilgoe (1978) surveyed 301 private sector manufacturing establishments in 1977 and concluded that the legislation had not had any significant impact on the level of recruitment[6].

As for the econometric studies, Burgess (1988) and Burgess (1993) found that strengthening of employment protection legislation (measured by the expected unfair dismissal payment) tended to reduce the speed with which employment levels adjusted. In contrast, Burgess and Nickell (1990) found no effect on employment or turnover.

b)   International comparisons

In the main, attention focuses again on the costs and constraints associated with hiring and firing. There are two main sources of information. One is survey evidence that captures the perceptions of labour

Figure 3.4   Unfair dismissal applications registered with Industrial Tribunals, 1977-1993

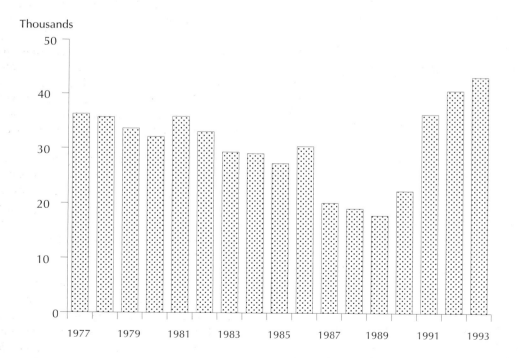

Includes all applications under unfair dismissal jurisdictions except joint unfair dismissal/redundancy payments applications, Great Britain.

Source: Central Office of Industrial Tribunals management information.

market actors (usually employers). The other is studies based on direct examination of regulatory systems. See Grubb and Wells (1993) for comments on the advantages and disadvantages of each approach.

Survey evidence on hiring and firing constraints

Comparative data for most EU member states is available from two surveys of employers, conducted in 1985/86 and 1989. Although the content of the questionnaires was standardised across countries, the surveys themselves were administered through national employers' organisations (e.g. the UK questionnaire was administered through the CBI). This means the surveys' coverage is restricted to the manufacturing and retail distribution sectors. It may also mean that survey respondents were not entirely representative of employers as a whole.

While some residual inconsistencies may remain, the surveys remain a very useful tool for assessing differences across countries in *perceived* constraints to flexibility on the extensive margin.

Employers were given a list of possible reasons why they were not employing more people in their firm, and asked to comment on the importance of each. One of these reasons was 'insufficient flexibility in hiring and shedding labour'. Responses to this question are recorded in Table 3.3.

Few UK employers regarded barriers to hiring and firing as significant, much less than in any other EU member state. At the other end of the spectrum, Italian employers thought such constraints were particularly severe. For the manufacturing sector, the perceived severity of these constraints appears to have diminished between 1985/86 and 1989. The principal exceptions to this pattern are Germany, the Netherlands and the UK - although, for the UK, this was from a very low base and within likely sampling error. With the exception of Belgium and the Netherlands, hiring and firing barriers were seen as less of a problem in retail distribution than in manufacturing.

Some checks can be made on the internal consistency of these results. Table 3.4 shows the relative importance in each country of 'insufficient flexibility in hiring and shedding labour', measured by this response's rank ordering compared to the other answers available.

Hiring and firing constraints were relatively unimportant in the UK. Most other countries consistently attached a higher ranking to the issue, especially France, Greece, and the Netherlands.

In the 1985/86 survey, employers were also presented with thirteen specific options designed to increase employment. They were asked to asked to rate the likely impact of each option on their business.

The results are presented in Table 3.5, in the form of a score. The higher the score, the greater the positive impact on employment. A notable feature of UK employers' responses are the low scores given to most of the options. This suggests there were relatively few constraints on UK employers' ability to expand employment levels, beyond those dictated by product demand, wage levels, technology etc.

Institutional analyses

Institutional constraints and the structure of regulation are an important factor influencing flexibility on the extensive margin. A number of recent studies have reviewed employment protection regimes in the EU and OECD.

Emerson (1988) considered the institutions and constraints affecting various aspects of the hiring and firing process. The broad conclusions of the analysis suggest that, compared to other European countries, the UK has few onerous restrictions on recruitment or individual and collective dismissal. This conclusion is supported if one looks at employers' perceptions of the constraints on their actions, or if one considers the content and application of regulations themselves. For example, Emerson suggests the UK is unusual in having unfair dismissal legislation that takes a pragmatic approach to individual dismissals, based upon what an Industrial Tribunal deems reasonable. In most other European countries, there are more prescriptive rules limiting employers' and regulators' discretion and/or the requirement to obtain approval from a third party (the government, trade unions, or a works council) before a dismissal can be authorised.

Comparisons with the USA in Emerson's study suggest, however, that labour market regulation is more pervasive in the UK than in the USA. For example, the USA has no generally applicable legislation governing individual dismissals. Grievances have been pursued through the civil courts (Mendelsohn (1990)).

Bertola (1990) constructed a rank ordering of job security provisions for 10 OECD countries. This was based on Emerson's (1988) findings, although the statistical criteria used to construct the ranking were not specified. Of the countries surveyed, Bertola considered Italy to have the most stringent employment protection regulations, with the USA being most liberal. The UK was ranked seventh.

Table 3.3   EU employers' perceptions of the scope for greater flexibility in hiring and firing

Percentage of employers who thought insufficient flexibility was an obstacle to employment[1]

Insufficient flexibility was:		Belgium	Denmark	France	FR Germany	Greece	Ireland	Italy	Luxembourg	Netherlands	Portugal	Spain	UK
Manufacturing													
Very important	1985/86	38	..	48	23	45	41	68	30	19	..	..	7
	1989	27	..	32	21	27	29	45	..	44	29	35	9
Important	1985/86	37	..	33	33	22	27	15	26	32	..	..	19
	1989	32	..	30	42	28	21	33	..	27	25	33	35
Not important	1985/86	35	..	15	27	19	30	17	44	45	..	..	58
	1989	25	..	26	33	26	37	22	..	28	46	15	54
No reply	1985/86	7	..	4	5	14	2	-	-	4	..	..	16
	1989	-	..	12	4	19	13	-	..	1	-	18	2
Score[2]	**1985/86**	**113**	**..**	**129**	**79**	**112**	**109**	**151**	**86**	**70**	**..**	**..**	**33**
	1989	**86**	**..**	**94**	**84**	**82**	**79**	**123**	**..**	**115**	**83**	**103**	**53**
Retail													
Very important	1989	60	..	26	28	..	..	15	..	55	23	19	5
Important	1989	31	..	25	28	..	..	42	..	17	13	27	32
Not important	1989	7	..	27	38	..	..	43	..	27	64	54	59
No reply	1989	2	..	22	6	..	..	-	..	1	-	-	3
Score[2]	**1989**	**151**	**..**	**77**	**84**	**..**	**..**	**72**	**..**	**127**	**59**	**65**	**42**

Notes

1   Employers who thought 'insufficient flexibility in hiring and shedding labour (i.e. necessary redundancies/dismissals and new recruitment may be difficult and costly)' was a reason for them not being able to employ more people in their firm.

2   Calculated as very important=2; important=1; not important=0. Thus the score can range from 0 to 200 in value.

..   indicates that data were not available.

-    indicates zero.

Source: CEC (1986), Table 17; CEC (1991), Tables 4a and 14a.

32

Table 3.4 EU employers' perceptions of the relative importance of inflexibility in hiring and firing

Rank ordering[1] of 'insufficient flexibility in hiring and shedding labour' in employers' perceptions of reasons why they have not been able to employ more people[2]

	Belgium	Denmark	France[3]	FR Germany	Greece	Ireland	Italy	Luxembourg	Netherlands[4]	Portugal	Spain	UK[3,5]
Manufacturing												
1985/86	4	..	1	4	1	4	2	4	2	..	..	7
1989	5=	..	3	5=	3	5	2	..	4	5	3	6
Retail												
1989	1	..	2	6	..	..	8=	..	3	7	7	7

Notes

1 Rankings are based on the scores as calculated in Table 3.3.

2 Employers were given a list of ten reasons 'which employers have given for not being able to employ more people', and asked to state the importance of each in relation to their firm. The 1989 survey increased the list to eleven, by adding 'other reasons', a category that attracted a significant number of responses in two countries (Italy and Portugal).

3 Retail sector employers in France and the UK were only given nine reasons to choose from.

4 'Other reasons' was omitted from the survey of Dutch retail sector employers.

5 Only nine reasons were given to UK manufacturing employers in the 1985/86 survey.

.. indicates no data available.

Source: CEC (1986), Table 17; CEC (1991), Tables 4a and 14a.

Table 3.5 EU employers' perceptions of the effectiveness of measures to stimulate employment

Employers' ratings[1] of the impact on employment of various possible changes in the labour market, 1985/86

Policy change	Sector	Belgium	France	FR Germany	Greece	Ireland	Italy	Luxembourg	Netherlands	UK
Shorter periods of notice in case of redundancies, dismissals and simpler legal procedures	Manufacturing	106	53	93	125	36	166	66	52	31
	Retail	127	63	::	87	::	::	::	38	42
More frequent use of temporary contracts (fixed term, interim work etc.)	Manufacturing	87	66	95	73	46	94	77	33	27
	Retail	88	60	::	68	::	::	::	23	19
Better trained jobseekers	Manufacturing	84	19	88	106	15	129	120	37	43
	Retail	81	24	::	62	::	::	::	19	39
Introduction of wider wage differentials according to skills and working conditions	Manufacturing	85	35	75	122	19	144	53	47	17
	Retail	97	34	::	95	::	::	::	31	34
Greater emphasis on productivity in determining wages and salaries	Manufacturing	107	42	83	165	32	131	113	37	-8
More flexible shop opening hours	Retail	71	58	::	25	::	::	::	17	48
Introduction of 'initial wage rates' (i.e. lower wages for new starters)	Manufacturing	66	47	53	99	38	106	73	28	38
	Retail	107	67	::	80	::	::	::	30	68
More flexible working time arrangements at company level	Manufacturing	88	74	61	89	16	82	76	39	19
	Retail	90	74	::	55	::	::	::	23	29
Reduction of redundancy payments that may have to be paid	Manufacturing	88	23	65	87	33	106	59	12	25
	Retail	103	31	::	59	::	::	::	8	27

Table 3.5   EU employers' perceptions of the effectiveness of measures to stimulate employment (continued)

Employers' ratings[1] of the impact on employment of various possible changes in the labour market, 1985/86

Policy change	Sector	Belgium	France	FR Germany	Greece	Ireland	Italy	Luxembourg	Netherlands	UK
(Higher) temporary employment subsidies for employing unemployed persons, who have particular difficulties in finding a job, (e.g. young people, women, older workers etc.)	Manufacturing	33	24	39	71	43	118	32	27	53
	Retail	80	38	..	39	..	..	..	29	63
Functional improvement of public employment offices (better services provided by official employment agencies regarding job-seekers, professional training etc.)	Manufacturing	53	9	52	39	15	80	94	24	14
	Retail	61	21	..	34	..	..	..	16	24
Reduction in standard weekly working hours without increasing total production costs (i.e. cost-neutral)	Manufacturing	58	29	74	18	37	-37	75	46	45
	Retail	24	19	..	50	..	..	..	21	35
Introduction of (more) profit-oriented components in contractual salaries	Manufacturing	98	42	58	75	36	10	50	25	2
	Retail	102	55	..	61	..	..	..	13	21

Notes

1   Employers were given a list of possible changes and asked 'which effect do you think each might have on your employment plans for the next twelve months?' Perceptions are measured by scores calculated as follows: significant positive effect=2; positive effect=1; no change=0; negative effect=-1. Scores can thus range from -100 to 200.

..   indicates that data were not available.

Source: CEC (1986), Tables 18 and 26.

CEC (1993) surveyed labour market regulation in EU member states. Its broad conclusion was that the regulatory regime in the UK is among the most liberal in the EU, alongside Ireland and Denmark. At the other extreme are the southern EU member states, Greece, Italy, Portugal and Spain. CEC (1993) also looked at recent changes in regulations. Some countries (e.g. Germany, Spain, Portugal) introduced measures during the 1980s designed to facilitate part-time or temporary work. In contrast, Ireland and Italy strengthened their employment protection regimes, while France relaxed and then tightened controls on dismissals.

OECD (1993) looked at a wider range of countries. The evidence presented suggests that employment protection appears to be somewhat more stringent in Austria and the Nordic countries than in the UK. On the other hand, regimes are more liberal in the USA, Canada, Australia and New Zealand.

Finally, Grubb and Wells (1993) examined the stringency of employment regulation within the EU (minus Luxembourg), through a more detailed analysis of the available material on regulatory systems. Their analysis went wider than protection from dismissal, including restrictions on working time and the use of temporary contracts. They computed a rank ordering of countries in terms of the stringency of their overall system of employment regulation. Table 3.6 lists this alongside Bertola's.

There are differences between the two rankings, notably the relative positions of Belgium and the UK[7]. While such rankings are inevitably judgemental, the evidence presented in these studies suggests that Grubb and Wells's ranking may be a more appropriate measure of the UK's relative position, especially when one includes the impact of voluntary regulation.

There is also a small amount of evidence on the impact of different systems of employment protection regimes, based on cross-country comparisons. This is summarised in Appendix 2.

The studies reviewed there tend to agree that strong employment protection regulations reduce both hiring and firing, 'smoothing' employment over the cycle. However, there is no consensus on whether regulation affects long-run levels of employment and unemployment. Lazear (1990) claims that job security damages employment, whereas Bertola (1990) finds no such effect.

c)   Summary and conclusions

- Flexibility on the extensive margin is about the ability of employers to vary the size of their workforce. In general, costs and other constraints associated with hiring and firing will add to the (expected) fixed costs of employment. This reduces flexibility on the extensive margin and may adversely affect employment levels in the long-run.

- There is insufficient data to reach firm conclusions on whether turnover of people or jobs has increased or decreased over time.

- The trend in recruitment and training costs is uncertain. Joint regulation of recruitment,

Table 3.6   Rankings of OECD countries by stringency of employment regulations

Ranking	Bertola (1990)	Grubb and Wells (1993)
1 (= most stringent)	Italy	Portugal
2	Belgium	Greece
3	France	Spain
4	Sweden	Italy
5	FR Germany	FR Germany
6	Japan	France
7	**UK**	Belgium
8	Netherlands	Netherlands
9	Denmark	Ireland
10	USA	Denmark
11 (= least stringent)		**UK**

however, declined considerably between 1980 and 1990.

- The incidence of joint regulation of employment levels has declined to a similar extent.

- British employers face relatively few constraints on their ability to make redundancies. Regulation of individual dismissals (unfair dismissal legislation) was progressively relaxed during the first half of the 1980s. Use of the legislation, however, has increased in recent years.

- The available evidence, some of which is now quite dated, suggests that the impact of these regulations has been relatively small, compared with other factors. The relatively light regulatory burden placed on UK employers in this area, however, makes it dificult to assess the effect of changes in the regulatory regime against a background of structural and cyclical change in the economy.

- The evidence suggests that British employers face relatively few constraints on their ability to exploit external flexibility.

- Constraints on engagements and dismissals in the UK appear relatively light when compared to other European countries. Both the content of the regulations themselves, and employers' perceptions of the constraints they face, confirm this. Regulatory regimes in the USA, Canada, Australia and New Zealand appear, however, to be more liberal than in the UK.

- Along with some other EU countries, the UK has liberalised its regulations during the 1980s. Some other countries appear to have moved in the opposite direction.

- The available evidence suggests that employment protection regulations may 'smooth' the level of employment over the cycle. There is no consensus on whether regulation reduces employment in the long run.

Footnotes to Chapter 3

1. The argument is that dismissals of new hires occur at some point in the future, so the costs are discounted. This means that the impact of firing costs on (future) dismissals is outweighed by the immediate disincentive for employers to dismiss their current workforce.

2. Essentially, the problem was that the panel of employers used to provide the data was set up in the early 1970s. Although the panel was topped up from time to time, its composition became increasingly unrepresentative of manufacturing as a whole, with 'sunset' industries over-represented and 'sunrise' industries under-represented.

3. Arrangements in the docks had statutory backing. Employers in Dock Labour Scheme ports were prevented by law from using anybody but Registered Dock Workers for dock work, and entry to the pool of Registered Dock Workers was effectively controlled by the trade unions.

4. Interestingly, this was the conclusion of earlier studies by Parker, Thomas, Ellis and McCarthy (1971) and Daniel and Stilgoe (1978).

5. Indeed, the median cost to employers of cases dismissed by the Tribunal exceeded the median cost of all applications (Banerji and Wareing (1994)).

6. A larger proportion of employers, however, said the legislation had forced them to change aspects of their behaviour, such as recruitment and disciplinary procedures, which may have increased administrative and managerial costs.

7. For the seven countries covered by both rankings, the rank correlation coefficient is 0.75.

Chapter 4
Working time

Firms can change their effective use of labour on the intensive margin, without recourse to the external labour market. One means of achieving this is through flexibility in working time. The demand for flexible working time arrangements will depend on the variability and uncertainty of product demand, and on the nature of the production process. For example, in the retail sector, employment needs to be closely tailored to peaks and troughs in shopping patterns over the day, week and year.

In order to structure the discussion, a distinction can be made between:

- Flexibility in **average hours worked over a given period of time** (usually a week or month). This form of adjustment commonly takes the form of overtime or short-time working, and tends to reflect peaks and troughs in product demand.

- Flexibility in **working time arrangements *within a given number of hours worked*** over the week or month. This form of flexibility encompasses a wide range of working arrangements, including part-time work, shift systems, flexitime and more

recent innovations like annual hours contracts. These forms of flexibility appear to be more closely associated with the needs of the production process and predictable variations in product demand.

This distinction is mainly for clarity. The two aspects are not completely separable. For example, some employers have restructured working patterns in order to reduce their dependence on overtime working.

There are other ways in which the section and the data could be structured. One could distinguish between 'traditional' forms of flexibility (overtime, short-time working, shift systems) and 'new' forms of flexibility (flexitime, compressed working weeks, annual hours contracts etc.). A similar distinction could be made between 'formal' flexibilities (specified working patterns that form part of the contract of employment) and 'informal' flexibilities (e.g. variable starting and finishing times). 'Traditional' and 'new', 'formal' and 'informal' flexibilities can be substitutes as well as complements.

There are also supply-side considerations. Employees may value a degree of choice (and, perhaps, flexibility) over their working arrangements.

Figure 4.1   Average hours worked by full-time manual employees, 1948-1990

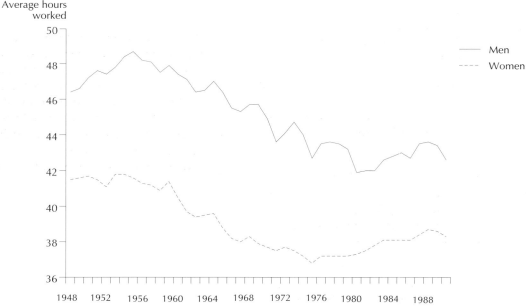

Notes

Full-time manual employees on adult rates, Great Britain.

Source: Employment Department.

Figure 4.2   Average hours worked by full-time employees, 1971-1994

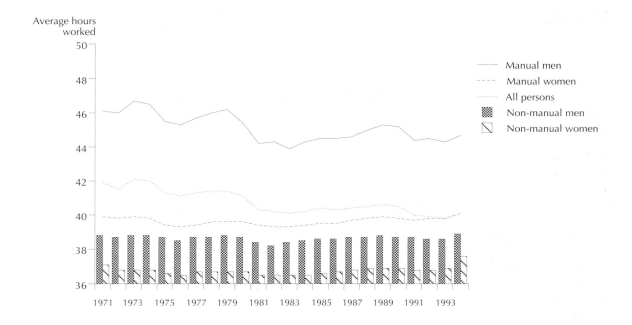

Notes

Full-time employees on adult rates (prior to 1984, men aged 21 and over, women aged 18 and over) whose pay for the survey period was unaffected by absence, Great Britain, April.

Source: New Earnings Surveys.

a)   Trends in average hours worked

A broad illustration of post-War trends in hours worked is available from the Employment Department's (now discontinued) October enquiry into the earnings of manual workers. The data, presented in Figure 4.1, only covers manual employees in selected industries, principally in the manufacturing sector.

Average working hours reached a post-War peak in the early 1950s before falling steadily until the second half of the 1970s. However, the downwards trend appears to have eased off (or even reversed itself) since then.

More comprehensive and reliable data on paid weekly hours is available on an annual basis from the New Earnings Survey (NES). Appendix 1 contains details on the design of the NES. Figure 4.2 graphs average hours worked by full-time employees since 1971.

There is some variability from year to year in the length of the average working week. However, the trend was definitely downwards during the 1970s. It is less clear if there has been any further trend fall since then. There are consistent differences between

groups of workers: men work longer hours on average than women, and manual employees tend to work longer hours than non-manuals. Figures 4.3 and 4.4 split average hours worked into paid overtime and other paid hours, which can be termed the basic working week.

The basic working week fell during the 1970s, with a more noticeable reduction in the basic hours of manual employees (especially men) in the early 1980s. Since then, however, it has not fallen further. Figure 4.4 shows that most of the year-to-year variability in average hours worked arises through variation in overtime hours[1]. Most of this variability is due to the overtime patterns of manual men; other groups of employees tend to work far less paid overtime.

Figure 4.3   The basic working week for full-time employees, 1971-1994

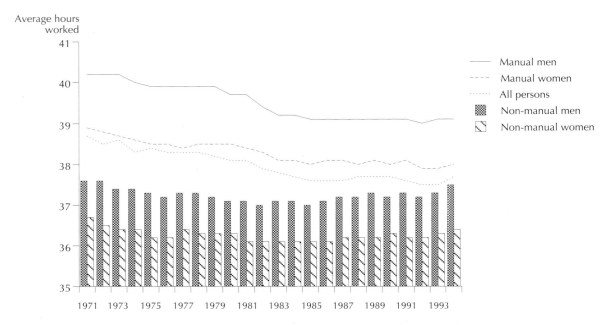

Notes

Full-time employees on adult rates (prior to 1984, men aged 21 and over, women aged 18 and over) whose pay for the survey period was unaffected by absence, Great Britain, April.

Source: New Earnings Surveys.

Figure 4.4   Average paid overtime hours worked by full-time employees, 1971-1994

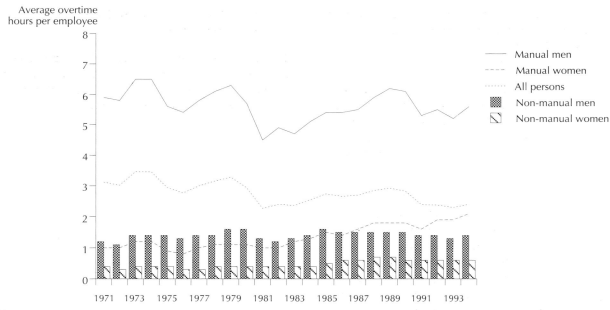

Notes

Full-time employees on adult rates (prior to 1984, men aged 21 and over, women aged 18 and over) whose pay for the survey period was unaffected by absence, Great Britain, April.

Source: New Earnings Surveys.

Figure 4.5   Average overtime and output growth, 1971-1994

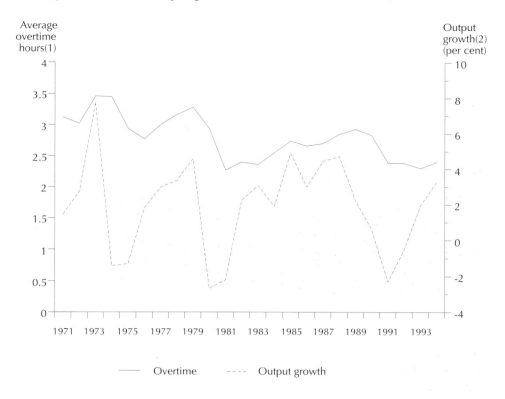

Notes

1   *Average overtime hours worked per full-time employee on adult rates (prior to 1984, men aged 18 and over, women aged 21 and over), Great Britain, April.*

2   *Annual percentage change in real GDP at constant factor cost, UK, second quarter.*

Source: New Earnings Survey, Central Statistical Office.

The role of overtime in adjusting total hours worked to peaks and troughs in demand is confirmed in Figure 4.5. Overtime hours clearly reflect movements in output.

More detailed information on overtime and short-time working is available on a quarterly basis for the manufacturing sector. The data covers operatives (manual workers) only, although the NES data suggests this is the most significant group in terms of paid overtime.

Total overtime hours worked, as well as hours lost due to short-time working, are graphed in Figure 4.6. Again, total overtime shows a clear cyclical pattern. Short-time working has not been significant, with the exception of the 1980/81 recession, when government short-time working programmes gave employers a financial incentive to offer short-time work rather than make redundancies.

Finally, Figure 4.7 demonstrates the strong cyclical role of overtime in manufacturing. There is a positive and significant relationship between overtime and output growth, with no evidence of any lag between the two series.

These results suggest that overtime is important (at least within manufacturing) as a short-run means of adjusting labour input to business needs, entirely consistent with the economic theory.

Figure 4.6   Overtime and short time working in manufacturing, 1976-1994

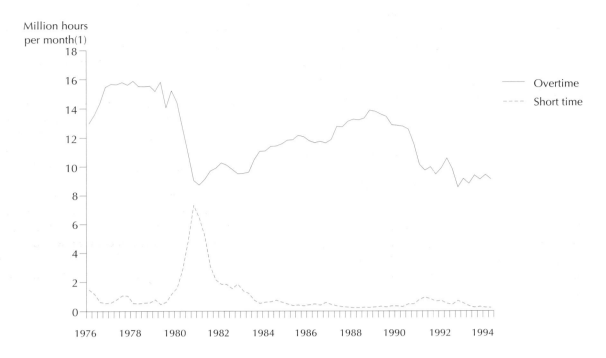

Notes

1   Data refer to manual workers (operatives) in manufacturing industry, Great Britain, seasonally adjusted.

Source: Employment Department.

Figure 4.7   Changes in output, employment and overtime in manufacturing, 1976-1994

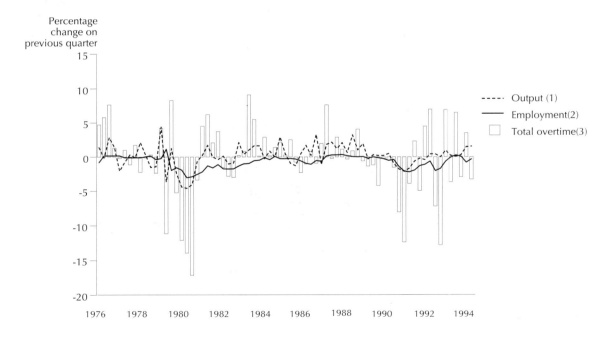

Notes

1   Manufacturing output, UK, seasonally adjusted.

2   Employees in employment, manufacturing, Great Britain, seasonally adjusted.

3   Overtime hours worked by manual workers (operatives) in manufacturing industry, Great Britain, seasonally adjusted.

Source: Employment Department, Central Statistical Office.

b) Flexible working time arrangements

The last decade has seen a widening in the distribution of hours worked. Figure 4.8 graphs the distribution of usual hours worked by employees and the self-employed in 1984, 1989 and 1994. The proportion working between 31 and 40 hours a week has declined considerably, with more people working both shorter and longer hours.

Part of this widening can be accounted for by increased female participation (as women are more likely to work part-time) and by strong growth in the number of self-employed (who work relatively long hours).

There is considerable diversity not just in the numbers of hours worked, but also in variables such as the number of days people work. For example, in Spring 1991, only two fifths of people in employment (61 per cent) usually worked for five days a week,

with 21 per cent working on either six or seven days of the week (Watson (1992)).

Such diversity is not new. Shiftworking has long been a source of temporal flexibility for employers. Figure 4.9 presents time series evidence, drawn from the NES[2].

Bosworth (1994) suggests that the incidence of shiftworking increased steadily over the post-War period, before peaking in the early 1980s. Since then, the proportion of employees covered by formal shiftworking arrangements has declined.

Certain new, more 'innovative' working time arrangements have often been linked to greater flexibility on the intensive margin. Examples include annual hours contracts, term-time working and jobsharing. There are only two comprehensive sources of information available, reported in Table 4.1.

Figure 4.8   Distribution of usual hours worked, 1984-1994

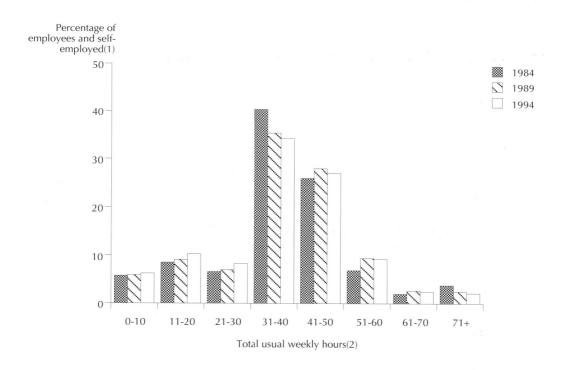

Notes

1 *Great Britain.*

2 *Includes paid and unpaid overtime.*

Source: Labour Force Surveys, Spring.

Figure 4.9   Full-time employees receiving shiftwork premia, 1973-1994

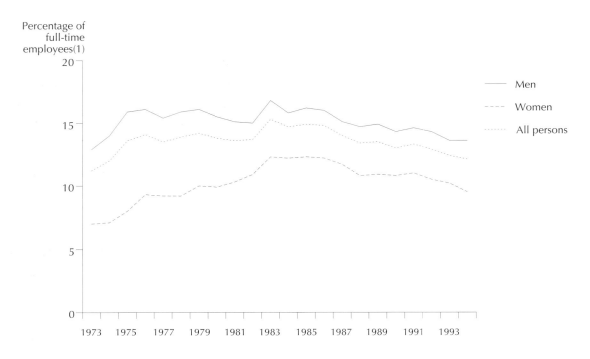

Notes

*1   Full-time employees on adult rates (prior to 1984, men aged 21 and over, women aged 18 and over) whose pay for the survey
    period was unaffected by absence, Great Britain, April.*

Source: Bosworth (1994), updated using New Earnings Surveys.

The table puts 'new' forms of flexible working time into context. Clearly, 'new' forms of flexibility are not as widespread as more 'traditional' means, such as overtime, part-time work, shift work, or flexible starting and finishing times (a potential source of 'informal' flexibility).

These surveys only report on the position since the beginning of the 1990s. There is no clear picture on longer term trends. However, the emphasis in the industrial relations and practitioner literature on annual hours, term-time working etc. as 'new' or 'novel' forms of work suggests that the incidence of flexible working patterns must have increased over the past ten to twenty years.

There is also evidence that employees value diversity in working time arrangements. The range of alternative working patterns available may therefore enhance the flexibility of labour supply.

Three surveys provide supporting evidence. The 1989 British Social Attitudes Survey (BSAS) asked employees if they wished to change their working hours. Table 4.2 summarises responses.

Nearly two thirds of employees said they were happy with the hours they worked, and did not wish to change them. Satisfaction was particularly high for people working part-time (i.e. 30 hours or less).

The survey results confirm that leisure is a 'good', in that people working long hours were more likely to say they would prefer shorter working hours. However, when given an explicit trade-off between pay and hours of work, most employees who said they wanted to work less hours opted to maintain their income. In total, only 11 per cent of employees said they would prefer a different combination of pay and hours of work (i.e. people who wanted to work longer hours, and people who would prefer shorter hours and less pay).

Another survey of employees, also conducted in 1989 and reported in Marsh (1991), came to similar conclusions. Nearly three quarters (73 per cent) opted not to change their hours when faced with a hypothetical change in working time and earnings. Twice as many respondents wanted to work longer hours (18 per cent) as shorter hours (9 per cent). This response was most common among women working part-time.

Finally, Wareing's (1992) survey, reported in Table 4.1, asked respondents if they were satisfied with

Table 4.1   The incidence of flexible working time arrangements

	Column percentages[1], Great Britain					
	Wareing (1992)[2]			Watson (1994)		
Data	1990 NOP Omnibus survey			Spring 1993 LFS		
Base	All in employment			All employees		
Form of working time arrangement:	Men and women	Men	Women	Men and women	Men	Women
Part-time work	21	5	43	25	6	45
Reservism (just work when asked/needed)	5	4	6	Not included		
Regular paid overtime	19	27	10	27 (1991)[3]	Not reported	Not reported
Shiftwork	15	18	11	18	21	14
Flexitime	8	8	8	12	10	14
Annualised hours	5	6	4	9	9	10
Compressed working week[4]	4	5	2	4	4	3
Term-time working[5]	*	*	1	1	Not reported	Not reported
Jobsharing	1	-	2	1	*	2
Flexible starting and finishing times	27	31	21	Not included		

Notes

1 *Totals may add up to greater than 100 per cent because respondents could name more than one category.*

2 *The results in this table are based on the first three waves of the NOP Omnibus survey. Other results quoted in Wareing (1992) may differ slightly, because they were based on a larger sample.*

3 *Percentage of employees who usually work basic hours and paid overtime (with or without unpaid overtime) (Watson (1992), Tables 1 and 2).*

4 *This was a single response in Wareing (1992). The LFS data combines two separate responses, a nine day fortnight and a four-and-a-half day week.*

5 *In the case of the LFS data, employees in the education sector are excluded. Watson (1994) states that term time workers are almost entirely women.*

* *indicates less than 0.5 per cent.*

- *indicates zero.*

Sources: Wareing (1992), Table 7; Watson (1994), Tables 2 and 3.

Table 4.2   Employees' preferences for working more or fewer hours, 1989

Column percentages, employees usually working 10 or more hours each week, Great Britain

Usual hours worked	More hours	Less hours	Respondent would prefer to work: Even if it meant less pay?			Happy with present hours
			Yes	No	It depends	
10-20	13	2	2	1	-	84
21-30	7	9	7	2	1	84
31-40	3	30	8	20	2	67
41-50	3	41	7	31	2	56
51-60	-	67	9	48	5	33
61+	-	67	12	53	-	33
All men[1]	4	36	5	29	1	60
All women[1]	5	24	9	12	2	71
All persons[1]	4	30	7	21	1	65

Notes

1   Excludes small number of don't know/no answer responses.

-   indicates zero.

Source: 1989 British Social Attitudes Survey.

their current pattern of working hours. Uniformly high proportions of employees - around 80 per cent - expressed satisfaction, irrespective of their particular working patterns.

Taken together, this evidence suggests current patterns of working time command a good deal of employee satisfaction. The flexibility employers have to structure working time expands choice and makes it easier for people to find a job that optimises their individual trade-off between paid work and other activities.

c)   International comparisons

For EU member states, comparable data on working time is available from the European LFS. This data reveals clear differences between the distribution of working time in the UK and other member states.

Figure 4.10 presents data for Spring 1990 on the incidence in each member state of short hours working (i.e. under 16 hours a week) and long hours working (over 48 hours).

The UK had relatively large proportions working both short hours and long hours. The high proportions working under 16 hours a week in the UK, the Netherlands and Denmark reflect the relatively high share of part-time work in these countries. Only Greece and Ireland had higher proportions working over 48 hours a week. A distinguishing feature of the UK is that long hours working is quite common among employees. Over 15 per cent of UK employees worked over 48 hours a week: elsewhere, only in Ireland (8.2 per cent) and France (5.3 per cent) was the figure above 5 per cent. Among non-employees (the self-employed and family workers), however, long hours working was common throughout the EU. The proportion of this group working over 48 hours was over a third in every member state except Italy and Spain. In Ireland, the figure was over two thirds (compared with 42.2 per cent for the UK).

Figure 4.10 looks at the tails of the distribution of working hours. A summary measure of the dispersion of the entire distribution, the standard deviation, is presented in Figure 4.11.

Across all those in employment, the UK had the greatest dispersion in usual hours worked, slightly higher than Ireland and the Netherlands. This is obviously a consequence of relatively large proportions of people with working hours at the top

Figure 4.10 Incidence of short and long hours working in EU member states, 1990

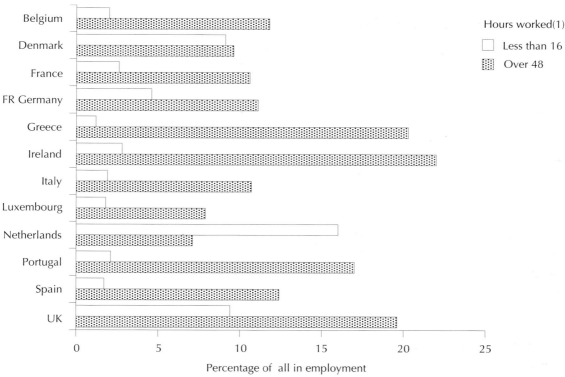

Notes

1 *Total usual weekly hours.*

Source: Watson (1993), Table 3.

Figure 4.11 Dispersion of working time in EU member states, 1990

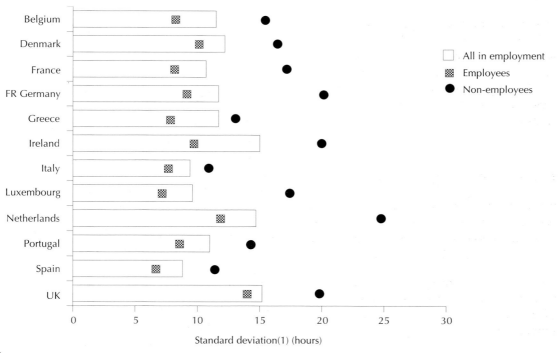

Notes

1 *Total usual weekly hours.*

Source: Watson (1993), Table 3.

and bottom ends of the distribution. Again, the UK is not out of step if one looks at non-employees.

CEC (1994) presents some evidence on recent trends. Between 1983 and 1992, average working time for employees fell in every member state. The fall in the UK was the second smallest (behind Italy), at about 1 hour per week. In most other countries, the fall in average working time was mainly due to a reduction in the 'normal' working week. However, in the UK, graphical analyses suggest that the reduction in the mean of the working time distribution has been accompanied by an increase in its dispersion (consistent with Figure 4.8).

There are also differences across the EU in the frequency of specific forms of 'flexible' working patterns. Figure 4.12 presents data on the incidence of shiftwork from a 1989 survey of employees.

A third of those in employment in the UK worked shifts on at least some occasions - along with Spain, one of the highest proportions in the EU.

CEC (1994) presents 1992 European LFS data which shows that the UK had relatively high proportions of employees with other 'flexible' working arrangements. The UK had the highest proportion of employees who worked nights (ahead of Denmark and Germany). Saturday working was more common in most countries, and the UK is not exceptional here. However, the UK also had the highest proportion of employees who worked on Sundays.

It is noticeable, however, that the proportions of UK employees who said they 'usually' worked nights or at weekends were fairly close to the EU average. The difference was in the higher proportion who 'sometimes' work at nights or weekends.

Most EU member states have regulations, laid down in statute and/or reinforced by collective agreements, that place limits on the hours employees can work. These conditions typically include a maximum length of working week, as well as minimum rest periods, maximum overtime periods etc. Their origin can be traced to an ILO Convention of 1919. In contrast, the UK is the only member state where there are no mandated limits on the length of the working day or week. As a result, Grubb and

Figure 4.12   Incidence of shiftwork in EU member states, 1989

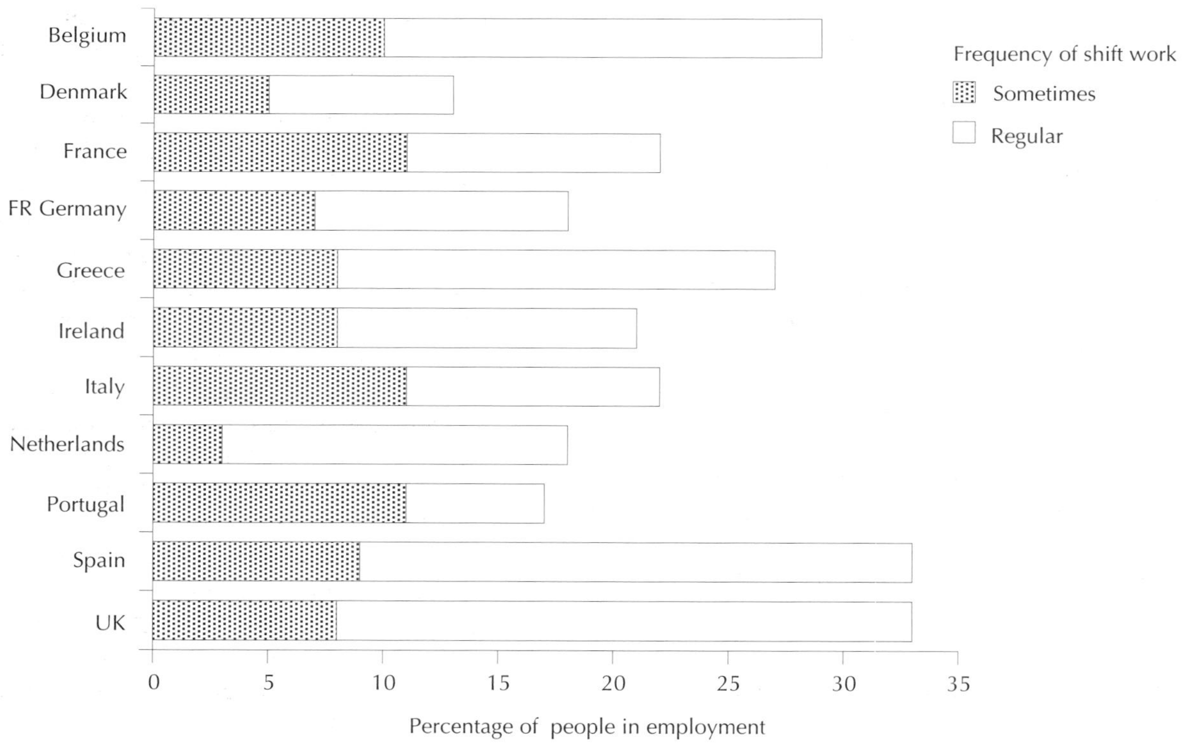

Percentage of people in employment

Source: CEC (1991).

Wells (1993) place the UK at the bottom (least stringent) of their rank ordering for regulation of working time.

Some very persuasive evidence on the impact of regulation is presented in Watson (1992) and CEC (1994). In most EU member states, there are particular 'spikes' in the distribution of hours worked. These 'spikes' tend to correspond with the provisions of regulations and collective agreements. The UK is the exception to this because there is no 'standard' working week defined in regulations. Hence Watson (1992) shows that, in 1989, the modal number of hours worked in the UK was 40 hours a week. But only 10 per cent of employees actually worked this number of hours. In other EU countries, the percentage working the modal number of hours varied from 30 per cent in Germany and the Netherlands (both at 38 hours) to as many as 83 per cent in Luxembourg (at 40 hours).

These analyses only covered employees. Figures 4.10 and 4.11 suggest the dispersion of working time is considerably greater among non-employees throughout the EU. This may be because regulations governing working time tend to exclude this group.

Grubb and Wells (1993) also examined the impact of working time regulations. They show that countries with the most stringent restrictions on normal working time (such as maximum working weeks) tended to have the shortest average working weeks. Similarly, restrictions on overtime and night work appeared to be effective in curtailing work above 'normal' hours and night working respectively. Interestingly, though, they found no evidence that restrictions on weekend working reduce the incidence of weekend work.

The trend in the regulation of working time within the EU since the end of the 1970s has been mixed. While the UK has removed residual restrictions, other countries reduced the maximum working week (e.g. France, Belgium). At the same time, there have been attempts to introduce greater flexibility within a regulated framework. Collective agreements on working time negotiated in Germany during the 1980s embodied this approach. However, there is still a considerable gap between the UK and the regulated regimes of other member states.

d)   Summary and conclusions

- Flexibility on the intensive margin can be achieved through changes in the number of hours worked. Analytically, one can distinguish between flexibility in the average number of hours worked (achieved through practices such as overtime or short-time working) and flexibility in working patterns *given* a specific number of hours worked.

- Average hours worked have been on a downwards trend for much of the post-War period, as the 'basic' working week has been reduced. This trend, however, levelled off in the 1980s.

- Most paid overtime is worked by male, manual employees. For this group, overtime hours form a significant proportion of total hours worked.

- The volume of overtime worked varies over the cycle. Overtime would appear to be an important means of securing short-term flexibility in the manufacturing sector.

- Short-time working has been uncommon in Britain, apart from a short period in the early 1980s, which may have been the result of government employment measures.

- There appears to be considerable diversity in working time patterns. There is a wide spread in terms of numbers of hours worked, numbers of days worked etc. The evidence also suggests that the distribution of working hours widened between 1984 and 1994.

- Considerable numbers of people have working time arrangements that may be conducive to flexibility on the intensive margin. These range from working time arrangements contingent on demand (e.g. annual hours contracts) to less formal modes, such as flexitime.

- Compared with other EU member states, the dispersion of hours worked by employees in the UK is relatively wide. This is not the case, however, when non-employees are included.

- The UK has a relatively high proportion of people working both long and short hours. In most other countries, the majority of employees work a 'standard' number of hours.

- The UK has relatively high proportions of employees working shifts, at nights, and at weekends. These arrangements appear to be more widely spread among the workforce on an occasional or periodic basis.

- The UK has fewer constraints on employers' and employees' freedom to structure working time than any other country in the EU. In this respect, the UK is similar to the USA[3]. The evidence suggests the scope for greater flexibility and diversity is taken up.

Footnotes to Chapter 4

1. Note this is overtime hours worked *per employee*, including employees who do not work any overtime.

2. The time series only includes full-time employees, and only counts people who received some form of premium payment for working shifts. Bosworth (1994) found that LFS data suggests that a slightly higher percentage of people in employment considered themselves to be working shifts.

3. The UK may even have a more liberal regime than the USA, given the existence of federal regulations setting down minimum overtime premia for people working over 40 hours a week.

Chapter 5
Functional flexibility

Functional flexibility is the degree of adaptability that firms possess in allocating labour between different parts of the production process, i.e. the efficiency of the internal allocation of labour.

In order to illustrate the concept, consider what a firm with full functional flexibility would look like. Assume the production process has a number of different, sequential parts to it. Alternatively, the firm could produce a number of outputs using the same plant and machinery. In a functionally flexible firm, employees could be readily re-assigned to different parts of the production process in response to predicted or unpredicted changes - such as sudden surges in demand, bottlenecks, seasonal patterns, absenteeism etc. A further development might be the development of autonomous work groups - a team of people who, between them, are responsible for carrying out some or all of the various stages in the production process, with members being competent to perform some or all of these tasks.

Functional flexibility will not be for everyone. Employers are likely to pursue it to varying degrees, depending on the costs and benefits involved. The benefits are likely to be greater productivity. The costs arise through the necessary investment in physical and human capital. The balance of these costs and benefits will vary depending upon the characteristics of the workforce and the production process. The question is whether there are other constraints on firms' ability to achieve functional flexibility.

a)   Functional flexibility in Britain

While the concept of functional flexibility is quite readily grasped, operational definitions are more difficult. Nevertheless, there is evidence that functional flexibility increased during the 1980s.

Daniel (1987) reports results for manufacturing establishments drawn from the 1984 WIRS, based upon a supplementary questionnaire administered to production managers. Respondents tended to be from relatively large, unionised workplaces. Daniel found that 43 per cent of the establishments interviewed had taken specific steps to increase the flexibility of their workforce, such as the relaxation of job demarcations, or the creation of new

multiskilled grades. Changes of this kind were most often associated with the introduction of organisational change (83 per cent of these establishments) and advanced technical change (52 per cent). Virtually all the establishments surveyed adopted some (admittedly limited) 'flexible' practices, such as machine operators also undertaking cleaning or maintenance work.

Other studies, based on less reliable or comprehensive sampling frames, tend to support these conclusions. Ingram (1991a) analysed data from the CBI's Pay Databank, which covers bargaining units in the private manufacturing sector. He found that about a third of wage negotiations each year included bargaining over working practices and other means of increasing productivity. The analysis, which covered the period between 1979 and 1989, found this proportion to be fairly stable from year to year. It is not possible to tell if this proportion was higher or lower than in earlier years.

Marsden and Thompson (1990) studied the contents of 137 agreements reported in the industrial relations press between 1980 and 1987. In total, these agreements were estimated to cover about 10 per cent of all manual workers in manufacturing industry, although there appears to have been a bias towards the engineering industry. The authors concluded that these agreements did represent a break with the productivity bargaining of the 1960s and 1970s. The most common changes introduced were more flexible deployment rules (48 per cent of cases), relaxation of job demarcation rules (30 per cent), and changes to grading structures (20 per cent).

Dunn and Wright (1994) analysed the contents of 50 collective agreements in both 1979 and 1990. The sample mainly covered large firms in the manufacturing sector. They also found evidence of an increase in the extent to which flexible working practices were part of collective agreements. By 1990, a third of the sample had flexibility agreements, and a number of others had adopted specific measures consistent with greater functional flexibility, such as simplifying grade structures and removing job demarcations.

In contrast, Cross (1988) found little evidence of formal agreements to change working practices on 'brownfield' sites. Of the 450 groups of manufacturing workers covered by this study, only 13 per cent were classed as having made such an agreement.

Most of the existing work only covers the manufacturing sector. Little is known about the extent or growth of functional flexibility in the service sector.

Another way of approaching the topic is to consider the existence of *constraints* to functional flexibility. Traditionally, excessive job demarcation has been seen as a particular problem in Britain. As noted above, many employers appear to have attempted to reduce job demarcations. They often appear to have (at least partially) succeeded.

Table 5.1   Constraints on managers' ability to organise work among non-managerial employees, 1990

Percentages of establishments with 25 or more employees reporting limits on the way management can organise work, Great Britain	
Type of constraint[1]	%
Union-related	16
Workforce-related	13
Management-related	8
Any workplace-related constraint	24
Any external constraint	7
Any constraint	32

Notes

1   *Managers could identify more than one constraint.*

Source: 1990 WIRS, Millward, Stevens, Smart and Hawes (1992), Table 9.3.

In the 1990 WIRS, managers were asked if there were constraints on their ability to organise work as they saw fit. Table 5.1 shows that only a third of managers reported any such constraints. For most employers, functional flexibility would appear to be possible if they want it. There is no clear evidence on trends over time[1].

The 1990 WIRS suggested that, where constraints existed, they were not always 'institutional' in form, i.e. related to trade union or employee opposition, or due to limits imposed by higher level management. Such responses appear to have been only slightly more common than 'economic' constraints associated with a lack of skills among the workforce, managerial expertise, or limits imposed by equipments or premises.

Thus, even if institutional constraints to flexibility were widespread at the beginning of the 1980s, they were not a barrier to functional flexibility in most workplaces by the end of the decade. It will not

have been in every employer's interests to pursue functional flexibility to the hilt. But where it has, increased functional flexibility may have contributed towards improved productivity. Indeed, Marsden and Thompson (1990) suggest that, while the bulk of productivity improvements are due to changes to working methods (such as new technology), changes in working practices may have been a necessary enabling factor.

b)   International comparisons

A lack of internationally comparable data means little can be said about the experience of other countries. OECD (1986) discusses some of the relevant issues, but presents little in the way of hard data. Its analysis suggests that constraints on functional flexibility, such as occupational demarcation, tended at that time to be most pronounced in the UK and the USA. At the other end of the spectrum was Japan, where there is a high degree of functional flexibility within large enterprises.

Lane (1988), in a pairwise comparison with Germany, identifies the lower proportion of skilled workers and the more rigid definition of job boundaries as factors inhibiting functional flexibility in Britain. Lorenz (1992) reaches similar conclusions, regarding functional flexibility as much further advanced in Germany and Japan than it is in either France or the UK.

This would seem to imply that the UK scores less well in terms of functional flexibility. In part this may be due to the scope for flexibility on the extensive margin.

c)   Summary and conclusions

- Functional flexibility is the ability of the firm to deploy labour on a wide range of tasks within the production process, in response to changes in demand and supply conditions.

- 'Full-blown' functional flexibility appears to be something of a rarity in Britain, perhaps because it involves costs as well as benefits for the employer.

- There is evidence, however, that manufacturing firms have taken steps during the 1980s to remove some of the barriers to functional flexibility, especially rigid job demarcation.

- More generally, by 1990, managers in less than a third of workplaces felt there were any constraints on their ability to organise work as they saw fit.

- Although the evidence to hand is very limited indeed, it seems likely that the degree of functional flexibility in the UK is relatively low by international standards, especially when compared to Japan and Germany.

Footnotes to Chapter 5

1. Daniel (1987) reports responses to a similar question put to production managers in 1984, on the constraints they faced in implementing technical change. The percentage facing constraints of some kind (34 per cent) was almost identical to the results from the 1990 survey displayed in Table 5.1. Daniel suggests this was a significant reduction when compared to earlier research from the 1960s and 1970s. However, the incompatibility of the 1984 and 1990 WIRS questions means that comparisons over time cannot be pursued any further.

Chapter 6
Labour mobility

In a flexible labour market, labour should be mobile. Labour mobility has a number of dimensions. It can be thought of as the degree to which people are prepared to move, in response to labour market phenomena, between jobs, industries, occupations and localities.

This chapter first considers 'job mobility' - movement between economic states, jobs, industries and occupations. It then concentrates on geographical mobility, an issue of interest to both researchers and policy-makers.

Three preliminary points need to be made:

- A degree of labour mobility is essential for labour market flexibility. But it is less clear *a priori* if there is a simple monotonic relationship between labour mobility and allocative efficiency. Movement between jobs (turnover) may help employment levels adjust to changing demand conditions, but it may also discourage investment in job-specific education and training.

- Most of the data presented in this section is drawn from the LFS. Each Spring, the survey asks respondents what they were doing one year previously. The LFS data used in this chapter compares peoples' situation at the time of the survey with that one year ago. Some people will change jobs, or move regions, more than once during the year preceding the survey. Hence this data will understate the actual degree of fluidity and mobility in the labour market.

- Due to constraints on data accessibility and changes over time in definitions of economic activity, most of the data presented in this chapter only covers the period between 1985 and 1994. The run of data does not cover a full cycle, and cyclical effects appear to be important. It is therefore difficult to draw firm conclusions about trends.

a) Job mobility

Changes of economic status

Mobility between economic states can include movements in and out of the labour force, as well as movements in and out of employment. However, the relationship between mobility and labour market flexibility is both complicated and ambiguous.

From the supply-side of the market, some conclusions can be drawn. The potentially damaging economic and social consequences of long-term unemployment suggest it is desirable for people to have a high exit rate *from* unemployment. It is less clear if relatively high exit rates from employment into unemployment or inactivity are also problematic. A degree of turnover among the working population - even if it involved a spell of unemployment or inactivity - could well speed up the reallocation of labour and be beneficial, provided the exit rate from unemployment was high enough.

There are also demand-side considerations. Entry rates into (and exit rates out of) employment will vary over the cycle. These rates may also reflect more deep-seated structural changes in the economy.

The discussion above suggests that changes in economic status are difficult to interpret in isolation. The LFS data tend to support this conclusion. Figure 6.1 charts the percentage of the population of working age whose economic status - in terms of being employed, unemployed or inactive - was different from a year previously.

Over the period 1985-1994, between 12 and 15 per cent of people of working age had a different economic status from the year previously. In absolute terms, the number of people involved varied between 4.5 million in 1990 and 5.2 million in 1987[1].

Table 6.1 may be more informative. It presents estimates of the *ex post* probability of someone having moved from one state to another.

For each of the three economic states identified, the most common outcome is for people to have the same status as one year previously. Thus, in any given year, over 90 per cent of people employed one year ago were in employment at the time of the survey; similarly, about three quarters of the economically inactive did not record a change of status; and 40 to 50 per cent of the unemployed also fall into this category.

The transition probabilities appear to vary over the cycle. There are no other clear patterns in the data. The underlying structure of movements in and out of inactivity, employment and unemployment seem to have remained fairly stable.

This conclusion, however, may not hold over a longer time period. Blanchflower and Freeman (1994) presented similar data to that in Table 6.1, but covering the period 1975-1990. Their results will be affected by changes in classification and other discontinuities, but broad comparisons may be

Figure 6.1   People changing economic status, 1985-1994

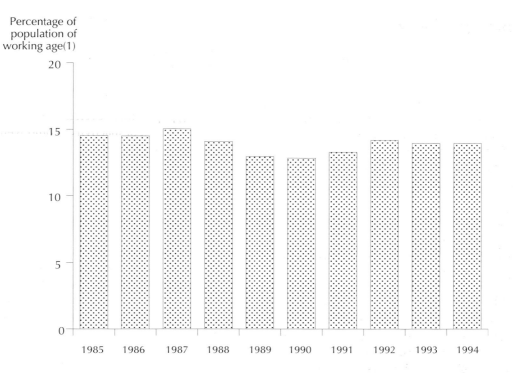

Notes

1. People of working age (men aged 16-64, women aged 16-59) whose economic status (in terms of employment, unemployment or inactivity) differed from one year previously, United Kingdom.

Source: Labour Force Surveys, Spring.

Table 6.1   Probabilities of changing economic status, 1985-1994

Economic status one year before survey[2](a)	Economic status at time of survey[2](b)	Transition probability = (b)/(a)									
		1985	**1986**	**1987**	**1988**	**1989**	**1990**	**1991**	**1992**	**1993**	**1994**
Employed	Employed	0.93	0.93	0.93	0.94	0.95	0.94	0.93	0.92	0.92	0.93
	Unemployed	0.04	0.04	0.04	0.03	0.03	0.03	0.04	0.05	0.04	0.03
	Inactive	0.03	0.03	0.03	0.03	0.03	0.03	0.03	0.04	0.04	0.03
Unemployed	Employed	0.31	0.31	0.34	0.39	0.40	0.41	0.36	0.32	0.32	0.34
	Unemployed	0.52	0.51	0.49	0.45	0.44	0.44	0.49	0.51	0.52	0.50
	Inactive	0.17	0.18	0.17	0.17	0.16	0.15	0.15	0.17	0.16	0.16
Inactive	Employed	0.17	0.17	0.18	0.19	0.20	0.20	0.18	0.18	0.16	0.17
	Unemployed	0.08	0.08	0.07	0.07	0.06	0.07	0.07	0.06	0.06	0.06
	Inactive	0.75	0.75	0.74	0.74	0.73	0.74	0.75	0.76	0.78	0.77

People of working age[1], United Kingdom

Notes

1   Men aged 16-64, women aged 16-59.

2   Definitions of economic activity at the time of the survey are based on ILO definitions, whereas economic status one year previously is self-assessed.

Source: Labour Force Surveys, Spring.

possible. On these estimates, the probability of the unemployed moving into employment seems to have declined over time. Blanchflower and Freeman also distinguish the self-employed from employees, and find that movements both into and out of self-employment increased considerably between 1979 and 1990. Thus, while mobility between economic states may not have changed greatly since 1985, there may have been more substantial changes during the late 1970s and early 1980s.

Discussion of job mobility now adopts a narrower focus, concentrating on movements of people between jobs that may or may not involve an intervening spell of short term unemployment or inactivity.

Job changes can facilitate the efficient reallocation of labour between firms, sectors and occupations. Measures of inter-firm mobility have been identified as an indicator of flexibility (OECD (1986), Boyer (1987)). 'Excessive' mobility, though, may not always be desirable on efficiency grounds. The arguments are set out in OECD (1986). In situations where employees need to acquire significant amounts of firm-specific human capital to reach maximum productive efficiency, too much movement between employers would not be in employers' or employees' interests. In these circumstances, internal labour markets may well evolve.

Taking one measure of inter-firm mobility from Chapter 3, turnover rates in UK manufacturing fell considerably during the 1960s and 1970s, before stabilising in the first half of the 1980s.

A measure of inter-firm mobility covering the whole economy is available from the LFS. This is the number of people in employment at the time of the survey, and in employment a year before, who had changed their employer in the mean time. This measure is only a proxy for the actual rate of inter-firm mobility, as it fails to identify people who changed employers more than once.

Table 6.2 shows that the number of people who were in employment at both dates, and who had moved jobs during the year, varied between 3.3 million in 1990 and about 2.1 million in 1993. While too short a period to be conclusive, the data does suggest the volume of job changes may be procyclical: more job opportunities encourage job-to-job quits, while people who lose their job get back to work more quickly.

Some indicative evidence on trends over a longer period is available from the General Household Survey (GHS). Figure 6.2 presents a time series of the percentage of workers who had started their present job within the previous 12 months[2].

Table 6.2   Job changes, 1987-1994

Base: People of working age[1] who were in employment both at the time of the survey and twelve months previously[2], United Kingdom

	1987	1988	1989	1990	1991	1992	1993	1994
Number of people changing employers (thousands):								
Men	1,360	1,567	1,777	1,789	1,555	1,277	1,124	1,157
Women	1,083	1,230	1,493	1,510	1,289	1,111	967	977
All persons	**2,442**	**2,796**	**3,270**	**3,299**	**2,844**	**2,386**	**2,091**	**2,135**
As a percentage of base:								
Men	10.1	11.4	12.6	12.5	10.8	9.0	8.1	8.5
Women	11.6	12.6	14.7	14.6	12.3	10.4	9.0	9.2
All persons	**10.7**	**11.9**	**13.5**	**13.3**	**11.4**	**9.6**	**8.5**	**8.8**

Notes

1   Men aged 16-64, women aged 16-59.

2   Excludes cases where data is not available or the question is not applicable, or where the respondent's workplace is outside the UK.

Source: Labour Force Surveys, Spring.

Figure 6.2 confirms that job mobility is indeed procyclical. Cyclical conditions apart, there is no evidence of any significant change in the 'underlying' level of job mobility.

Inter-industry mobility is of particular relevance when the structure of the economy is changing. If there are sizeable flows of labour between industries, adjustment may be more easily accomplished. On the other hand, if employees find it difficult, or are unwilling, to change industry, mismatch and structural unemployment may be the result.

Figure 6.3 charts the number of job changes that also involved a change of industry. 'Industry' is defined here at the one-digit, Divisional level of the 1980 SIC. The degree of industrial disaggregation clearly affects estimates of inter-industry mobility: a higher level sectoral analysis (between manufacturing and services) would produce fewer changes of industry; a finer disaggregation (two-digit, say) would produce more.

As with overall job changes, there is a procyclical pattern to the data. Depending upon the year, between 42 and 48 per cent of all job moves involved a change of industry Division.

Table 6.3 presents estimates of mobility by industry Division. To allow for differential rates of employment growth, a mobility score has been constructed which measures the overall scale of movement in and out of each industry.

The mobility score shows the same time-series pattern as the job change data graphed in Figure 6.3. Women were more likely to change their industry of employment than men. In addition, there were consistent differences between industries. Mobility was relatively high in parts of manufacturing industry (Divisions 2 and 4) as well as in parts of the service sector (Divisions 6 and 8). Mobility was noticeably low in Division 9, which includes most white-collar public sector industries.

Table 6.4 shows that considerable numbers of people changed their occupation each year - between 10 and 15 per cent of all people in employment at the time of the LFS who were also employed a year before. Note changes of occupation are self-defined. Analyses using occupational classification systems produce somewhat smaller estimates of overall occupational mobility (see Employment Department (1991), pp. 443-444). Again, there is a distinct, possibly procyclical, pattern to the data[3].

Figure 6.2   Job mobility in Britain, 1971-1991

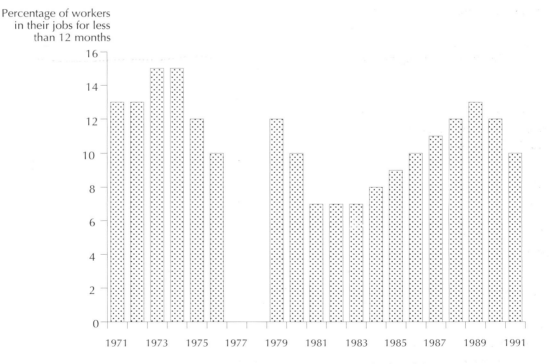

Percentage of workers in their jobs for less than 12 months

Notes

This data was not collected in the 1977, 1978 and 1992 surveys.

Source: General Household Survey.

Figure 6.3   Numbers of job changes between industries, 1985-1993

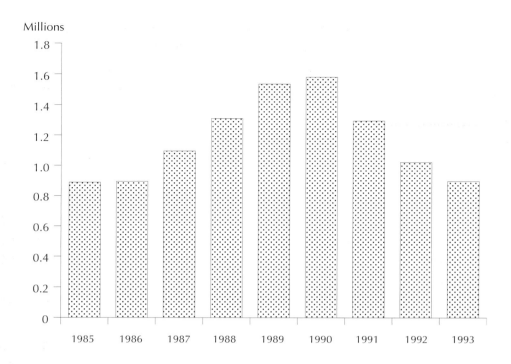

Notes

People of working age (men aged 16-64, women aged 16-59) in employment at the time of the survey and one year previously, who had changed industry (measured at the 1980 SIC Divisional level), United Kingdom.

Source: Labour Force Surveys, Spring.

The table also provides an indication of the extent to which changes of occupation occurred through external as opposed to internal labour market channels. The external labour market seems to have been the more important route for occupational change, especially for women (although it is not possible to identify whether changes of employer and occupation took place at the same time).

These findings suggest that occupational mobility is a quantitatively significant phenomenon[4]. While occupational mobility is clearly related to human capital formation, the data presented here is not a direct measure. Occupational mobility can be 'downwards' (possibly involving the depreciation or scrapping of human capital) as well as 'upwards'. Further analysis of these occupational moves would be needed to distinguish between the various effects.

b)   Geographical mobility

The spatial mobility of labour has received particular and continuing attention, both from social scientists and policy makers. Insufficient geographical mobility has often been diagnosed as one of the causes of regional economic disparities. This has in turn led to regional policies designed to encourage firms to locate in economically disadvantaged areas. In other words, compensating for labour immobility by providing incentives for relatively mobile capital (and hence jobs) to relocate.

Geographical mobility may bring efficiency gains. The quantity and quality of job matches is likely to be affected by the geographical restrictions that potential workers place on their job search activities[5]. Searching for work over a wide area - and being prepared to move to take up employment - involves financial and non-financial costs. The balance of costs and benefits is likely to vary widely between individuals.

The analysis of geographical mobility has often concentrated on the behaviour of the unemployed, and the extent to which they are prepared to travel or migrate in search of work. However, mobility among the employed and the inactive is also important.

Table 6.3   Job changes between industries, 1985-1993

Base: People of working age[1] who were in employment both at the time at the survey and twelve months previously[2], United Kingdom

Industry (1980 SIC Division):	Mobility score[3]:								
	1985	1986	1987	1988	1989	1990	1991	1992	1993
0 Agriculture, fishing, forestry	*	*	*	*	4.9	5.8	*	*	*
1 Energy and water supply	*	*	*	*	*	5.3	*	*	*
2 Mineral extraction etc.	5.5	4.8	6.3	6.7	8.4	8.0	7.4	5.9	4.8
3 Metal goods, engineering etc.	4.4	4.2	5.6	6.2	7.4	7.2	5.9	4.6	4.0
4 Other manufacturing	5.1	5.3	5.9	7.9	8.5	8.9	7.4	5.3	4.8
5 Construction	4.2	4.5	5.0	6.0	6.1	6.5	5.2	4.5	3.9
6 Distribution, hotels and catering, repairs	5.4	5.3	6.2	7.0	8.1	8.0	6.6	5.3	4.7
7 Transport and communications	4.3	4.2	5.2	6.9	7.7	7.8	6.1	4.7	4.5
8 Banking, finance, business services	5.5	5.6	6.8	7.4	8.0	8.0	6.6	4.9	4.6
9 Other services	3.0	2.9	3.5	3.9	4.5	4.5	3.8	3.1	2.7
All industries									
Men	3.6	3.5	4.5	5.1	5.8	5.8	4.8	4.1	3.7
Women	4.4	4.4	5.0	5.9	6.7	6.9	5.6	5.0	4.3
All persons	**3.9**	**3.9**	**4.7**	**5.4**	**6.2**	**6.3**	**5.2**	**4.5**	**3.9**

Notes

1   *Men aged 16-64, women aged 16-59.*

2   *Excludes cases where data is not available or the question is not applicable, or where the respondent's workplace is outside the UK.*

3   *The mobility score for an industry is calculated as the arithmetic mean of the inflow and outflow rates from that industry over the twelve month period, i.e. by the expression*

$$M_i = \frac{1}{2} \left[\frac{N_{it\text{-}1,jt}}{N_{it\text{-}1}} + \frac{N_{it,jt\text{-}1}}{N_{it}} \right]$$

where M_i is the mobility score, N is employment, i and j are industry subscripts, and t is a time subscript, such that $N_{it,jt\text{-}1}$ represents the number of people employed in industry i at the time of the LFS who had been employed in industry j ($j{\neq}i$) one year before the survey. The score is expressed here as a percentage.

*   *indicates cases where the absolute numbers involved are less than 30,000, and therefore unreliable.*

Source: Labour Force Surveys, Spring.

Table 6.4   Job changes between occupations, 1986-1994

Base: People of working age[1] who were in employment both at the time at the survey and twelve months previously[2], United Kingdom

	1986	1987	1988	1989	1990	1991	1992	1993	1994
Number of people changing occupation[3] (thousands):									
Men	1,264	1,366	1,715	1,962	1,980	1,629	1,312	1,191	1,182
Women	1,020	1,133	1,414	1,671	1,701	1,433	1,207	1,079	1,089
All persons	**2,284**	**2,497**	**3,128**	**3,633**	**3,681**	**3,062**	**2,519**	**2,269**	**2,271**
As a percentage of base:									
Men	9.4	10.1	12.5	13.9	13.8	11.3	9.2	8.6	8.7
Women	11.2	12.1	14.5	16.5	16.4	13.6	11.3	10.0	10.2
All persons	**10.1**	**10.9**	**13.3**	**15.0**	**14.9**	**12.3**	**10.1**	**9.2**	**9.4**
Percentage of people changing occupation who also changed employer[4]:									
Men	64.5	69.0	63.6	65.2	65.0	63.8	61.7	59.4	60.2
Women	73.1	73.8	66.5	69.4	68.2	67.4	65.4	63.0	64.6
All persons	68.3	71.3	67.1	67.2	66.5	65.4	63.4	61.1	62.3

Notes

1   *Men aged 16-64, women aged 16-59.*

2   *Excludes cases where data is not available or the question is not applicable, or where the respondent's workplace is outside the UK.*

3   *Changes of occupation are self-defined.*

4   *Changes of occupation and employer need not have taken place at the same time.*

Source: Labour Force Surveys, Spring.

Actual, observed migration flows can be used as a quantitative indicator of labour mobility. While some people migrate for reasons unconnected with the labour market, all migration has a direct or indirect impact on the labour market, whatever its motivation[6].

This section concentrates on the *inter-regional* mobility of labour. There are three reasons for this choice of geographical area:

•   Data is most readily available at the regional level;

•   Inter-regional mobility has been the most intensively studied form of mobility;

•   Restricting the analysis to moves between regions should exclude most commuting and short-distance moves unconnected with the labour market.

Nevertheless, economic disparities exist within, as well as between, regions. So intra-regional labour mobility is a potentially important source of flexibility. Indeed, significant barriers to mobility can exist within much smaller areas[7].

There are two principal sources of data on inter-regional migration within Britain - the National Health Service Central Register (NHSCR), and the LFS. Neither is entirely satisfactory. The NHSCR data records all migrants, including children and the retired, and may understate migration among the most mobile. The LFS data is based on comparisons of people's residence at the time of the survey with their stated region of residence one year previously, so it is not true flow data. It is also subject to sampling error. Appendix 1 has further information on both data sources.

Figure 6.4 presents estimates of the overall rate of inter-regional migration. The chart presents a time series drawn from the NHSCR for the period 1975-1992, as well as two time series drawn from the LFS. Although each series estimates migration as a percentage of the population, the age coverage is different in each case. There is also a difference in timing. The NHSCR series measures migration flows over a calendar year, whereas the LFS series measure changes of region from Spring to Spring.

The NHSCR data shows that the gross inter-regional migration rate varied between 1.4 and 1.8 per cent. Whereas the migration rate appears to have been on a downwards trend during the second half of the 1970s, it picked up significantly in the second half of the 1980s before easing off in the early 1990s[8].

Since the LFS data are on different bases, the series cannot be directly compared. However, the trend over time of each appears broadly consistent with the NHSCR series. The main exceptions to this are the sharp increase in the migration rate recorded in the 1989 LFS and a significant fall from 1992 onwards.

The NHSCR series suggests that the aggregate inter-regional migration rate may be procyclical. Upturns and downturns in the series seem to fit changing conditions in both housing and labour markets.

The data in Figure 6.4 measured *gross* inter-regional migration. Table 6.5 presents estimates of *net* inter-regional migration rates. Net migration flows (i.e. immigrants minus emigrants) are typically more modest as most regions experienced substantial inflows of population as well as outflows.

In most regions, net migration rates have been within a band of ±0.5 per cent. The exceptions are East Anglia and the South West, where net in-migration rates have tended to be higher.

In general, the distribution of net migration rates has remained reasonably stable. East Anglia, the South West, the East Midlands and Wales have tended to be net 'importers' of people, whereas the West Midlands, the North West and the North have consistently been net 'exporters'. The South East, the largest single region, had positive net migration rates during the first half of the 1980s, but significant net outflows since 1987. In contrast, Yorkshire and Humberside and Scotland - two regions where out-migration has tended to exceed in-migration - have seen a change in their relative position since the end of the 1980s.

Figure 6.4   Regional migration within Britain, 1975-1994

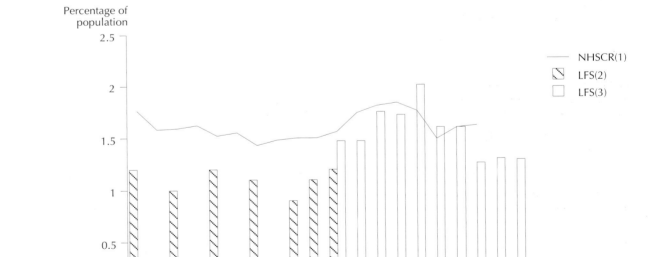

Notes

1   Migration as a percentage of the population, all ages.

2   Migration as a percentage of the population aged 16 or over.

3   Migration as a percentage of the population of working age (men aged 16-64, women aged 16-59).

Sources: CSO Regional Trends; OECD (1990b); Labour Force Surveys, Spring.

With the possible exception of the South East, the pattern of net inter-regional migration rates bears some resemblance to regional economic disparities. Crude comparisons can be drawn by examining the correlations between net migration rates and average earnings and unemployment.

Figure 6.5 shows that net migration rates have tended to be negatively correlated with average earnings, i.e. regions with high earnings are associated with net out-migration. On the face of it, these results are counter-intuitive: high wage regions ought to attract migrants. A possible explanation is that regions with relatively low earnings may be more successful in creating employment, and this will tend to attract migrants[9].

Figure 6.6 shows that net migration rates also tend to be negatively correlated with regional unemployment rates, i.e. high unemployment regions have net out-migration. This is consistent with standard theory. Note that the correlation became more pronounced during the late 1970s and early 1980s, as aggregate unemployment rose and overall migration rates declined.

Table 6.6 presents LFS data that puts inter-regional migration into context. While between 9 and 12 per cent of the population of working age changed their address during the course of a year, only about a fifth of these moves involved a change of region. The majority of changes of address are short-distance moves which may have little to do with the labour market[10].

Table 6.6 also presents estimates of job-related changes of address. LFS respondents who had changed address were simply asked if their move was 'job-related'. Responses were entirely subjective, and it is unclear how they should be interpreted (see Appendix 1); their presentation here is merely as a rough-and-ready guide to the potential strength of labour market influences on migration decisions. In fact, only a minority (between a fifth and a sixth) of changes of address were described as job-related. The proportion rises to around a third of inter-regional moves.

Table 6.5   Net migration flows between regions, 1975-1992

Net inter-regional migration flows (immigrants minus emigrants)[1] expressed as a percentage of the (mid year) population					
Region	1975	1979	1984	1989	1992
South East	-0.18	-0.07	0.04	-0.24	-0.21
East Anglia	1.23	0.97	0.67	0.34	0.38
South West	0.80	0.69	0.76	0.47	0.44
West Midlands	-0.31	-0.25	-0.25	-0.21	-0.12
East Midlands	0.13	0.34	0.13	0.18	0.24
Yorkshire and Humberside	-0.04	-0.12	-0.12	0.10	0.04
North West	-0.18	-0.28	-0.36	-0.05	-0.15
North	0.00	-0.16	-0.26	-0.03	0.03
Wales	0.29	0.18	0.11	0.42	0.12
Scotland	0.21	-0.15	-0.19	0.12	0.14
Dispersion of distribution[2]	0.46	0.40	0.37	0.24	0.21
Dispersion of distribution (excluding South East)[2]	0.46	0.42	0.39	0.22	0.19
Stability of distribution[3]	0.91	0.87	0.80	0.91	1.00
Stability of distribution (excluding South East)[3]	0.92	0.90	0.85	0.90	1.00

Notes

1   Migration flows within Great Britain, calendar years.

2   Unweighted standard deviation.

3   Pearson correlation coefficient between inter-regional migration rates in 1992 and those in earlier years.

Sources: NHSCR data reported in various CSO Regional Trends; OPCS Population Trends.

Figure 6.5   Correlation between inter-regional migration and earnings, 1975-1992

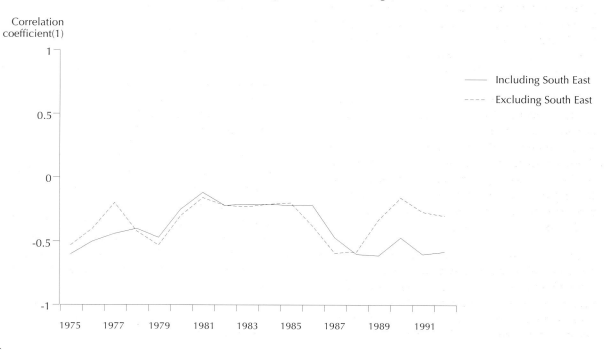

Notes

1   *Pearson correlation coefficient calculated across 9 standard regions between inter-regional net migration rates and average earnings (hourly earnings excluding overtime of all full-time employees whose pay for the survey period was unaffected by absence).*

Sources: NHSCR records, New Earnings Surveys.

Figure 6.6   Correlation between inter-regional migration and unemployment, 1975-1992

Notes

1   *Pearson correlation coefficient calculated across 9 standard regions between inter-regional net migration rates and unemployment rates (claimant unemployment adjusted for seasonality and discontinuities, expressed as a percentage of the workforce, April).*

Sources: NHSCR records, Employment Department.

The inability of unemployed people to move in search of work (or to take up a job offer) has long been regarded as an important cause of regional imbalances. This may be due to institutional barriers, such as public sector housing allocation policies, or because of the high financial and other costs that may be associated with long-distance moves. Table 6.7, however, shows that people unemployed a year before the LFS were more likely to have moved regions than people who had been in employment.

People who were inactive one year ago were the group most likely to have moved regions: young people entering or leaving higher education may account for much of the migration observed among this group.

Hughes and McCormick (1987) also suggest there is an occupational dimension to geographical mobility. People in manual occupations are less likely to move between regions than non-manuals. This may be due in part to differences in housing tenure: manual workers are more likely to occupy social rented housing, where transfer between areas can be difficult.

On balance, the data presented suggests that inter-regional migration rates are responsive to economic factors. This conclusion is supported by recent econometric studies, reviewed in Appendix 3. Net migration flows, in general, help to alleviate regional disparities in unemployment rates. However, the numbers involved are small. If other variables remained unchanged, migration on this scale would take many years to even out regional disparities. Furthermore, most of this adjustment appears to be taking place in the market for non-manual, rather than manual, workers (Evans and McCormick (1994)). This suggests that wage flexibility and capital mobility are also important if regional labour markets are to function efficiently.

While the evidence suggests that geographical mobility makes a significant (although modest) contribution to the flexibility and adaptability of the labour market, it is less clear if there has been any significant change in behaviour. Pissarides and Wadsworth (1989) found that labour market signals were less influential in shaping migration decisions in 1984 than they were in 1977, but this may reflect different cyclical conditions[11].

c)   International comparisons

Job mobility

Due to a lack of systematic and comparable data, international comparisons of job mobility are restricted to analyses of two partial and indirect sets of measures. These are measures of flows into and

Table 6.6   Changes of address and region, 1985-1992

	1985	1986	1987	1988	1989	1990	1991	1992	1993	1994
Number of moves (thousands)										
Changes of address	3,693	3,740	3,929	3,974	3,837	3,272	3,339	3,267		
Changes of address and region	480	484	578	570	671	538	539	426	440	435
Job-related changes of address	659	669	692	671	707	673	664			
Job-related changes of address and region	208	221	249	234	254	230	233			
As a percentage of the population of working age[1]										
Changes of address	11.31	11.39	11.88	11.98	11.47	9.78	9.94	9.46		
Changes of address and region	1.47	1.47	1.75	1.72	2.01	1.61	1.61	1.26	1.30	1.29
Job-related changes of address	2.02	2.04	2.09	2.02	2.11	2.01	1.98			
Job-related changes of address and region	0.64	0.67	0.75	0.71	0.76	0.69	0.69			

Notes

1   *Men aged 16-64 and women aged 16-59. Excludes cases where data is not available, and where people were resident outside Great Britain a year before the survey.*

Source: Labour Force Surveys, Spring.

Table 6.7   Inter-regional mobility by economic status, 1985-1992

Base: People of working age[1] who were resident in Great Britain a year before the survey and had moved regions within Britain by the time of the survey[2]

Economic status one year before the survey[3]	1985	1987	1990	1992
Employed	1.24	1.53	1.41	1.06
Unemployed	1.73	2.08	2.03	1.51
Economically inactive	2.02	2.25	2.16	1.88
All persons	**1.47**	**1.75**	**1.60**	**1.27**

Notes

1   Men aged 16-64, women aged 16-59.

2   Excludes cases where data is not available and where people were resident outside Great Britain a year before the survey.

3   Definitions of economic activity one year before the survey are self-assessed.

Source: Labour Force Surveys, Spring.

out of unemployment, and measures of turnover and job tenure.

Data on flows into and out of unemployment for fifteen OECD countries is graphed in Figure 6.7, drawn from a variety of sources: for most EU countries, the Labour Force Survey; for other countries, national sources.

Some clear differences seem to emerge. Certain countries (the USA, Canada, Australia) have high inflow and outflow rates. A number of other countries (Japan, Norway, Sweden) have more moderate inflow rates, but high outflow rates. Most other countries, principally EU member states, have relatively low inflow and outflow rates. Within this broad categorisation, the UK has relatively high inflow and outflow rates when compared to other EU member states. However, in this aspect, the UK labour market appears to be significantly less fluid than those of the USA, Canada and Australia.

The other set of partial indicators are those relating to turnover and job tenure. Recent comparisons of turnover rates are not available. OECD (1986) presented data for eight OECD countries - the G7 economies (minus Canada) plus Finland and Sweden - which came from national sources. In a number of instances, including the UK, the data only covered manufacturing industry[12]. Precise comparisons are therefore difficult to make, but the data nonetheless did reveal some sharp differences between countries: the USA and Finland had relatively high rates of turnover, and Japan and France had relatively low rates, while the UK held a middle-ranking position.

As Higuchi (1993) points out, turnover data does not indicate whether a few people change jobs very often or a larger number of people change jobs occasionally. Another partial indicator of the degree to which people change jobs is job tenure. OECD (1993) presents recent data for a number of countries, based on national sources, which is charted in Figure 6.8.

Average job tenure was shortest in Australia, the Netherlands and the USA, followed by Canada and the UK. In contrast, job tenure was longest in Japan, Germany and France.

More recent comparisons are available for EU member states (except Ireland). CEC (1994) presents data from European LFS's which shows that, in 1992, labour turnover in the UK (measured by the proportion of the employed who had been in their jobs for less than a year) was the fourth highest in the EU behind Spain, Denmark and the Netherlands. Turnover was lowest in Belgium, Italy and Greece.

There is, therefore, a fair degree of consistency between these results. The UK appears to lack the degree of movement in and out of work seen in Australia, the USA, Canada, and (possibly) the Nordic countries. Compared to other EU member states, however, job mobility in the UK appears relatively high. There is little solid evidence on trends.

Comparisons of industrial mobility can be made for EU member states (minus Italy). CEC (1994) calculated the rate of movement among the employed between industrial sectors (broadly

Figure 6.7   International comparisons of flows into and out of unemployment, 1979-1990/91

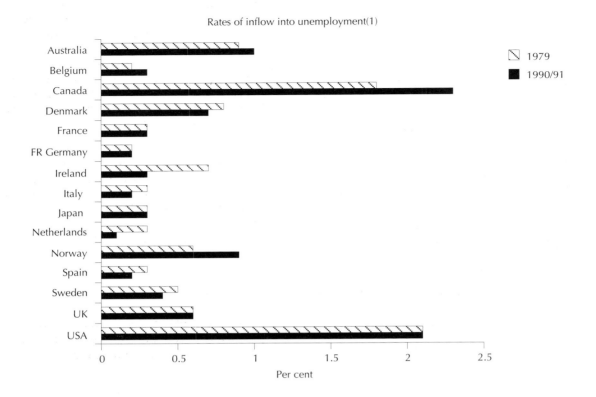

Rates of inflow into unemployment(1)

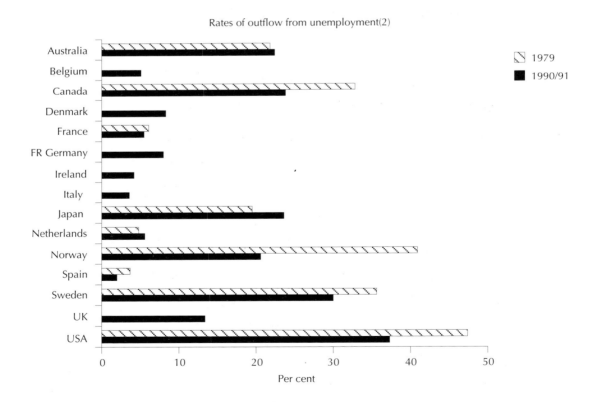

Rates of outflow from unemployment(2)

Notes

1   Total inflows into unemployment as a percentage of the population aged 15-64 (minus total unemployment).

2   Total outflows as a percentage of total unemployment.

Source: OECD (1993).

66

equivalent to SIC Divisions) over the period 1984-1992. On this measure, inter-industrial mobility in the UK was greater than anywhere else in the EU. Mobility was lowest in Belgium, Germany, Greece and Ireland.

There is less evidence on occupational mobility. OECD (1986) summarised the evidence available at the time. Comparisons between countries are inevitably complicated by differences in data sources, occupational classifications, and the time period over which mobility was measured. However, if occupational mobility is measured over the medium term (i.e. five to ten years), then it appears to have been greatest in the USA, followed by the UK and Germany. A comparison of occupational mobility over a single year (along the lines of Table 6.4) also suggested that occupational mobility was greater in the USA than in the UK. No recent analysis of trends is available.

Geographical mobility

Information on geographical mobility from a variety of countries was brought together in OECD (1990b). Table 6.8 summarises the main conclusions.

An important factor to bear in mind is the size of the 'regions' themselves. The Norwegian and Swedish

mobility rates appear to be high by international standards, but they measure flows between a large number of relatively small areas. At the other extreme is Australia, where the unit of measurement is the (generally much larger) state or territory. Given this, it seems likely that, 'mile for mile', mobility is greatest in the USA. Inter-regional mobility in the UK does not appear to be especially high or low. Mobility, however, may be greater in the UK than in France and Germany, and mobility rates in Italy seem to be very low[13].

Data presented in OECD (1990b) also suggests that, in most countries, net migration flows help to narrow regional disparities in unemployment. The majority of the evidence for other countries surveyed in that study suggests that adjustment through migration alone would take a long time. This is consistent with the evidence for Britain.

d)   Summary and conclusions

- Labour mobility is essential if labour is to be allocated and reallocated efficiently between industries, occupations and localities.

Figure 6.8   International comparisons of average job tenure, 1991

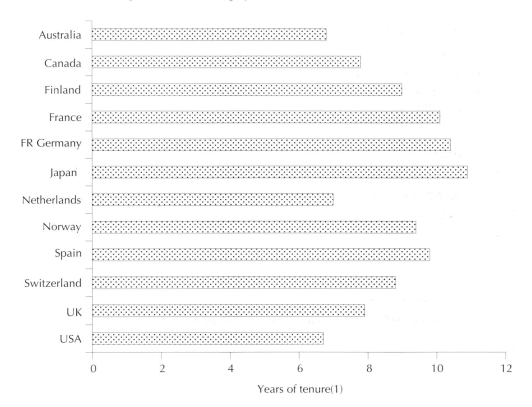

Notes

1   *Data are based on national sources, and measure time spent in current job (uncompleted spells). 1991, except Norway (1989); FR Germany, Japan and Netherlands (1990); and Spain (1992).*

Source: OECD (1993), Table 4.1.

- Most of the information on mobility in Britain is drawn from the LFS. This imposes two limitations on the analysis, and the conclusions that can be drawn from it. First, the LFS compares people's activity at two points in time, a year apart. It is not a true flow measure. Second, consistent and readily accessible data is only available from 1985 onwards. Conclusions about long-term trends can only be tentative.

- Large numbers of people change their economic status every year, between 12 and 15 per cent of people of working age.

- Among people in work, there are significant numbers of job moves (changes of employer) each year. Nearly half of all job moves involved a change of industry. Many also involved a change of occupation, although occupational mobility can occur without a change of employer.

- Time-series data suggests that, in the course of a year, between 1.4 and 1.8 per cent of the population move between regions. The overall migration rate appears to be procyclical. There is no evidence of an underlying trend in the time series.

- Net flows (immigrants minus emigrants) appear to be more modest, usually less than 0.5 per cent of the population. Certain regions - the South West, East Anglia, and the East Midlands - have tended to have net inflows of population. Other regions - the West Midlands, the North West, the North, Yorkshire and Humberside, and Scotland - have tended to have net outflows. These patterns may have changed slightly during the late 1980s and early 1990s.

- Both informal and econometric analyses suggest that net inter-regional migration flows respond to economic signals. These operate both in the labour market (through wage and unemployment disparities) and through house prices. However, regional labour market imbalances would take a long time to equalise on the basis of migration alone.

- Compared to other EU countries, mobility in and out of employment and unemployment appears to be relatively high in the UK. However, job mobility is not as great as in North America or Australia.

- Over the period 1984-1992, the UK had the highest rate of inter-industry mobility in the EU.

- Similar patterns are evident for geographical mobility. Compared to the UK, labour in the USA and Australia appears more likely to move around the country. Again, though, the UK compares favourably with other EU member states.

Table 6.8   Geographical mobility in selected OECD countries

Country	Relative size of geographical unit over which inter-regional migration flows measured	Assessment of relative *level* of inter-regional migration flows	Assessment of *trends* in numbers of inter-regional migrants
Australia	Large	Medium	Slight decline during early 1980s
Canada	Large	Medium	Decline from mid 1970s onwards
Finland	Medium	Medium	Decline from mid 1970s onwards
France	Medium	Low	Data only available from 1984 onwards
FR Germany	Medium	Low	Declining trend
Italy	?	Low	Declining trend
Japan	Small	High	Declining trend, flattening out in early 1980s
Norway	Small	High	Decline from mid 1970s onwards
Sweden	Small	High	Declining trend from mid 1970s, some recovery in 1980s
UK	Medium	Medium	Broadly flat
USA	Large	High	Some decline during mid 1970s

Source: Based on data presented in OECD (1990b), Table 3.3.

Footnotes to Chapter 6

1. To give an illustration of the degree to which the LFS data may understate the actual degree of movement between economic states, one should note that, in a typical year, the claimant unemployment count records between 3 and 4 million separate inflows.

2. This measure will include people who started work within 12 months of the survey, but who were unemployed or inactive 12 months before the interview (these groups are excluded from Table 6.2).

3. For comparison, Harper (1993) estimated that 9.6 per cent of men aged between 16 and 65 changed their occupation between 1975 and 1976. The data used, the National Training Survey, ought to be broadly comparable with the LFS.

4. Table 6.4 may understate the degree of occupational mobility if those employed at the time of the survey, but unemployed or inactive one year previously, were more likely to change their occupation on returning to employment. Unfortunately, the lack of data on the previous occupation of many unemployed and inactive people precluded a more detailed investigation.

5. This argument can also be applied to firms. The wider the area over which a firm advertises a vacancy, the more chance it has of finding a 'perfect' match.

6. Many migrants who, at the time of moving, are outside the labour force (children, inactive people of working age) will sooner or later become additions to, or subtractions from, the potential labour force. In addition, migration leads to changes in the size and composition of local populations. This in turn affects the level and structure of labour demand. For example, significant numbers of elderly people retire to particular locations (e.g. South coast towns). While these people may have no intention of re-entering the labour market, their presence will affect the labour market in those areas by changing the demand for particular types of work (nursing, other forms of personal services).

7. Local labour market studies in London, the West Midlands and Bristol found that immobility, even within urban areas, was a significant issue (see Meadows, Bartholomew and Cooper (1988), Cooper (1989), and Griffin, Knight and Wood (1991)).

8. The low figure for 1990 is an underestimate due to the computerisation of NHSCR records in that year (Hornsey (1993)).

9. Due to the small number of regions over which the correlation coefficients are calculated, the margins of error surrounding them are large. In most years, the null hypothesis that the two series are uncorrelated cannot be rejected at the 95 per cent level (the 95 per cent confidence intervals are approximately ±0.6).

10. NHSCR data suggests that the number of moves each year *between* FHSA areas *within* standard regions does not greatly exceed the number of inter-regional moves (Hornsey (1993), Figure 2). Hence the majority of changes of address must be short distance moves within FHSA areas.

11. Studies with a time-series dimension do not report tests of structural stability.

12. The UK data is graphed in Figure 3.1.

13. Some corroborating evidence can be found in Neven and Gouyotte (1994). Using 1985 data, they found that inter-regional mobility in the UK was significantly higher than anywhere else in the EU. They also found migration rates in Italy to be unusually low.

Chapter 7
Wage determination

This chapter reviews evidence on trends in price (wage) flexibility at the microeconomic level. In particular, it considers various aspects of wage determination which may be indicators of wage flexibility - how wages are determined, how they are related to performance, and the factors that influence pay outcomes. The data used primarily relates to firms or individuals. Relative wage flexibility is dealt with in Chapters 8 to 10.

For stylistic purposes, in this and subsequent Chapters, the terms pay, wages and earnings are used interchangeably.

a)   The institutional structure of wage determination

Wage outcomes are likely to be affected by the way in which wages are determined. In recent years, a number of studies have examined the link between wage determination and macroeconomic performance, notably Calmfors and Driffill (1988), Soskice (1990), and Layard, Nickell and Jackman (1991). These studies examined the correlation across countries between bargaining structures and labour market indicators, especially unemployment.

Two aspects of wage determination systems were identified as important. One is the degree of *centralisation*, i.e. the extent to which negotiation and decision-making is concentrated in the hands of a small number of actors. The other is the degree of *co-ordination* between actors. Centralised systems are necessarily co-ordinated. But decentralised systems can also be co-ordinated if one or both sets of actors (employers and unions) act with a common purpose or strategy. Soskice (1990) identifies Japan as a country with decentralised but co-ordinated wage bargaining, due to a high degree of co-operation between the major Japanese employers.

One view is that wage-setting will be most flexible where wages are decentralised. This is based on the assumption that wage determination is best left to those economic agents most closely affected by market conditions. These are generally individual employers (because they pay the wages and are the ones who will go out of business if increases are excessive) and employees (since some of them will

lose their jobs if pay increases are not justified by market conditions). This suggests that greater scope for pay determination at the level of the individual or plant is consistent with greater wage flexibility. In contrast, industry or nationwide collective agreements take no account of individual employers' and employees' market position.

The alternative view, set out in the studies referred to above, is that centralised and/or co-ordinated systems are better able to deliver aggregate real wage flexibility[1].

A descriptive picture of the degree of centralisation/decentralisation can be assembled from data on wage determination - in particular, the spread of collective bargaining and the forms it takes. It is more difficult to identify quantitative measures of co-ordination.

Centralisation/decentralisation

There is no single, authoritative source of time series data that collects detailed information on wage determination and covers the whole economy. However, evidence from two main sources of data - WIRS and the NES - permits an analysis of trends over time.

A detailed description of pay determination at the workplace is available from WIRS, through a series of questions asked about the most recent pay settlements reached at the establishment. This data is summarised in Table 7.1.

For 1984 and 1990, this information can also be presented in terms of the percentage of *employees* whose pay was determined by the above arrangements. Data on this basis is reported in Table 7.2.

Between 1980 and 1984, there was a moderate increase in the proportion of establishments with collective bargaining, 'but ... these [shifts in pay bargaining] arose much more as a result of a structural change in the economy than as a result of change in particular types of workplace' (Millward and Stevens (1986), page 225). This was the result of a decline in the number of private sector establishments relative to the number of public sector workplaces (where collective bargaining at that time was virtually universal).

Between 1984 and 1990, there was a substantial fall in the incidence of collective bargaining. The proportion of establishments with collective bargaining fell from 66 per cent in 1984 to 53 per cent in 1990. The decline was even more substantial if measured in terms of the proportion of employees covered by collective bargaining: down from 71 per cent in 1984 to 54 per cent by 1990.

Table 7.1   Establishment-based estimates of basis for most recent pay increase at the workplace, 1980-1990

	Manual employees			Non-manual employees		
Percentages of establishments with 25 or more employees employing the relevant category of worker, Great Britain						
	1980	1984	1990	1980	1984	1990
Result of collective bargaining	**55**	**62**	**48**	**47**	**54**	**43**
Most important level:						
Multi-employer	32	40	26	29	36	24
Single employer, multi-plant	12	13	13	11	13	15
Plant/establishment	9	7	6	4	4	3
Other answer	1	1	2	2	1	1
Not result of collective bargaining	**44**	**38**	**52**	**53**	**46**	**57**
Locus of decision about increase[1]:						
Management at establishment		20	31		30	37
Management at higher level		11	15		15	17
National Joint Body		5	4		2	5
Wages Council		3	2		1	*
Not stated		1	*		*	*

Notes

1   *Respondents in establishments where there was no collective bargaining could give more than one response to this question, so the sum of the percentage estimates for each of the locus of decision categories can add up to more than the percentage of establishments not covered by collective bargaining.*

*   *indicates fewer than 0.5 per cent.*

Source: WIRS series, Millward, Stevens, Smart and Hawes (1992), Table 7.1.

National-level bargaining remains influential. Although multi-employer agreements declined sharply in importance between 1984 and 1990, they are still regarded as the most important bargaining level. Interestingly, the survey results do not suggest any major shift towards bargaining at the plant/enterprise level. But where collective bargaining was absent, management at establishment level become increasingly influential in deciding wage increases.

The second major source of information on the extent of collective bargaining is the NES. Every year, the survey contains a question asking whether a particular individual's pay is affected by one or more of a list of major collective agreements. The list includes most public sector agreements, and the main private sector national agreements.

Figure 7.1 shows that the percentage of full-time employees whose pay was directly affected by one of these agreements *excluding* Wages Council orders has fallen considerably over the past twenty years. In 1972, as many as 65 per cent of all full-time employees had their pay affected by one of these agreements, but this proportion fell substantially during the 1970s and again between 1985 and 1990. By 1992, less than two in five full-time employees had their pay affected by one of these agreements. The trend over the period since 1980 is broadly consistent with WIRS.

This question only picks up specified collective agreements. In addition, a special question was added to the survey in 1973, 1978 and 1985, asking if an employee's pay was affected by any multi-employer agreement (national agreements with or without supplementary agreements).

The proportion of full-time employees whose pay was affected by a collective agreement of any kind

Table 7.2   Employee-based estimates of basis for most recent pay increase at the workplace, 1984-1990

Percentages of employees[1] in establishments with 25 or more employees employing the relevant category of worker, Great Britain

	Manual employees		Non-manual employees		All employees	
	1984	1990	1984	1990	1984	1990
Result of collective bargaining	**79**	**64**	**72**	**60**	**75**	**62**
Most important level:						
Multi-employer	43	30	49	36	46	33
Single employer, multi-plant	19	18	15	19	17	18
Plant/establishment	16	15	8	4	12	9
Other answer	1	1	*	1	*	1
Not result of collective bargaining	**21**	**36**	**27**	**40**	**24**	**38**
Locus of decision about increase[2]:						
Management at establishment	11	22	18	27	15	24
Management at higher level	6	11	8	11	7	11
National Joint Body	3	3	1	4	2	3
Wages Council	2	1	1	*	1	1
Not stated	-	1	-	1	-	1

Notes

1   *Employee estimates are calculated by assuming that the pay determination arrangements which apply to the largest manual and non-manual groups within the workplace in fact apply to all manual and non-manual employees at the workplace. They should therefore be regarded as approximate estimates of employee coverage.*

2   *Respondents in establishments where there was no collective bargaining could give more than one response to this question, so the sum of the percentage estimates for each of the locus of decision categories can add up to more than the percentage of employees not covered by collective bargaining.*

*   *indicates fewer than 0.5 per cent.*

-   *indicates zero.*

Source: 1984 and 1990 WIRS.

fell from 73 per cent in 1973 to 64 per cent by 1985. Of particular interest is the decline in multi-level bargaining (i.e. national agreements plus supplementary agreements at company, plant or local level) among manual workers.

The NES data in Figure 7.1 is corroborated by the fact that, since 1985, national agreements covering over 1.2 million employees have ended[2]. Most significant of these was the demise of the national engineering agreement, which *covered* around 600,000 employees and *affected* the pay of around a million.

The collective evidence therefore points to a significant degree of decentralisation during the last twenty years, with a particularly sharp fall in the incidence of both multi-employer bargaining and of

collective bargaining *per se* during the second half of the 1980s[3].

It is not possible to estimate with precision the proportion of employees whose pay is subject to collective bargaining. However, the 1990 WIRS suggested that only 54 per cent of employees were covered by collective bargaining. WIRS covers employees in establishments with 25 or more employees, about 70 per cent of all employees. Given that unionisation is far less prevalent in smaller workplaces[4], the incidence of collective bargaining among the other 30 per cent of employees is almost certainly much lower than the WIRS estimates. Thus it is highly likely that less than half of all employees now have their pay determined by collective bargaining.

Figure 7.1   Coverage of major collective agreements, 1972-1992

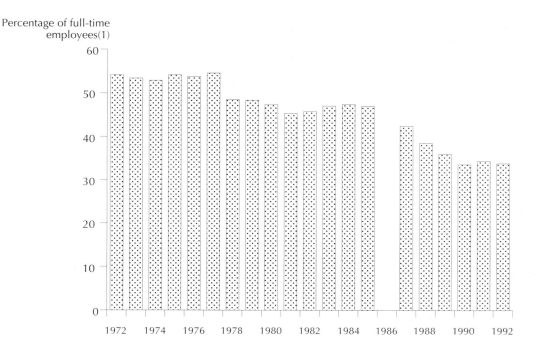

Table 7.3   Estimates of whether employees' pay is affected by a collective agreement, 1973-1985

Percentages of full-time employees on adult rates[1] whose pay was not affected by absence during the survey period, Great Britain, April

		Pay was affected by:			
		National agreement plus supplementary agreement etc.	National agreement only	Company, district or lower level agreement	No collective agreement
All full-time employees	1973	22	41	10	27
	1978	20	39	11	30
	1985	13	40	11	36
Manual employees	1973	31	40	10	19
	1978	29	36	13	23
	1985	19	37	14	31
Non-manual employees	1973	11	43	9	38
	1978	12	43	8	37
	1985	8	43	8	40

Brown (1993) reaches similar conclusions. Using NES and WIRS data, together with other sources, he estimates the proportion of full-time employees covered by collective bargaining to have been 65 per cent in 1968, peaking at 72 per cent in 1973, and falling to 64 per cent in 1984 and 47 per cent in 1990.

The trend towards decentralisation may date from as far back as the 1950s, when some of the highly centralised wage-setting institutions established during World Wars I and II began to fragment (Brown and Walsh (1991)). However, the pace of decentralisation seems to have accelerated in recent years.

Co-ordination

Less quantitative information is available on the co-ordination of wage setting. With the exception of various statutory and voluntary incomes policies introduced between the 1950s and the end of the 1970s, there has been no formal or informal economy-wide wage co-ordination.

At an industry level, the decline in national collective agreements has led to less co-ordinated bargaining on the part of unions and employers. Indeed, WIRS data shows that membership of employers' associations fell from a quarter of establishments in 1980 to an eighth by 1990.

Brown and Walsh (1991) point out that statistical evidence on the extent of decentralisation may understate the degree of co-ordination. They suggest that, in many large companies, decentralised bargaining units often determine pay with a close eye to the centre. However, it is difficult to resist the conclusion that wage setting has become increasingly unco-ordinated since the last statutory incomes policy ended in 1979.

b)   Performance related pay

Payment and reward systems may also facilitate pay flexibility. Where individuals' pay is related to individual or company performance, this should create incentives for employees to raise their effort, efficiency, and productivity. Weitzman (1984), (1985) has also stressed the virtues of profit-related pay as a means of generating greater aggregate wage flexibility (hence stabilising output and employment over the cycle).

The generic term PRP is used here to describe all payment systems that, to some extent, link an individual's pay or overall financial remuneration to some measure of individual, group or organisational performance. There are many variants of PRP.

Nevertheless, some (inevitably arbitrary) labelling is necessary.

The typology below was developed for the IPM/NEDO survey (see below). PRP schemes were grouped under the following headings:

- **individual payment by results (IPBR)** or piecework, where an individual's earnings are totally or partially based directly on individual performance, usually in terms of the quantity or value of output produced[5];

- **group payment by results (GPBR)**, where the output or sales-related performance pay is divided between group members according to a pre-determined formula;

- **plant or enterprise-wide bonuses**, in which all employees or production members receive a bonus on the same basis;

- **merit pay**, where the employee receives a level of bonus or basic pay linked to an assessment and/or appraisal of performance;

- **financial participation**, where the employee receives a reward in terms of cash or an option over shares, the size of which will normally depend upon company performance over a fixed period. Both profit-sharing schemes and share option schemes fall under this heading.

This classification takes a broad view of PRP. In particular, it includes all forms of financial participation.

The NES is the best source of data on individual earnings, but there are major defects in its coverage of PRP. The only performance-related sub-category of total earnings identified is one called 'individual PBR' consisting of 'piecework, bonuses (including profit-sharing), commission, productivity and other payments'. While many incentive payment schemes ought to be included in this category (most IPBR and GPBR schemes and many plant/enterprise bonuses and profit-sharing schemes), some will not to be included. In particular, employers are unlikely to classify many merit pay schemes under this heading as merit pay awards are often consolidated into basic pay or are used to determine an individual's position on a pay scale.

Figure 7.2 plots the proportions of full-time employees whose earnings included *some* element of incentive pay on the NES definition. Manual employees are more likely to receive incentive payments than non-manuals, and men are more likely to receive them than women.

The graph suggests that PRP schemes became more common during the second half of the 1970s. This

Figure 7.2   Full-time employees in receipt of incentive pay, 1974-1994

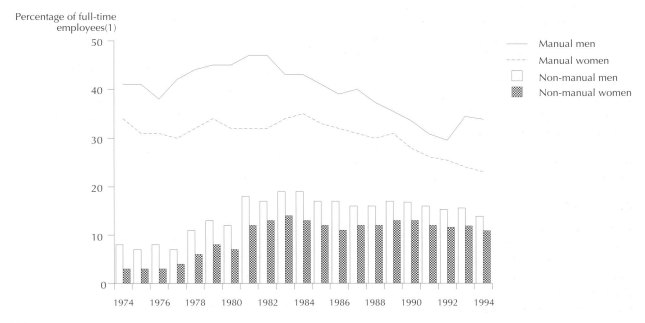

Percentage of full-time employees(1)

Notes

1   Full-time employees on adult rates (prior to 1984, men aged 18 and over, women aged 21 and over) whose pay for the survey period was unaffected by absence, Great Britain, April.

Source: New Earnings Surveys.

may have been due to incomes policies which allowed exemptions for 'productivity-enhancing' payments[6]. On the face of it, the graph suggests that the proportion of manual employees in receipt of incentive payments continued to increase until 1984 before falling in the second half of the decade, whereas there was an increase for non-manual employees between the mid 1970s and early 1980s that has not been reversed. The problem is that the NES measure of PRP tends to exclude those types of PRP - merit pay and financial participation schemes - where growth over the 1980s has been most rapid. In contrast, types of scheme that appear to be falling out of favour, such as IPBR, tend to be included in the NES. Thus the NES probably understates the growth of PRP among employees during the 1980s.

The 1984 and 1990 WIRS contain a (limited) amount of information on payment systems. In both years, managers were asked whether there was any payment by results (PBR) for manual and junior non-manual staff. Over the period 1984-1990, the percentage of workplaces with PBR[7] for manual staff rose slightly from 31 per cent to 32 per cent. There was a slightly greater increase in the proportion of workplaces using PBR for junior non-manual staff, up from 16 per cent to 19 per cent. As with the NES, though, the question wording suggests that financial

participation and merit pay schemes may not be reported.

The 1990 WIRS questions were therefore extended to include merit pay and cover a wider range of occupational groups. The results, presented in Table 7.4, suggest that PRP is widespread. Over half (52 per cent) of establishments reported using at least one method of individual or group-related PRP for at least some of their staff. IPBR and merit pay were more common than GPBR or plant/enterprise bonuses, the latter mainly being used for manual employees.

For the trading sector, data was collected on the whole range of PRP, including financial participation. Table 7.4 indicates that the trading sector was somewhat more likely in 1990 to use both individual and group-based forms of PRP in any case[8]. In addition, though, more than half of all establishments in this sector said that some form of financial participation was available to at least some employees[9].

For financial participation only, additional comparisons can be drawn with 1984. The proportion of trading sector establishments with cash or share-based profit-sharing schemes rose from 18 per cent in 1984 to 43 per cent by 1990. Over the

Table 7.4   The incidence of performance related pay, 1990

Form of PRP:	All establishments	Trading sector establishments[2]
Percentages of establishments with 25 or more employees that used the relevant payment system for at least one occupational group[1], Great Britain		
Individual PBR or merit pay	45	53
Group/establishment or organisational PBR	17	20
Any PBR or merit pay	52	61
Financial participation		55
Financial participation (excluding executive share schemes)[3]		53
All incentive payments		76
All incentive payments (excluding executive share schemes)[3]		75

Notes

1   *These questions were only asked of occupational groups with 5 or more employees present at the workplace.*

2   *Questions on financial participation were only put to respondents in trading sector (ie. industrial and commercial) establishments.*

3   *Excluding discretionary or executive share option schemes.*

Source: 1990 WIRS.

same period, the proportion with some form of employee share ownership scheme rose from 23 per cent to 32 per cent.

In addition to these regular data sources, supporting evidence is provided from three one-off studies.

A survey of payment systems carried out for the Institute of Personnel Management (IPM) and the National Economic Development Office (NEDO) in 1991 (see Appendix 1) found that PRP was widely used. Only 14 per cent of organisations said they did not make any use of PRP.

Figure 7.3 summarises results for each type of PRP. It suggests there are clear differences in the types of system applied to manual and non-manual employees, although a significant proportion of employers have extended merit pay and financial participation to all employees.

A quarter of organisations had IPBR for at least some of their manual employees. The survey also revealed that a significant number of organisations had group incentive schemes. However, it was rare for this type of scheme to be applied to the whole workforce in an organisation.

The most common forms of PRP were merit pay and financial participation. Two fifths (40 per cent) of the organisations surveyed used merit pay for at least some non-manual employees, with a further 22 per

cent having extended its use to all employees. Similarly, 19 per cent of organisations used some form of financial participation for non-manual employees, while a further 23 per cent had extended it to all their employees.

The survey also collected retrospective information on organisations' activity during the previous ten years (1981-1991). This information suggested that IPBR schemes had fallen out of favour during the 1980s: a quarter of all schemes extant at the beginning of the 1980s had been withdrawn. In contrast, the 1980s saw strong growth in merit pay and financial participation schemes. Although the majority of merit pay schemes were over ten years old at the time of the survey, a rush of new schemes were recorded in the second half of the 1980s. There were many extensions to the scope of existing schemes. This was also the period when the introduction of financial participation schemes accelerated. Over two thirds of all schemes extant at the time of the survey were less than ten years old.

The second *ad hoc* data source is a survey of organisations carried out in 1991, which formed part of an IPM study of performance management systems (see IPM (1992)). Most of the respondents were large employers, so the results are again probably representative of large organisations only. Although the survey focused on performance management, questions were asked about PRP. The

Figure 7.3   Employers' use of performance related pay, 1991

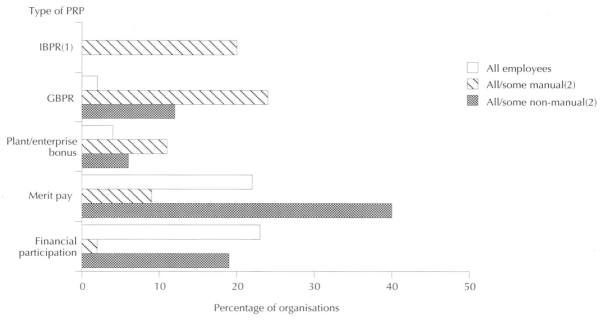

Notes

1   The incidence of IPBR for non-manuals and all employees is not reported.

2   Cases where a performance related payment is made to this group only, not to all employees.

Source: Cannell and Wood (1992).

survey found that 74 per cent of employers used at least one form of PRP, which is consistent with findings from other studies.

Finally, the 1992 Employment in Britain survey provided some additional evidence on employee coverage (see Gallie and White (1993)). It found that 27 per cent of employees were receiving some form of incentive payment, which included all forms of bonus or commission. Financial participation schemes covered 15 per cent of employees. In addition, 18 per cent of employees received formal appraisals which they perceived as affecting their earnings. This can be taken as an approximate measure of merit pay. These figures cannot simply be added together to produce an estimate of the proportion of employees covered by PRP, as some employees receive more than one form of payment. However, the survey's results do suggest that some sort of link between pay and performance now forms part of the pay of a substantial proportion - probably at least a third - of all employees.

c)   Factors influencing pay

A more general measure of wage flexibility might be the degree to which pay is linked to economic conditions. This section focuses on one such

measure: managers' own perceptions of the main factors determining the size of pay rises.

Data is available from the 1984 and 1990 WIRS. The surveys asked the main management respondent what, in their judgement, were the most important factors behind the most recent pay increase at the establishment. There were some differences between the two surveys in the way the questions were asked, and in the responses available to respondents. However, if the responses are aggregated into a small number of categories, the data can be regarded as comparable. These categories are as follows:

- **Cost of living**;
- **Labour market**, includes fear of redundancy and (in 1990) recruitment and retention, as well as cases where wage settlements were based on what other employers were paying;
- **Economic performance**, includes profitability, product market conditions, ability to pay, and fear of plant closure;
- **Linked to other settlement**, where managers explicitly linked the settlement (either formally or informally) to another settlement;
- **Other influences** covers a wide range of issues, including the threat and use of industrial action and individual merit, and as such is more difficult to interpret.

Table 7.5 shows that, in 1984, the single most common factor influencing the size of pay increases for manual employees was economic conditions - mentioned by 38 per cent of respondents - followed by the cost of living and other influences. Labour market influences were relatively weak, mentioned by only 16 per cent of managers. The pattern had changed by 1990: the relative importance of the cost of living had increased significantly (from 31 per cent to 50 per cent of all respondents), whereas economic performance was a factor in only 30 per cent of cases. There was also a significant increase in the percentage of managers influenced by labour market factors. A very similar pattern is evident in the data for non-manual employees. 'Other influences' score more highly for non-manual workers: this category includes merit pay, which is more common among non-manual employees.

In large part, the changes between 1984 and 1990 reflect changes in the economic environment. Inflation averaged 5 per cent in 1984, and had fallen sharply over the previous three years. In 1990, inflation was on a rising trend, increasing during the year from 7.7 per cent to a peak of 10.9 per cent. Other cyclical factors were also important: in 1984, a slack labour market and fear of redundancy or plant closure were likely to have been the main labour market pressures on pay; in 1990, skill shortages and recruitment and retention problems were of greater significance.

The role of cyclical factors is also apparent in the CBI's pay databank. Data is collated from over a thousand 'settlement groups' each year. Ingram (1991b) reported data for each pay round[10] between 1979/80 and 1988/89. Managers were asked to specify the direction of wage pressures, so upward and downwards pressures can be separately identified. The survey, however, only covers the private manufacturing sector.

Figures 7.4 presents the results. The most significant upward pressure on wage settlements over this period was the cost of living, especially when inflation was high and/or rising at the start and end of the 1980s. Similarly, profits increased in importance as profitability improved over the decade. Recruitment and retention was rarely mentioned by managers during the early 1980s, yet it rapidly became an important source of wage pressure as the labour market tightened.

Turning to downward pressures, low or falling profits appear to have been a more influential source of downward pressure on wage settlements than high or increasing profits were in pushing up settlements. The inability to raise prices, possibly a measure of product market competition or demand, also scored highly throughout the 1980s. Risk of redundancy exerted far less discipline on pay settlements as the decade wore on.

For manufacturing at least, comparability remained a factor behind many wage settlements. Throughout the 1980s, around half (or more) of wage settlements involved some sort of comparison: either with other

Table 7.5   Factors influencing the size of the most recent pay settlement, 1984-1990

Percentage of establishments with 25 or more employees where managers identified the factors below as having influenced the size of the most recent pay settlement for manual/non-manual employees, Great Britain

Factor[1]:	Manual employees[2]		Non-manual employees[2]	
	1984	1990	1984	1990
Cost of living	31	50	31	48
Labour market	16	30	13	30
Economic performance	38	30	40	29
Linked to other settlement	15	14	17	12
Other influences	32	25	42	36
Not stated	14	7	9	7

Notes

1   Managers could identify more than one factor.

2   Excludes the few non-union public sector establishments in the sample, plus non-union establishments where pay was determined by a Wages Council, employers' association or national joint negotiating body.

Source: 1984 and 1990 WIRS.

Figure 7.4   Pressures on wage settlements, 1979/80-1988/89

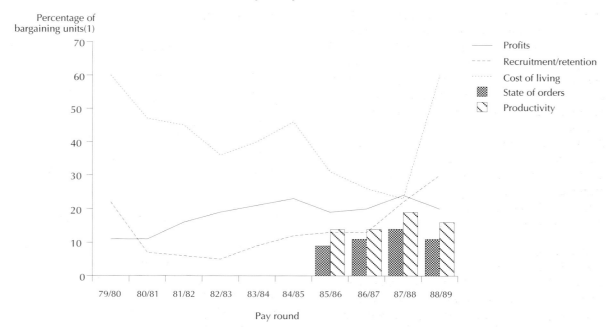

Upward pressures

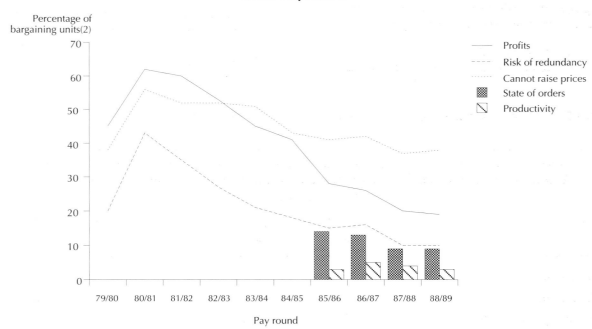

Downward pressures

Figure 7.4   Pressures on wage settlements, 1979/80-1988/89 continued

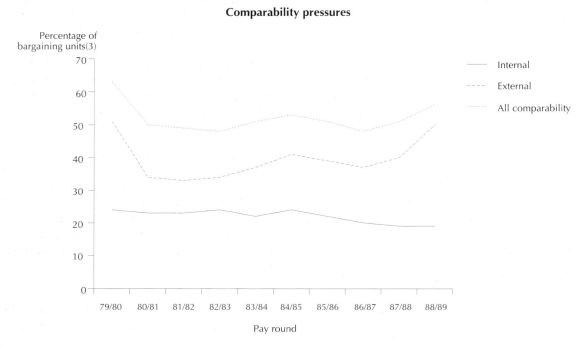

Comparability pressures

Notes

1   *Private sector employers in manufacturing industry citing these factors as 'very important' upward pressures on wages.*

2   *Private sector employers in manufacturing industry citing these factors as 'very important' downwards pressures on wages.*

3   *Private sector employers in manufacturing industry citing comparability as a 'very important' pressure on wages.*

Source: Ingram (1991b).

groups in the firm; or with other firms in the same industry or the same locality; or with national pay rises. This is a weaker definition of comparability than used in the WIRS data, as there is no requirement for any formal link between the wage settlement in question and other settlements.

Apart from the comparability measures, the CBI and WIRS results are broadly similar. WIRS data for the private manufacturing sector was compared with the CBI results, and there was a good degree of concordance between the two sets of responses. The only real difference was that WIRS found economic performance mentioned more often than in the CBI data. But there is a limit to how far comparisons between the surveys can be made.

Perceptions of pressures on wage settlements appear very much influenced by the economic environment. Cost of living became a major factor when inflation was high and/or rising, while recruitment and retention considerations outweighed the fear of redundancy as the labour market tightened towards the end of the 1980s. On the whole, the key factors influencing wage settlements appear to be the cost of

living, the firm's economic performance, and labour market conditions. There is, however, insufficient data to tell if any one of these factors became more significant during the 1980s, once allowance is made for changing economic conditions[11].

d)   International comparisons

The institutional structure of wage determination

International experience has been especially important in influencing the debate about the effects of alternative systems of wage determination. This debate, however, has not in general been conducted on the basis of detailed, comparable and quantitative measures of bargaining institutions. This is because of the difficulties involved in obtaining consistent measures of centralisation and co-ordination.

OECD (1994c) collated estimates of collective bargaining coverage for most OECD countries. These are presented in Figure 7.5. The data is based on national sources, so estimates will not be entirely consistent across countries.

The evidence suggests that, by 1990, the incidence of collective bargaining in Britain was below the OECD average. In a number of countries, (Australia, Austria, Belgium, Finland, France, Germany, Sweden), collective bargaining covered over 80 per cent of employees. There is often little correspondence between unionisation and collective bargaining coverage. This is because, unlike the UK, many countries have institutional mechanisms that extend the provisions of collective bargaining to other groups of workers. These mechanisms are especially important in Australia, Austria, Belgium, France and Portugal.

Less data is available on trends, but the available information is summarised in Figure 7.6. The fall in the coverage of collective bargaining during the 1980s was greater in Britain than in any other country (with the possible exception of New Zealand, not included in Figure 7.6).

The trend towards decentralisation observed in the UK is not unique. Katz (1993) reviewed recent developments in six countries - Australia, Germany,

Italy, Sweden, the UK, and the USA - and found evidence of greater decentralisation in all of them. Decentralisation, however, has taken different forms in different countries. In Sweden, for example, the 1980s and 1990s saw industries and individual companies begin to opt out of the highly centralised confederal wage agreements. Similarly, the Australian award system has been reformed to create greater scope for enterprise-level agreements. Only in the UK and the USA has there been a significant move away from collective bargaining.

In accounting for this trend, Katz found changes in the organisation of work to be the most persuasive explanation. Decentralisation can then result in benefits for both employers and employees[12]. OECD (1994c), however, suggests that the trend towards decentralisation has not been universal. Some countries, such as Norway, appear to have moved in the opposite direction.

OECD (1994c) also looks at co-ordination mechanisms. It confirms that wage determination in the UK is unco-ordinated, alongside Canada,

Figure 7.5   International comparisons of collective bargaining coverage, 1990

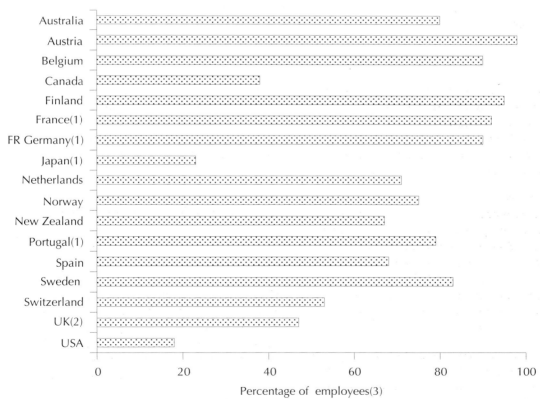

Notes

1   1990 except for France (1985), Germany (1992), Japan (1989) and Portugal (1991).

2   Excluding Northern Ireland.

3   Excluding groups debarred from collective bargaining .

Source: OECD (1994c).

Figure 7.6   International comparisons of changes in collective bargaining coverage, 1980-1990

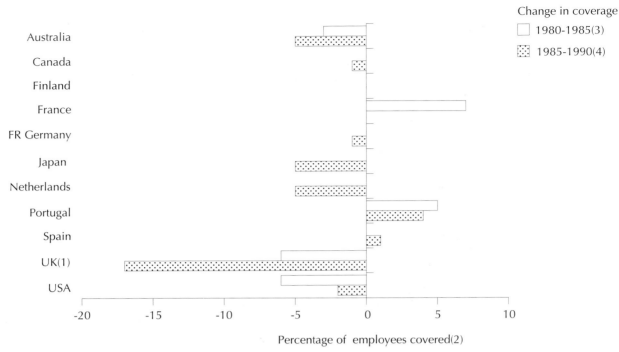

Percentage of employees covered(2)

Notes

1   Excluding Northern Ireland.

2   Excluding groups debarred from collective bargaining.

3   Except Australia (1974-1985); Canada (1980-1986); France (1981-1985); Portugal (1981-1985); Spain (1980-1983); UK (1978-1985).

4   Except Canada (1986-1990); Germany (1985-1992); Japan (1985-1989); Portugal (1985-1991); Spain (1983-1990).

Source: OECD (1994c).

Switzerland and the USA[13]. Most other countries have some form of overt or covert co-ordination (e.g. employer collusion).

Performance related pay

There is less evidence available on PRP. A 1985/86 survey of employees in EU member states collected information on one aspect of PRP, profit-sharing. The results, graphed in Figure 7.7, show that coverage in the UK was relatively high: only France and Luxembourg had higher proportions covered by these arrangements.

Indicative data from seven countries is also available from the 1989 International Social Survey Programme (ISSP). Employees covered by these surveys were asked to identify the most important factor influencing the pay of employees at their workplace. One of these was personal performance[14].

Figure 7.8 shows that personal performance was seen as the most important determinant of individual pay. In all seven countries, it was the most common response to this question. Again, the UK's rating is relatively high: 57 per cent of private sector employees thought that personal performance was the most important influence on workplace pay, equal with the Netherlands and second only to the USA.

Although the data available is very limited in scope, *perceptions* of a link between pay and performance appear to be relatively strong in the UK. Vaughan-Whitehead (1990) suggests there has been some movement towards PRP (especially financial participation) throughout most of the EU. However, it is not possible to tell if these developments have been as pronounced elsewhere as in Britain.

Factors influencing pay

Again, the evidence is limited. Boyer (1988) suggests that labour market factors had little influence on wage determination in the UK until the early 1970s, with the implication that such factors subsequently increased in importance. Boyer suggests that the economic climate has, in various ways, been an important influence on pay outcomes in Belgium,

Figure 7.7   Profit-related pay in EU member states, 1985/86

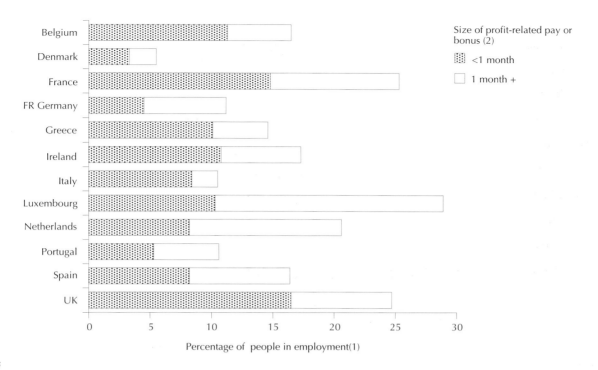

Notes

1   People in employment in 1984 who personally received some bonus or profit-sharing because of the performance of the company.

2   As months of salary.

Source: CEC (1986), Table 8.

Figure 7.8   International comparisons of the impact of personal performance on employees' pay, 1989

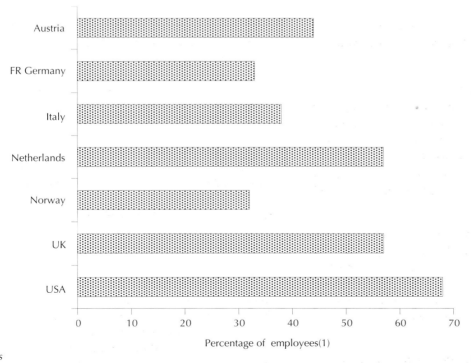

Notes

1   Percentages of respondents who thought personal performance was the most important factor in determining individual pay at their workplace. Private sector employees (except for the USA, where the data refers to all employees).

Source: Black (1994).

Germany, Ireland and Italy. In France and Spain, external labour market factors played little or no role.

Using a different approach, Flanagan (1989) presents an internationally comparable econometric test of the factors affecting wage outcomes: in particular, the balance between 'insider' and 'outsider' variables. For a number of countries with differing institutional frameworks (France, Germany, Italy, Japan, Sweden, the UK and the USA), wage equations were estimated for various periods between the mid 1970s and the mid 1980s. These equations included price terms, insider variables (overtime, employment expectations) and an outsider variable (unemployment). When both sets of variables were included in these equations, none of the insider variables were statistically significant in any country. Unemployment, in contrast, exerted a more consistent and significant effect. Although this is a simple test, it suggests that wage determination in the UK may not be that different from other advanced economies. It also suggests that external labour market factors are a significant influence on wage outcomes.

e)   Summary and conclusions

- Wage flexibility refers to the degree and speed with which pay responds to demand and supply conditions. It is likely to be affected by the way in which pay is determined.

- At the micro level, decentralised wage setting should make economic agents set pay levels with a close eye to the market and its consequences. An alternative view, however, is that centralised and/or co-ordinated systems are better placed to exploit wage flexibility at the macro level.

- The available evidence suggests that wage determination in Britain has become increasingly decentralised. By 1990, it is likely that less than half of employees were covered by collective bargaining arrangements. Coverage fell substantially during the second half of the 1980s. A number of industry-wide national agreements were abandoned or fell into abeyance.

- Systems that link pay to individual, group or organisational performance are now widely used by employers. The evidence suggests that a substantial majority of medium and large employers make some use of PRP - the proportion could be 75 per cent or more for larger organisations.

- The most common forms of PRP are merit pay, financial participation and IPBR. Somewhere between a half and three quarters of medium to large organisations may make some use of merit

pay, while over a half of organisations in the private sector probably have some form of financial participation.

- In terms of employee coverage, there are major gaps in the data. The 1994 NES recorded 20 per cent of full-time employees in receipt of incentive pay, but this is almost certainly an underestimate. The Employment in Britain survey suggests it could be a third or more[15]. The actual proportion of employees receiving some form of PRP may therefore fall within a wide range.

- The evidence suggests that the 1980s saw a rapid expansion of merit pay and financial participation, partially offset by a decline in the incidence of IPBR (piecework) schemes.

- Managers thought that cost of living increases were the single biggest factor affecting wage settlements during the 1980s. Labour market factors (risk of redundancy, skill shortages, recruitment and retention) were also significant factors, as was economic performance (profitability and productivity).

- It is difficult to tell, however, if labour market considerations have become more important in wage-setting, because the perceived importance of such factors varies over the cycle.

- Compared with other OECD countries, wage determination in the UK appears to be unco-ordinated and relatively decentralised. Perhaps only the USA (and possibly Canada and New Zealand) are further down this road. In addition, although there appears to have been a trend towards greater decentralisation in many OECD countries, only in the UK and the USA has this led to a decline in collective bargaining.

- Although data is in short supply, the evidence suggests that PRP is at least as common in the UK as in other OECD economies.

Footnotes to Chapter 7

1. See Calmfors (1993) for an overview of the theoretical issues and a brief summary of the empirical evidence to date.

2. See Beatson (1993), Box 1.

3. Gregg and Yates's (1991) survey of industrial relations in large companies provides supporting evidence. Their results point to a significant degree of decentralisation among unionised companies during the second half of the 1980s. This did not occur during the first half of the decade. The low response rate, however, must qualify the weight that can be attached to these results (see the Technical Note to Beatson (1993) for further comments).

4. BSAS asks employees if there is a union at their workplace recognised by management for negotiations over pay and conditions of employment - not necessarily one they are able to join themselves. The 1990 survey found that 68 per cent of employees in workplaces with 25 or more employees reported the presence of a recognised union or staff association. For workplaces with less than 25 employees the corresponding figure was 38 per cent.

5. The survey also identified one other form of PRP. This was measured day work, essentially a variant of IPBR, where pay is fixed at a higher rate than for a time-rate worker on the understanding that the employee maintains a specified level of performance. Cannell and Wood (1992) do not report separate analyses for measured day work, but its use appears to have been confined to the public sector, where some employers (especially local authorities) used it for their manual employees.

6. Bowey *et al's* (1982) research into incentive payment schemes introduced during the late 1970s suggested that, in a significant minority of cases, one of the objectives of the payment system was to provide employees with pay increases above those set by the incomes policy.

7. PBR is defined as where payment varies by the amount or value of work done, and not just by the hours worked.

8. See Beatson (1993) for more information on public-private sector differences in the incidence of PRP.

9. Little difference is made if executive share schemes are excluded from the analysis. Most financial participation schemes tended to cover all or most of the workforce at the establishment, although employee take-up was in some cases relatively low.

10. The pay round covers the period from August 1 to July 31 of the following year.

11. Suppose one could model managers' assessments of pay outcomes by a linear model of the form

$$W_{it} = \sum_i \beta_{it} X_{it}$$

where W is the pay increase and the X's are factors such as cost of living, economic performance, comparability etc. The data presented in this chapter has measured changes in the relative weight of the combined βX's. It is less clear whether the changes observed have arisen solely because of variation in the X variables (e.g. inflation), or if there has also been some underlying change in the β's too, e.g. a reduction in the weight given by managers to comparability.

12. The economic pressures that break down centralised bargaining systems are explicitly modelled by Freeman and Gibbons (1993). They identify the costs of centralised bargaining as well as the benefits. Broadly speaking, these costs are microeconomic inefficiencies which have to be set against the advantages of aggregate real wage flexibility. Freeman and Gibbons suggest that the more variable economic environment of the 1980s and 1990s has increased the relative costs of centralisation. They cite Sweden as an example. Henrekson, Jonung and Stymne (1994) also seem to support this interpretation of events in Sweden.

13. Soskice (1990) suggests that Swiss employers do in fact co-ordinate their wage decisions.

14. Measured by 'How well the employee does his/her job'.

15. A study of payment systems in Reading and Leicester (Casey, Lakey and White (1992)) found that managerial assessment of performance was a factor in deciding the pay rise of 42 per cent of employees.

Chapter 8
Relative wage flexibility: regions

In practice, labour markets are differentiated along a number of dimensions. These include geography, product market (industry), and human capital. Relative wage flexibility enables sub-markets to adjust to changes in demand and supply conditions.

Framework of analysis

Labour markets can adjust through prices and quantities, and this applies both at aggregate and disaggregated levels. Figure 8.1 illustrates the issues involved in the case of two interdependent labour markets, A and B. These could be two regions (North and South, say), two industrial sectors (manufacturing and services), or two occupational groups (skilled and unskilled).

Both labour markets are initially in equilibrium. Demand and supply are in balance, and there is no involuntary unemployment in either A or B. Wages are equalised at W_0. Note this is the wage with all

Figure 8.1   Relative wage flexibility in interdependent labour markets

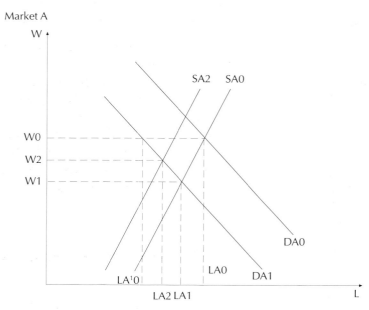

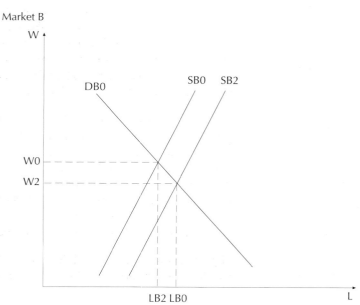

other variables held constant, i.e. the *ceteris paribus* wage differential. Actual wages could vary between A and B because of differences in factors such as the cost of living, working conditions, human capital, and the relative attractiveness of geographical locations.

Suppose demand fell in market A and labour demand shifted inwards to DA_1. If wages were flexible, the wage in A would fall to W_1, with employment at LA_1. Involuntary unemployment in either market would again be eliminated. The relative wage between A and B, however, would have changed.

Alternatively, suppose that relative wages between A and B are rigid for some reason. If the wage remained at W_0, then unemployment in market A would be $(LA_0-LA'_0)$. If the wage did fall to W_1 in A, but the wage in B also fell, there would be excess demand in market B. If wages remained stuck at some intermediate point, involuntary unemployment in A could co-exist with excess demand in B.

This is only a short-term analysis. In the longer term, there is a degree of labour mobility. The supply curves would therefore shift from SA_0 and SB_0 to SA_2 and SB_2, and equilibrium would be restored at a new wage rate W_2, with *ceteris paribus* wage differentials again equalised.

In theory, then, relative wage flexibility facilitates adjustment towards an equilibrium, rather than the properties of the equilibrium itself. But the adjustment process can take time if there are costs and constraints associated with mobility. This is quite feasible for geographical or occupational mobility, although it may be easier for individuals to move between industries. Flexible relative wages provide a price signal to encourage mobility. Quantity imbalances (unemployment, excess demand) are the other form of market signal.

While movements in relative wages may be an indicator of wage flexibility, the discussion above suggests their interpretation may be difficult. For one thing, there is the need to take account of other factors, which means looking at controlled (*ceteris paribus*) as well as uncontrolled wage differentials. Appendix 4 reviews relevant evidence on *ceteris paribus* wage differentials. In addition, changes in relative wages need to be related to market adjustment. The relative wage (W_A/W_B) in Figure 8.1 would be unity in equilibrium. If relative wages were flexible, it would fall in response to less demand in A, before increasing again as the market moved back into balance. These movements may be difficult to identify when so many other factors are changing at the same time.

Introduction

This study looks at relative wage flexibility along three key dimensions. This chapter considers regional wage flexibility, while industries and human capital are covered in Chapters 9 and 10 respectively.

Regional economic disparities - in terms of prosperity, employment, infrastructure - have long been regarded as a persistent feature of the British economy and a potential economic problem. As a result, a variety of regional policies designed to reduce the scale of these disparities have been implemented over the past fifty years.

Wage rigidity is often cited as a cause of persistent regional disparities in unemployment rates. While *ceteris paribus* wage differentials should be equalised across regions in long-run equilibrium, regional wage relativities may need to widen in the short to medium term (Pissarides and McMaster (1990)).

The evidence on regional wage flexibility is dealt with in three stages:

- the aggregate data on the regional distribution of earnings is analysed, and changes in regional wage relativities are identified;
- these changes are then related to regional unemployment and labour market adjustment;
- finally, there is a brief review of evidence from econometric analyses of regional wage determination.

a)   Trends in the distribution of earnings by region

The analysis in this section concentrates on developments since 1974, due to changes in regional boundaries arising from a reorganisation of local government. Time series of average earnings by standard region on a consistent basis have been produced[1] and real earnings have been calculated using the *national* Retail Price Index (RPI).

Previous studies have suggested that regional earnings had been converging since at least the 1960s (Moore and Rhodes (1981), Pissarides and McMaster (1990)). Figure 8.2 displays coefficients of variation (weighted by size of region)[2] for full-time employees[3]. In line with previous studies (Walsh and Brown (1991)), measures of dispersion including and excluding the South East are reported.

Higher earnings in the South East widen the earnings distribution. Furthermore, although

Figure 8.2 Dispersion of regional earnings, all full-time employees, 1974-1993

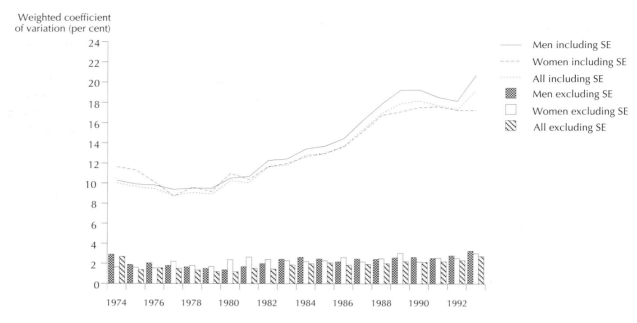

Notes

Real average hourly earnings excluding overtime, full-time employees on adult rates whose pay for the survey period was unaffected by absence, Great Britain, April.

Source: New Earnings Surveys.

Figure 8.3 Dispersion of regional earnings, manual employees, 1974-1993

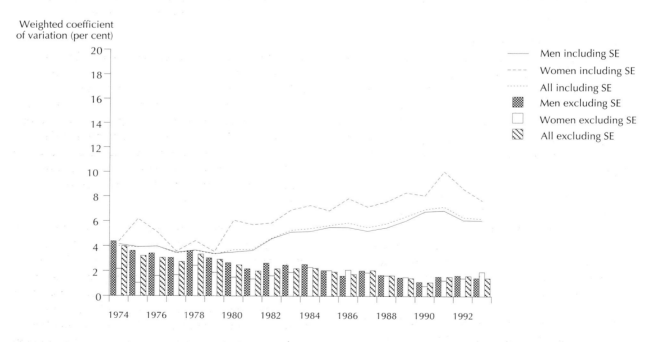

Notes

Real average hourly earnings excluding overtime, full-time employees on adult rates whose pay for the survey period was unaffected by absence, Great Britain, April.

Source: New Earnings Surveys.

Figure 8.4   Dispersion of regional earnings, non-manual employees, 1974-1993

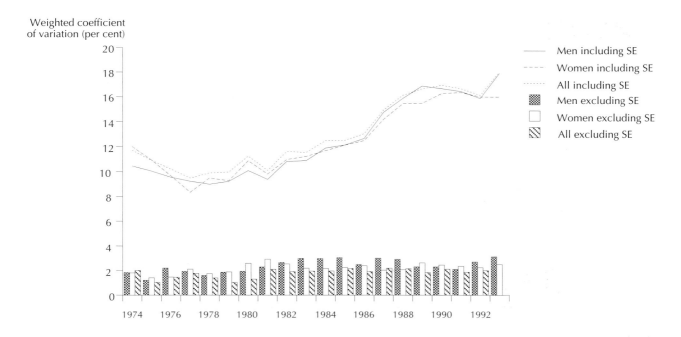

Notes

Real average hourly earnings excluding overtime, full-time employees on adult rates whose pay for the survey period was unaffected by absence, Great Britain, April.

Source: New Earnings Surveys.

regional earnings dispersion increased during the 1980s, this was very much a consequence of faster earnings growth in the South East.

The problems of regional wage inflexibility are often held to be most acute for manual workers. Possible explanations have included the greater proportion of manual employees who are covered by national agreements[4] and the greater proportion of manual workers who are council house tenants (Minford and Stoney (1991), McCormick (1991)). Separate analyses are therefore presented for manual and non-manual employees.

Figures 8.3 and 8.4 show that the dispersion of earnings across all regions is greater for non-manuals than manuals, but only because of earnings in the South East. The earnings distribution has widened because the earnings of non-manual employees in the South East have 'pulled away' from the rest of the country.

However, this does not mean the remainder of the earnings distribution was static. Regional earnings relativities could have changed without much of an increase in overall dispersion.

Table 8.1 presents 'league tables' ranking the earnings of manual, non-manual and all full-time

employees over time. While they illustrate changing relativities, they do not provide any information on changes in the *size* of inter-regional wage differentials.

For all full-time employees, average hourly earnings have been highest in Greater London and second highest in the rest of the South East (RoSE) throughout the period. However, there has been a considerable degree of re-ordering among the other regions. Relative earnings have increased in East Anglia (since 1984), the South West, Scotland and the North West. On the other hand, the relative position of the West Midlands and Wales appears to have deteriorated since 1979.

In 1974, hourly earnings for manual employees were higher in the West Midlands than in Greater London, although Greater London topped the table by 1979. Real earnings in RoSE were relatively low over the period 1974-1984. It was only during the second half of the 1980s that manual earnings in RoSE drew above those of other regions. East Anglia and the North West have tended to move up the distribution, whereas the West Midlands and Wales have tended to move down it.

89

Table 8.1   Ranking by region of average hourly earnings of full-time employees, 1974-1993

Real hourly earnings excluding overtime of full-time employees on adult rates[1] whose pay for the survey period was unaffected by absence, Great Britain, April

Rank	1974	1979	1984	1989	1993
MANUAL EMPLOYEES					
1	W MIDS	LONDON	LONDON	LONDON	LONDON
2	LONDON	NORTH	NORTH	ROSE	ROSE
3	WALES	WALES	WALES	NORTH	NORTH
4	NORTH	W MIDS	N WEST	N WEST	N WEST
5	ROSE	YORKS	SCOT	E ANGLIA	YORKS
6	E MIDS	N WEST	ROSE	WALES	W MIDS
7	N WEST	E MIDS	W MIDS	W MIDS	S WEST
8	YORKS	ROSE	YORKS	YORKS	E ANGLIA
9	SCOT	SCOT	E ANGLIA	E MIDS	SCOT
10	S WEST	E ANGLIA	E MIDS	S WEST	WALES
11	E ANGLIA	S WEST	S WEST	SCOT	E MIDS
NON-MANUAL EMPLOYEES					
1	LONDON	LONDON	LONDON	LONDON	LONDON
2	ROSE	ROSE	ROSE	ROSE	ROSE
3	W MIDS	N WEST	SCOT	S WEST	SCOT
4	S WEST	YORKS	N WEST	SCOT	S WEST
5	WALES	W MIDS	W MIDS	N WEST	N WEST
6	NORTH	E MIDS	YORKS	E ANGLIA	W MIDS
7	E ANGLIA=	SCOT	S WEST	W MIDS	NORTH
8	N WEST=	S WEST=	E ANGLIA	YORKS	E ANGLIA
9	E MIDS	WALES=	E MIDS	WALES	E MIDS
10	YORKS	NORTH	WALES	E MIDS	YORKS
11	SCOT	E ANGLIA	NORTH	NORTH	WALES
ALL FULL-TIME EMPLOYEES					
1	LONDON	LONDON	LONDON	LONDON	LONDON
2	W MIDS	ROSE	ROSE	ROSE	ROSE
3	ROSE	W MIDS	SCOT	S WEST	S WEST
4	WALES	WALES	N WEST	N WEST	N WEST
5	NORTH	NORTH	W MIDS	SCOT	SCOT
6	S WEST	N WEST	S WEST=	E ANGLIA	W MIDS
7	N WEST	YORKS	NORTH=	W MIDS	NORTH
8	E MIDS	SCOT	WALES	YORKS	E ANGLIA
9	YORKS=	E MIDS	YORKS	NORTH	YORKS
10	SCOT=	S WEST	E ANGLIA	WALES	WALES
11	E ANGLIA	E ANGLIA	E MIDS	E MIDS	E MIDS

Notes

1   See Appendix 1 for details of the correction made.

=   indicates a tie.

Source: New Earnings Surveys.

For non-manual employees, Greater London and RoSE have consistently had the highest earnings. In contrast, non-manual employees in the North have tended to have relatively low earnings, even though manual earnings in the region have been relatively high (the reverse is true in the South West). Scotland, the North West and (since 1979) the South West have moved up the distribution, whereas the West Midlands and Wales have, again, slipped down the table.

Table 8.2 presents a more formal measure of change, Spearman's rank correlation coefficients. While, in most cases, the ordering of regions has remained relatively stable over short periods, the values in the three right hand columns suggest that the effects of these changes accumulate over time.

b)   Regional earnings and unemployment

Regional unemployment differentials have been more pronounced. Figure 8.5 presents estimates of the weighted coefficient of variation of regional unemployment rates[5]. For all but the most recent years, the coefficient of variation greatly exceeds that of the regional earnings distribution.

An alternative measure of dispersion is also presented in Figure 8.5, the (weighted) mean absolute deviation of regional unemployment rates. In absolute terms, the distribution of regional unemployment rates widened considerably in the early 1980s, before beginning to narrow in the late

Table 8.2   The stability over time of the rank ordering of regional earnings, 1974-1993

Real hourly earnings excluding overtime of full-time employees on adult rates[1] whose pay for the survey period was unaffected by absence, Great Britain, April						
Spearman's rank correlation coefficient for regional earnings between:						
1974-1979	1979-1984	1984-1989	1989-1993	1974-1993	1979-1993	1984-1993
Male manual	0.84	0.79	0.53	0.73	0.58	0.40	0.48
Female manual	0.48	0.72	0.68	0.85	0.31	0.51	0.46
All manual	0.84	0.76	0.64	0.76	0.34	0.37	0.50
Male non-manual	0.46	0.74	0.83	0.90	0.56	0.48	0.75
Female non-manual	0.82	0.66	0.82	0.89	0.60	-0.09	0.72
All non-manual	0.34	0.80	0.85	0.85	0.47	0.32	0.80
All men	0.67	0.89	0.78	0.95	0.53	0.51	0.84
All women	0.76	0.72	0.89	0.97	0.57	0.25	0.85
All persons	**0.87**	**0.67**	**0.78**	**0.95**	**0.48**	**0.21**	**0.88**

Notes

1   *See Appendix 1 for details of the correction made.*

Source: New Earnings Surveys.

Table 8.3   The stability over time of the rank ordering of regional unemployment rates, 1974-1993

Claimant unemployment (adjusted for seasonality and discontinuities) expressed as a percentage of the workforce, Great Britain, April						
Spearman's rank correlation coefficient for regional unemployment rates between:						
1974-1979	1979-1984	1984-1989	1989-1993	1974-1993	1979-1993	1984-1993
Men	0.99	0.87	0.91	0.80	0.75	0.72	0.90
Women	0.98	0.86	0.90	0.56	0.53	0.57	0.66
All persons	**0.99**	**0.86**	**0.91**	**0.76**	**0.72**	**0.71**	**0.87**

Source: Employment Department.

Figure 8.5   Dispersion of regional unemployment rates, 1974-1993

Relative dispersion

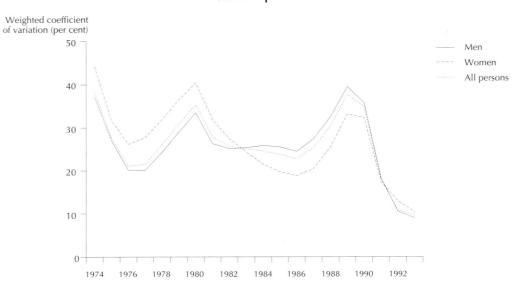

Absolute dispersion

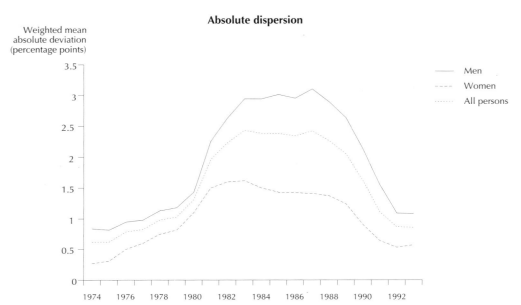

Notes

Claimant unemployment (adjusted for seasonality and discontinuities) expressed as a percentage of the workforce, Great Britain, April.

Source: Employment Department.

1980s. Whichever measure is used, though, the dispersion of regional unemployment rates has narrowed greatly in recent years.

Not only has the distribution of regional unemployment rates tended to be wider than that of regional earnings, its rank ordering has remained more stable.

Table 8.3 suggests that the rank ordering of regional unemployment rates changed little between the mid 1970s and the end of the 1980s, although there are indications of a more significant change between 1989 and 1993, as unemployment differentials narrowed. This is mainly due to a sharp rise in claimant unemployment in Greater London. Evans and McCormick (1994) suggest these recent changes in the regional pattern of unemployment rates have been the most pronounced for at least 70 years.

Figure 8.6 Correlation across regions between average earnings and unemployment rates, all full-time employees, 1974-1993

Including South East

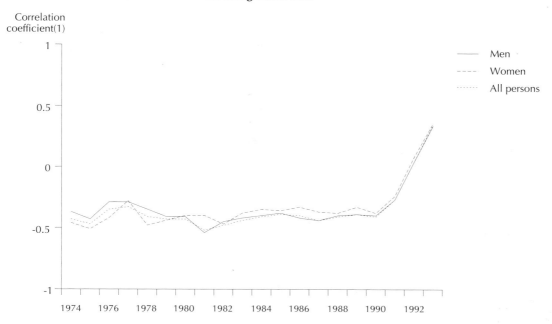

Excluding South East

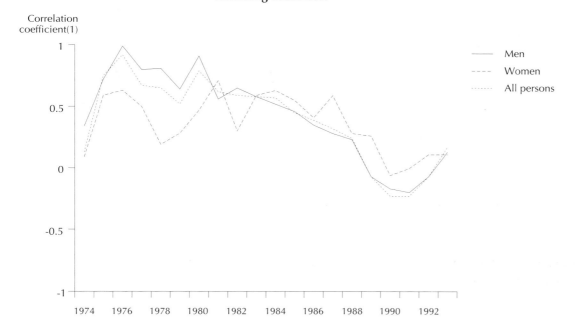

Notes

1 *Correlation coefficient calculated across standard regions between: average earnings (real average hourly earnings excluding overtime for full-time employees on adult rates whose pay for the survey period was unaffected by absence); and claimant unemployment (adjusted for seasonality and discontinuities, expressed as a percentage of the workforce); April.*

Sources: New Earnings Surveys, Employment Department.

Figure 8.7 **Correlation across regions between average earnings and unemployment rates, full-time manual employees, 1974-1993**

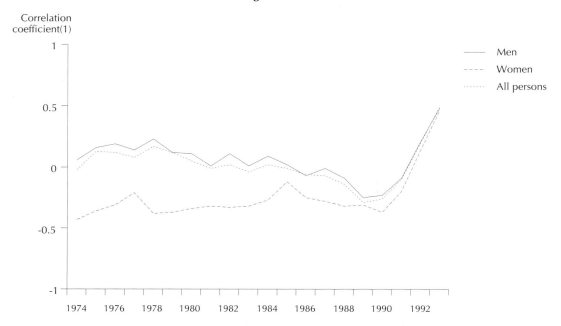

Including South East

Excluding South East

Notes

1   *Correlation coefficient calculated across standard regions: between average earnings (real average hourly earnings excluding overtime for full-time manual employees on adult rates whose pay for the survey period was unaffected by absence); and claimant unemployment (adjusted for seasonality and discontinuities, expressed as a percentage of the workforce); April.*

Sources: *New Earnings Surveys, Employment Department.*

Figure 8.8   Correlation across regions between average earnings and unemployment rates, full-time non-manual employees, 1974-1993

Including South East

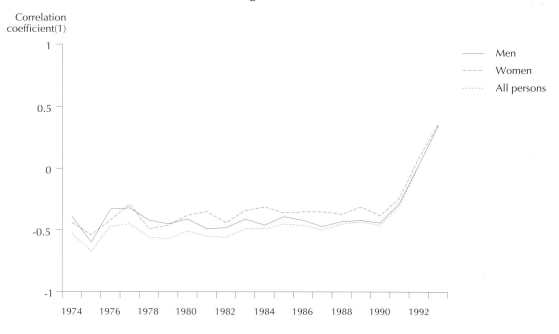

Excluding South East

Notes

1   *Correlation coefficient calculated across standard regions between: average earnings (real average hourly earnings excluding overtime for full-time non-manual employees on adult rates whose pay for the survey period was unaffected by absence); and claimant unemployment, (adjusted for seasonality and discontinuities, expressed as a percentage of the workforce); April.*

Sources: New Earnings Surveys, Employment Department.

Figure 8.6 provides some descriptive data on the relationship between regional wages and unemployment by plotting the correlation coefficients between regional earnings (male, female and total) and the regional unemployment rate.

Outside the South East, earnings have tended to be positively correlated with the unemployment rate. However, the size of the correlation coefficient fell steadily during the 1980s. By 1990, regional earnings outside the South East were uncorrelated with the unemployment rate. Illustrations of this are the way that relative earnings in East Anglia (a low unemployment region) steadily increased after 1979, whereas Wales (where unemployment in 1979 was relatively high) has seen relative earnings fall.

Figures 8.7 and 8.8 present similar calculations for manual and non-manual earnings. In general, there has been a strong positive correlation between manual earnings outside the South East and unemployment, greater than for non-manual earnings. In both cases, though, the correlation declined during the second half of the 1980s.

c) Econometric studies

The analysis above suggests there has been some realignment of relative earnings, in response to widening unemployment differentials. But inferences based on movements in aggregate variables and pairwise correlations are necessarily tentative. They take no account of the dynamics of labour market adjustment, or of other relevant variables (such as regionally-biased demand shocks). Econometric methods ought to shed more light on these issues.

Table 8.4 presents summary information on the studies reviewed in this section.

Hyclak and Johnes (1992) provide specific estimates of regional wage flexibility. This is measured by the coefficient on the regional unemployment rate in their wage equations; the greater the (negative) sign of this coefficient, the more responsive regional earnings are to regional unemployment.

Figure 8.9 graphs estimates for each standard region. All these estimates were statistically significant (at

Table 8.4   Econometric studies of regional wage determination

Study	Time period[1]	Dependent variable(s)	Method of analysis
Hyclak and Johnes (1992)	1971-1985	Average male earnings	Time-series Phillips curves estimated for each region
Egginton (1988)	1971-1987	Average male earnings, actual and 'normalised'[2]	Time-series wage equations estimated for each region
Blackaby and Manning (1990b)	1970-1986	Ratio of actual to 'expected', average male gross weekly earnings[3]	Time-series wage equations estimated for each region
Pissarides and McMaster (1990)	1961-1982	Average male manual earnings	Pooled cross-section, time-series wage equation
Jackman and Savouri (1991)	1974-1989	Average hourly earnings excluding overtime, full-time employees	Pooled cross-section, time-series wage equations estimated for different categories of employee: men and women, manual and non-manual, manufacturing and non-manufacturing
Blackaby and Manning (1992)	1972-1988	As Blackaby and Manning (1990b)	Pooled cross-section, time-series Phillips curve

Notes

1   All these studies use annual data.

2   'Normalised' earnings in a region were calculated by multiplying average national earnings in each industry by regional employment weights.

3   'Expected' earnings calculated as in Egginton (1988). Two series were calculated: one controlling for industry; the other for occupation.

the 10 per cent level), and varied from -0.42 for the West Midlands to -0.82 for East Anglia.

Figure 8.9 suggests there is a positive correlation between regional wage rigidity and unemployment, i.e. regions where earnings were slowest to adjust suffered the largest increases in unemployment.

Egginton (1988) attempted to correct the earnings data for inter-regional differences in the composition of employment. In most cases, the growth of 'normalised' earnings was an accurate indicator of actual earnings growth. Excess supply, represented by the regional short-term unemployment rate (the proportion of the workforce unemployed for less than 6 months), did exert a restraining influence on wage growth in a number of regions, but the estimates were often not very well determined.

Blackaby and Manning (1990b) followed a similar approach. They also found that unemployment

exerted a negative effect on regional earnings, although the precise mechanism varied between alternative model specifications.

Given the potential difficulties associated with pure time-series modelling - especially the lack of a long time series - a number of studies have pooled cross-section and time-series data. Pooling assumes that the relationships between regional earnings and other variables are the same across all regions, and this assumption needs to be tested[6].

Pissarides and McMaster (1990) estimated a dynamic wage equation incorporating an error correction mechanism. The more sophisticated dynamics enabled them to distinguish between short-run and long-run effects. In the long-run, relative wages were positively correlated with relative unemployment - a compensating differentials story. However, this positive correlation did not

Figure 8.9   Real wage flexibility and changes in regional unemployment

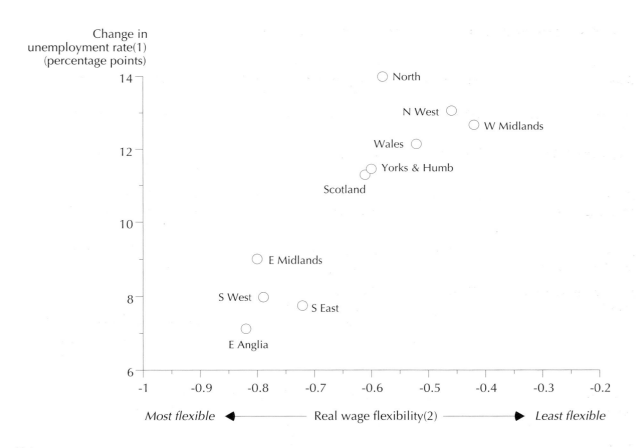

necessarily hold during periods when the labour market was out of equilibrium.

Jackman and Savouri (1991) found that local labour market conditions (measured by the regional unemployment rate) had a restraining effect on the earnings of male manual employees, especially in manufacturing. However, regional unemployment had no significant effect on the earnings of non-manual employees or women. These findings appear reasonably robust to a number of alternative specifications.

Jackman and Savouri suggest their findings may reflect differences in the geographical scale of occupational labour markets: the labour market for manual workers may be local in nature, whereas the market for non-manual workers is essentially national in scope, due to greater labour mobility[7]. In the case of women, they suggest that compositional effects and changes in supply outweigh other factors.

There was little evidence to suggest that regional earnings had become more responsive to unemployment in recent years. Jackman and Savouri tested for this by inter-acting their regional unemployment variable with a dummy variable for the post-1985 period. A significant negative effect was only found for male manual employees outside manufacturing.

Blackaby and Manning's (1992) model specification bears some similarities to Hyclak and Johnes (1992), although pooling meant the authors were able to use more general model specifications. The steady-state results suggest that the short-term unemployment rate exerts a negative effect on regional earnings. There is also a feedback to unemployment, with higher regional earnings pushing up unemployment. Blackaby and Manning also examined the stability of their results and found no evidence of instability.

All of these studies used aggregated, regional-level data. Some of them make corrections for inter-regional differences in the industrial or occupational composition of employment. However, none controls adequately for human capital and other personal and workplace characteristics that are known to influence wages at the individual level. Changes in aggregate wage behaviour could reflect complex compositional effects, or changes in other explanatory variables.

Appendix 4 reviews the available evidence on *ceteris paribus* regional wage differentials. The evidence suggests such differentials can be significant. They appear to resemble the patterns evident in the raw data, with wages being highest in the South East and those in other regions much closer to each other.

There is still evidence of increasing dispersion and some degree of realignment in these differentials.

There is also evidence of a negative relationship between wages and regional unemployment (Blackaby and Manning (1990a), Blackaby, Bladen-Hovell and Symons (1991), Blanchflower and Oswald (1993)). Furthermore, Blanchflower and Oswald's results indicate that wages may have become more responsive to unemployment during the 1980s.

One reason why regional earnings differentials may persist, even after controlling for other factors, is regional differences in the cost of living. No official data exist on regional price levels. However, a number of studies have used alternative, independent cost of living indices[8]. These suggest that regional differences could be an important source of wage variation.

d)   Sub-regional analyses

Discussion so far has focused entirely on standard regions, but these are not local labour markets. The geographical size of the labour market is likely to vary by industry and occupation but, for most of the labour force, the appropriate unit of analysis is likely to be a smaller, sub-regional area (with the possible exception of Greater London). Geographical areas such as Travel to Work Areas (TTWAs) would be more appropriate, but reliable earnings data at such a local level is not generally available.

Freeman (1988) explored the relationship between earnings and unemployment at the county level. For the period 1979-1985, he regressed average earnings of male manual workers on county unemployment, plus variables to capture education levels and industrial structure. The result was an estimated wage-unemployment elasticity of -0.92 (i.e. a 1 per cent increase in the local unemployment rate was associated with average earnings being 0.92 per cent lower). Although the relatively simple specification means the results must be treated with caution, they are consistent with the region-based analysis of Jackman and Savouri (1991), who also found that manual earnings are most sensitive to local economic conditions.

Manning (1994) provides a more sophisticated analysis of wage determination at county level, using pooled cross-section, time-series data for the period 1976-1992. The results are for male earnings only. They indicate that the relationships between earnings and unemployment estimated using region-level data are also evident at the county level, with estimated wage elasticities of about -0.1[9].

Manning found, however, that counties could not be treated in isolation. There was evidence to suggest that earnings at county level were influenced by county-specific and national factors, as well as by developments in neighbouring areas.

At an even more disaggregated level, Molho (1991) presents earnings data derived from tax records that are disaggregated to the Local Labour Market Area (LLMA) level, spatial units similar in size to TTWAs. Figure 8.10 suggests that, at the sub-regional level, there has been a moderate increase in the dispersion of earnings.

However, the strength of this effect is insufficient to reject the hypothesis that, as with the regional data, most of the increase in wage dispersion has been due to earnings in the South East pulling away from the rest of the country.

e)   International comparisons

Regional earnings data for nine countries (the G7 economies plus Australia and Sweden) was brought together in OECD (1990b). Regional wage dispersion has tended to be greatest in France, Japan and the USA. During the 1970s, regional wage differentials narrowed in the UK and in every other country covered by the study. But the increase in wage dispersion seen in the UK during the 1980s appears to have exceeded that of any other country: indeed, wage differentials continued to narrow in Australia, Canada, Germany, and Sweden. By 1987, regional wage dispersion in the UK was on a par with the USA[10].

Figure 8.11 presents estimates of the stability of regional wage distributions, measured by the correlation coefficient between the regional wage structure in 1987 and that in earlier years. In most countries, regional earnings distributions were quite stable during the 1970s and 1980s. The relative position of regions appears to have changed most in Australia, Canada and Italy.

OECD (1990b) also presents estimates of the correlation across regions between earnings and unemployment. These measures are similar to those presented in Figures 8.6 to 8.8. The correlation coefficients for 1987 are graphed in Figure 8.12.

Figure 8.10   The dispersion of earnings at local labour market level, 1975/76-1987/88

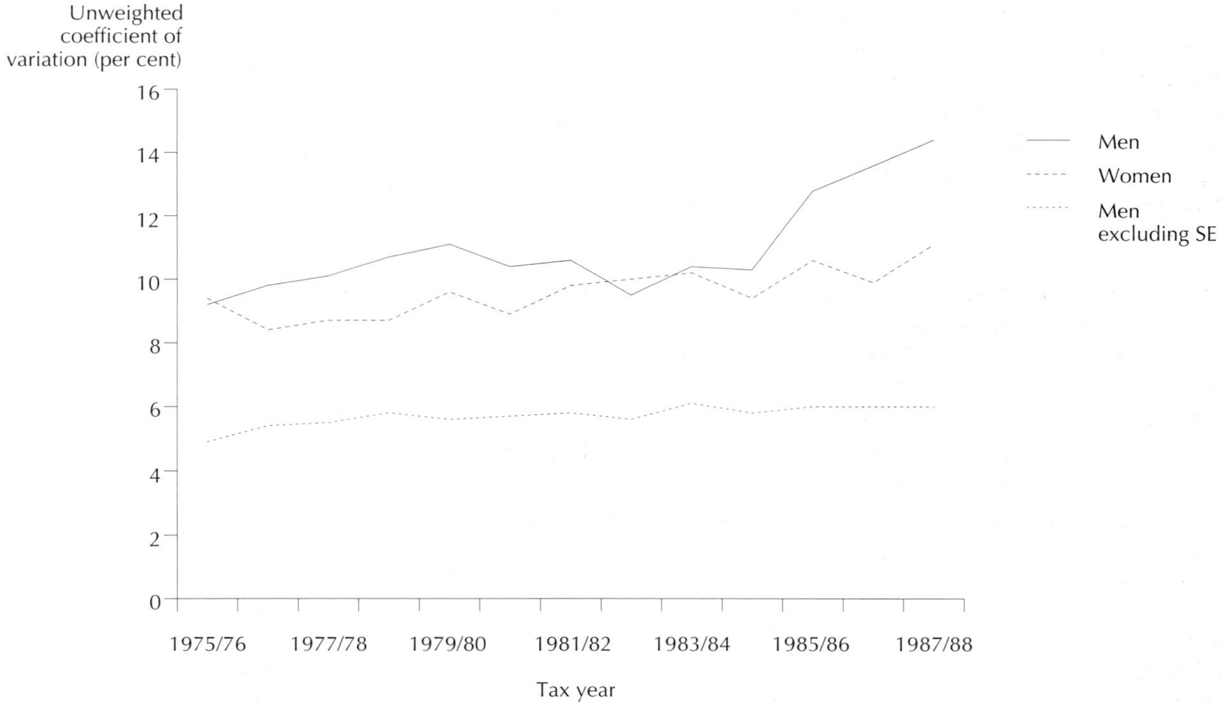

Notes

The earnings variable used is average gross monthly earnings.

Source: Molho (1991).

The coefficient for the UK was substantially more negative than for any other country. In Italy and Germany there was a sizeable positive relationship[11]. This does not necessarily mean that regional wages in the UK are more responsive to labour market shocks than elsewhere (CEC (1993)). It does, however, suggest that the UK regional wage structure is not unusually rigid.

Comparable information from the EU-wide Labour Costs Survey is available for the manufacturing sector. CEC (1993) presents regional analyses based on the 1988 survey. Another measure of dispersion was used, the gap between the region with the highest hourly labour costs and that with the lowest. On that basis, regional labour cost dispersion was greatest in Portugal (60 per cent difference), followed by France (56 per cent), Italy (40 per cent), Spain (35 per cent), the UK (30 per cent), and finally Germany (27 per cent). These results differ from those reported in OECD (1990b), but the different measures of dispersion and different variables used mean that a satisfactory explanation would require further analysis of the raw data. CEC (1993) presents comparisons with the 1981 survey. The distribution of regional labour costs appears to have widened

significantly between 1981 and 1988 in France and the UK, whereas there was little change in Italy and Germany.

The relationship in 1988 between regional labour costs and regional unemployment rates varied across the EU. There was a negative relationship between the two variables in France, Italy, the UK, and Spain, but there was a positive relationship in Portugal and virtually no correlation between the two variables in Germany[12]. Again, these results are not wholly consistent with the OECD estimates in Figure 8.12.

There is also some econometric evidence comparing regional wage flexibility across countries. Johnes and Hyclak (1989) estimated time-series Phillips curves for each region in the UK, Germany and Italy. These were similar to those estimated in Hyclak and Johnes (1992), save for the addition of a union militancy term. The time period covered by the analysis was 1973-1985. The region-specific estimates of wage flexibility were found to be negative and reasonably significant in every region in each of the three countries. Regional earnings in Germany, however, were found to be more responsive to unemployment than earnings in either the UK or Italy.

Figure 8.11 International comparisons of the stability of regional wage distributions, 1970-1987

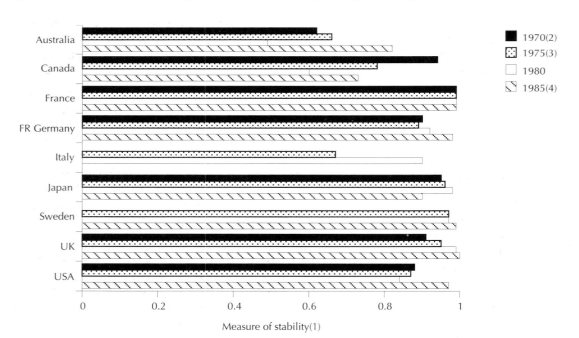

Measure of stability(1)

Notes

1 Measured by the correlation coefficient across regions between average earnings in 1987 and average earnings in the year in question.

2 Except for the UK (1971).

3 Except Italy (1976).

4 Except Italy (1984).

Source: OECD (1990b), Table 3.5.

100

Figure 8.12 International comparisons of the correlation between regional earnings and unemployment, 1987

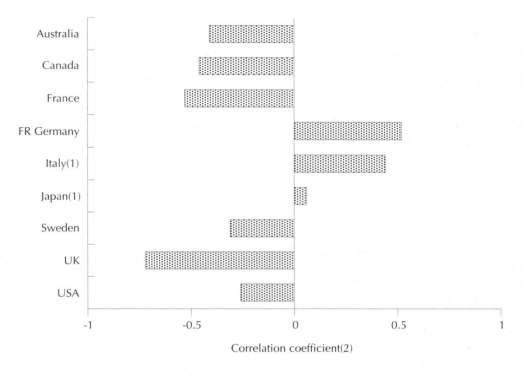

Correlation coefficient(2)

Notes

1   *1987 except Italy (1984) and Japan (1985).*

2   *The correlation across regions between average regional earnings and the regional unemployment rate.*

Source: OECD (1990b), Table 3.6.

Blanchflower and Oswald (1992) estimated 'wage curves' for nine OECD countries. These measured the relationship between individual earnings and regional unemployment using individual-level (ISSP) data. A statistically significant negative relationship was found in every case except the Netherlands[13].

f)   Summary and conclusions

- Outside the South East, there is little regional variation in average earnings. Although the trend towards convergence has been halted, the regional earnings distribution has widened because wage growth in the South East has tended to outstrip that in the rest of the country.

- There are also occupational differences: the earnings of non-manual employees are more dispersed than those of manuals.

- Nevertheless, there have been changes in the regional wage structure since the end of the 1970s. Some regions, the West Midlands and Wales in particular, have seen earnings decline relative to other regions. But other regions, such as East Anglia and the South West, have seen a relative increase in wages. All regions, however, have seen average earnings grow in real terms.

- Regional earnings may have become better aligned with regional unemployment rates. Although the regional bias of the last recession is probably the main reason why unemployment rates converged so rapidly, regional wage realignment may have been a contributory factor[14].

- Econometric studies suggest that earnings do respond to supply and demand conditions in regional labour markets. There is less evidence available on whether or not earnings have become more responsive in recent years.

- There are significant *ceteris paribus* inter-regional wage differentials. These may be explicable in terms of cost of living and/or compensating differentials, but they may also represent residual barriers to adjustment.

- In absolute terms, regional wage differentials are still very low outside the South East. In 1993, average hourly earnings for manual employees in the North (where earnings were the highest outside the South East) were only 6 per cent higher than in the South West (where earnings were lowest).

- In contrast, even though the regional distribution of unemployment rates has narrowed, unemployment differentials are still relatively large. Unemployment rates are likely to vary most by region for manual workers, where wage dispersion is narrowest[15].

- In these circumstances, it appears difficult to accept that there is too much regional variation in earnings, or that wages are too sensitive to labour market conditions.

- Regional wage dispersion during the 1970s and 1980s tended to be greatest in France, Japan and the USA. During the 1970s, the regional distribution of earnings narrowed in all the main OECD economies. While the dispersion of earnings across regions widened during the 1980s in a number of countries, this trend was most pronounced in the UK.

- Econometric evidence suggests there is a negative relationship between wages and regional unemployment in most major OECD countries.

Footnotes to Chapter 8

1. Two minor adjustments had to be made to the earnings data to produce a consistent time series on current definitions. See Appendix 1 for details.

2. The weighted coefficient of variation is calculated as:

$$CV = \frac{1}{W_{GB}} \frac{1}{\sqrt{\sum\limits_{i=1}^{i=k} S_i}} \sqrt{\sum\limits_{i=1}^{i=k} S_i (W_i - W_{GB})}$$

where w is the wage, w_{GB} is the national wage, s is the number of full-time employees, and i=1...k is the number of regions.

3. The earnings variable used is average hourly earnings excluding overtime, but very similar results are obtained if either total weekly earnings or total hourly earnings are used instead.

4. Table 7.3 contains NES data that supports this hypothesis. Table 7.2, however, suggests the opposite: by 1990, a greater proportion of non-manual employees were covered by multi-employer agreements than manual employees. This apparent discrepancy may be due to changes in wage setting arrangements in the late 1980s. The majority of employees covered by national agreements that were dissolved over this period are likely to have been manual workers.

5. Estimates excluding the South East are not presented, as calculations on this basis produce broadly similar results.

6. Hyclak and Johnes (1992) found their data could not reject the pooling assumption.

7. Reflected in the significance of regional house prices in the male non-manual earnings equation.

8. See Blackaby and Manning (1990a), Blackaby, Bladen-Hovell and Symons (1991), Blackaby and Murphy (1991), and Blackaby and Manning (1992).

9. In the case of manual earnings, there was some evidence of a non-linear relationship between earnings and unemployment.

10. Although the data in OECD (1990b) did not point to a very significant widening of the US regional earnings distribution, Phillips (1992) presents calculations which suggest that inequality across 'economic regions' may have doubled during the 1980s.

11. Statistically significant in the case of Italy.

12. The measure used was the Spearman's rank correlation coefficient. The results were Germany = 0.03; France = -0.39; Italy = -0.59; UK = -0.31; Spain = -0.79; Portugal = 0.79.

13. Based on the results for wage equations that *included* regional dummies, (except Switzerland, where a wage equation of this form was not reported because only a single year's data was available). The Dutch wage equation without regional dummies did produce a negative and significant coefficient on the unemployment variable.

14. This pattern of regional wage adjustment would appear to be consistent with the predictions of the model estimated by Pissarides and McMaster (1990).

15. LFS data on unemployment rates by previous occupation was examined but found to be unsatisfactory for this kind of analysis. One objection is that they are based on previous occupation, and this may not be the same as the respondent's 'typical' occupation. In addition, though, data on previous occupation is not collected for many of the unemployed - people with no previous occupation, or people who have not been in employment for some time.

Chapter 9
Relative wage flexibility: industries

The analysis of relative wage flexibility across industries is presented in two parts:

- A descriptive analysis of the distribution of wages across industries;

- A review of the econometric evidence on *ceteris paribus* inter-industry wage differentials, and the extent to which earnings in different industries are responsive to demand and supply.

The conclusions that can be drawn from analyses of the industrial earnings distribution are influenced by views about how the industrial wage structure is determined in the first place. Lawson, Tarling and Wilkinson (1982) identify three competing explanations:

- In neoclassical models, *ceteris paribus* wage differentials should only reflect non-pecuniary compensating differentials. Lawson, Tarling and Wilkinson suggest that this implies an industrial wage structure which is stable over time. But this is very much a long run position. During the intermediate period, there need be no such presumption. So, even if the wage structure reflects compensating differentials in the long run, there can be short to medium term fluctuations as demand and supply conditions change.

- In contrast, 'Keynesian' models of wage determination stress the institutional aspects of wage-setting. The key feature is the interdependence of wage-setting across sectors. Wage shocks are transmitted quickly from industry to industry through formal or informal comparability mechanisms. Hence the observed wage structure is highly stable. This prediction would furthermore seem to hold in all but the short run.

- Finally, there are non-competitive models of wage determination that do not require the industrial wage distribution to be stable over time, such as efficiency wages, insider-outsider, or union bargaining models.

These alternative theoretical positions still leave room for ambiguity. It is far from clear how to differentiate the 'stability' seen as inherent in neoclassical and 'Keynesian' models from the potential 'instability' of other models. Equally, it is difficult to see how short run fluctuations in the wage structure are to be distinguished from long term effects. This means different conclusions could be drawn from the same stylised facts.

a)   Trends in the distribution of earnings by industry

There are some important limitations on analyses of long-term trends in the distribution of earnings. Changes in the way earnings data has been collected, and who it covers, have been compounded by changes to the system of industrial classification (the SIC). Long term comparisons are restricted to certain types of employee (mainly manual workers) in certain industries (typically concentrated in the production and manufacturing sectors).

Tarling and Wilkinson (1982) assembled data covering the period from 1948 to 1980, drawn from the Department of Employment's average earnings enquiry and the October enquiry into manual earnings. The data covers much of the manual labour force, and most of manufacturing industry, but excludes most private service industries.

Tarling and Wilkinson reported two measures of the stability of the industrial earnings distribution. One was the value of R^2 from a regression of the wage structure at any single year on that in the base year, 1948[1]. The other was the rank correlation coefficient between the wage structure in any single year and that in 1948. By 1980, both measures took values of around 0.25, suggesting there had been a good deal of change over time. Tarling and Wilkinson noted the role of the incomes policies periodically applied by governments during the 1960s and 1970s. The impact of these policies, and their unwinding, certainly contributed to the degree of short run variability in the data.

Haskel and Martin's (1991) comparison of the wage structure for unskilled workers covers roughly the same period, 1948-1979. The data, drawn from the Census of Production, was aggregated to industry groups within the production and manufacturing sectors. In contrast to Tarling and Wilkinson, their results suggest the industrial wage structure was highly stable over the period in question. The correlation coefficient measuring the relationship between the wage structures in 1948 and 1979 was 0.82[2]. Hence there are conflicting views about the *degree* of stability. Haskel and Martin also found that employment growth in these industries varied much more than relative earnings. Thus, in the long term at least, quantities have adjusted rather than prices.

Elliott and White (1993) present a more detailed analysis of trends, covering the period 1970-1982. Their analysis used NES data covering all industries. Some limited compositional controls were also introduced through separate analyses of the wage structure for men and women, as well as for different occupational groups.

The main measure of stability used was the rank correlation coefficient, comparing earnings in any given year with the base year, 1970. There was a good deal of stability in the wage distribution over this period: rank correlation coefficients tended to remain at values of 0.6 or higher. The results depend upon the *measure* of pay used. Table 9.1 presents estimates of the rank correlation coefficients between 1970 and 1982 for different measures of average earnings.

In general, the results for women were broadly similar whichever measure of earnings was used[3]. Those for men differ more.

Elliott and White also present estimates of the dispersion of the industrial earnings distribution around the mean. Figure 9.1 graphs the (unweighted) coefficients of variation.

The picture is quite complex, varying to some extent between men and women, and between occupational groups. However, the general tendency was for a narrowing of the distribution during the mid 1970s, followed by a widening towards the end of the decade.

While changes to the industrial classification pose some problems, an update on trends since the early 1980s is required. Figure 9.2 presents estimates of industrial wage dispersion since 1985.

The industrial distribution of earnings has continued to widen. At this broad level of aggregation, however, the wage distribution appears to have been highly stable. The correlation coefficient between earnings[4] in 1985 and 1994 was 0.986, while the comparable rank correlation coefficient was 0.955[5].

Table 9.2 presents data on relative earnings in each industry Division for 1985 and 1994. It demonstrates the relatively small changes in rank ordering that have taken place over the period. On average, earnings have grown fastest in banking, finance and business services, the energy sector, and other services.

Earnings *growth*, however, is not so stable in the short run. There is little correlation across industries between real annual earnings growth in one year and that in the next, i.e. sectors where real earnings grow slowly one year can often see earnings grow quickly the next. This effect was present in Tarling and Wilkinson (1982), who pointed to the effects of incomes policies. However, a degree of short run variability has also been found for a period when earnings have not been regulated.

Table 9.1   The stability of the industrial earnings distribution, 1970-1982

Measure of stability[1] calculated for full-time employees, Great Britain, April							
Measure of earnings:	SEG4 (Junior non-manual)		SEG6 (Skilled manual)		SEG8 (Unskilled manual)	
	Men	Women	Men	Women	Men	Women
Gross earnings:						
Weekly	0.50	0.95	0.50	0.90	0.73	0.79
Hourly	0.16	0.92	0.77	0.94	0.88	0.65
Residual earnings[2] (1973-1982):						
Weekly	0.54	0.93	0.87	0.86	0.67	0.75
Hourly	0.49	0.92	0.87	0.79	0.61	0.65

Notes

1   The Spearman's rank correlation coefficient between earnings in 1970 and 1982, calculated across the 10 Divisions of the 1980 SIC.

2   Average earnings excluding overtime, shiftwork and incentive payments. Hourly earnings were calculated using total hours worked minus overtime hours.

Source: Elliott and White (1993), Table 4.

Figure 9.1   Dispersion across industries of average earnings, 1970-1982

Men

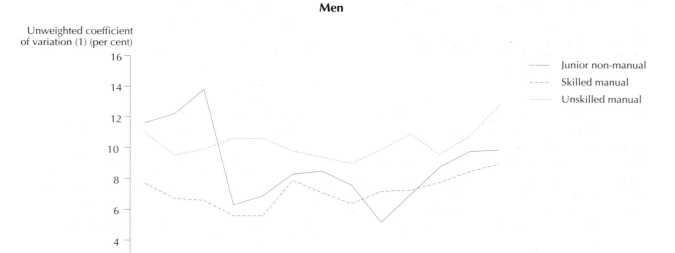

Unweighted coefficient
of variation (1) (per cent)

Junior non-manual
Skilled manual
Unskilled manual

Women

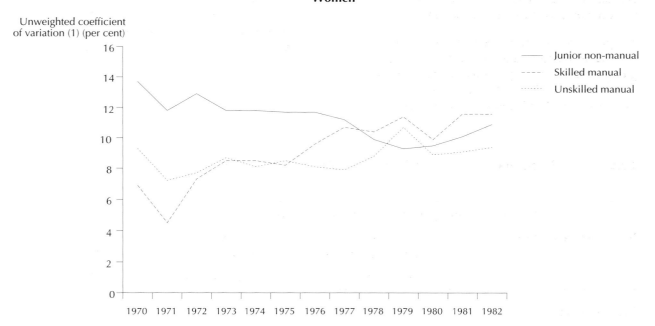

Unweighted coefficient
of variation (1) (per cent)

Junior non-manual
Skilled manual
Unskilled manual

Notes

1   *Coefficient of variation of average earnings, computed across the 10 Divisions of the 1980 SIC.   The measure of earnings used is gross weekly earnings of full-time employees, Great Britain, April.*

Source: Elliott and White (1993), Table 7.

Figure 9.2   Dispersion across industries of average earnings, 1985-1994

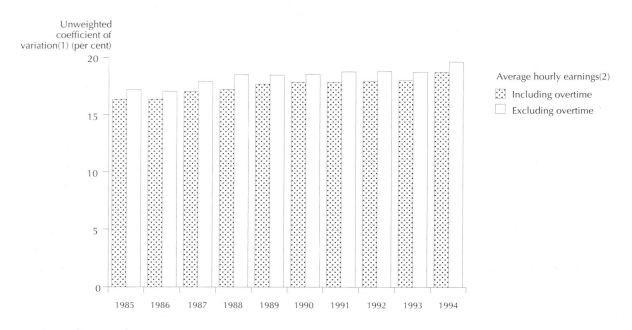

Notes

1   *Coefficient of variation of average earnings, computed across the 10 Divisions of the 1980 SIC.*

2   *Average hourly earnings of full-time employees on adult rates whose pay for the survey period was unaffected by absence, Great Britain, April.*

Source: New Earnings Surveys.

Table 9.2   Relative earnings by industry Division, 1985-1994

Real hourly earnings excluding overtime of full-time employees on adult rates whose earnings for the survey period were unaffected by absence, Great Britain, April			
Industry Division (1980 SIC):	**1985**	**1994**	**Average real earnings growth, 1985-1994 (per cent per annum)**
0 Agriculture, forestry, fishing	63.0	61.7	2.5
1 Energy and water supply	124.5	130.9	3.3
2 Mineral extraction etc.	105.8	101.4	2.3
3 Metal goods, vehicles etc.	100.0	97.8	2.5
4 Other manufacturing	91.8	87.0	2.1
5 Construction	91.5	90.5	2.6
6 Distribution, hotels and catering, repairs	80.4	77.7	2.4
7 Transport and communication	101.0	94.4	2.0
8 Banking, finance, business services	121.1	125.3	3.1
9 Other services	103.9	106.4	3.0
All industries	**100.0**	**100.0**	**2.8**

Source: New Earnings Surveys.

b)   Econometric studies

The descriptive analyses above are insufficient on their own to determine whether the industrial wage structure is 'flexible' or 'inflexible'. Short run variability in real earnings growth could be a sign of relative wage flexibility, with wages in different sectors growing at different rates in response to market conditions. But such an observation is also consistent with other explanations, such as differential lags in the speed with which earnings respond to the whole economy 'going rate'.

An immediate issue is the extent to which inter-industry wage differentials reflect compositional differences in the workforce. Evidence from recent studies of *ceteris paribus* inter-industry wage differentials is summarised in Appendix 4. These studies suggest that inter-industry wage differentials persist once human capital and other factors are controlled for. The dispersion of these differentials, however, is considerably reduced. Product and labour market conditions would appear to play a significant role in accounting for the remaining variation.

Results from a number of studies shed some light on sectoral wage determination. In terms of relative wage flexibility, a key issue is the extent to which earnings in individual industries are responsive to demand and supply conditions.

Key details on each of the four studies considered here are given in Table 9.3. Three of them - Lawson (1982), Pissarides and Moghadam (1989), and Lee and Pesaran (1993) - use a common methodology, estimating separate time series wage equations for each of the industries in their sample. The measures of responsiveness to labour market conditions varied, but in all three studies results were mixed:

- Lawson (1982) found that, in 12 of the 40 industries covered, the unemployment rate had no noticeable effect on earnings. In another 19, the coefficient on unemployment was statistically insignificant. This left only a minority of industries where unemployment exerted any significant independent effect.

- Lee and Pesaran (1993) found that the coefficient on aggregate unemployment was statistically insignificant in eight sectors, while in four it was significant and *positive*. In just four sectors - agriculture, business and the private service sector - was the coefficient on aggregate unemployment significant and negative. In much of the production sector, internal influences (productivity and profitability) and wage developments in other sectors (comparability) appear to have been more influential factors.

- Pissarides and Moghadam (1989) used extra measures of sector-specific conditions, but the results were no more consistent. The relative vacancy rate was statistically significant in just

Table 9.3   Econometric studies of sectoral wage determination

Study	Time period[1]	Number of industries covered	Method of analysis	Demand/supply variables used
Lawson (1982)	1954-1978	40	Time series[2]	Aggregate unemployment rate
Pissarides and Moghadam (1989)	1963-1982	16, mainly manufacturing	Time series[2]	Industry-specific relative vacancy and unemployment rates, aggregate vacancy rate
Henley (1989)	1970-1982 1983-1989	47 68	Pooled cross-section time series	None - flexibility measured by coefficient on lagged dependent variable
Lee and Pesaran (1993)	1957-1990	16	Time series[2]	Aggregate unemployment rate

Notes

1   All these studies used annual data.

2   In other words, a separate time series wage equation was estimated for each industry in the sample.

four sectors, where its coefficient was negative, contrary to expectations. The authors concluded that industry-specific influences on wage determination were relatively weak in most of the sectors studied.

Henley's (1989) study used another approach. Henley argued that industrial wage flexibility reflects the degree, and speed, with which actual earnings converge to their equilibrium levels. The speed of adjustment was therefore measured by the degree to which earnings growth in one period is a function of earnings growth in previous periods. The less serially correlated earnings growth is, the quicker wages return to their equilibrium levels.

The results suggest that industrial earnings were highly flexible, especially over the 1983-1989 period[6]. Yet, as Elliott and White (1993) point out, this short-run flexibility was insufficient to change the rank order of industrial earnings greatly from one year to the next.

Stability and short run flexibility are not inconsistent. Henley's model allowed earnings in individual industries to grow at different rates, reflecting differences in human capital formation, technological change or institutional features such as bargaining arrangements. Similarly, Lawson's (1982) results suggest there is an element of short-run variability to real earnings growth. What is not clear is whether these short run variations are the result of labour markets adjusting to sector-specific shocks, or whether they are the result of the vagaries of incomes policies and wage shocks being transmitted from one industry to another.

c)   International comparisons

Freeman (1988) analysed trends in industrial wage dispersion across the OECD area. Figure 9.3 presents estimates of the dispersion of hourly compensation per employee[7].

Figure 9.3   International comparisons of wage dispersion across industries, 1975-1986

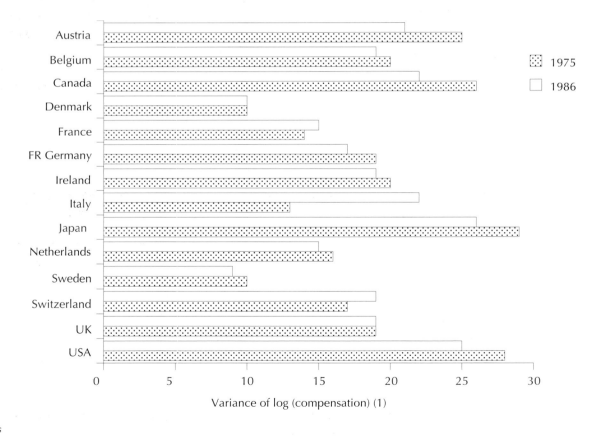

Variance of log (compensation) (1)

Notes

1   Hourly compensation per employee, computed across industrial sectors.

Source: US Bureau of Labor Statistics data, cited in Freeman (1988), Table 2.

Freeman identified a group of 'high and increasing' countries, comprising Canada, Japan, the USA and Austria. The UK, along with Australia, New Zealand and Norway, formed an 'increasing' group. At the other end of the spectrum, France and Italy were identified as countries with 'declining' industrial wage dispersion, while Denmark, Finland and Sweden had the narrowest inter-industry wage differentials. The latter finding is no doubt a consequence of the tradition of 'solidaristic' wage bargaining in these countries.

No information is available which gives a reliable picture on trends since the mid 1980s.

Two of the econometric studies of wage determination reviewed earlier in this chapter included international comparisons. Pissarides and Moghadam (1989) estimated time-series earnings equations for a number of (manufacturing) industries in four countries - Finland, Sweden, the UK, and the USA. Although both corporatist and non-corporatist economies were covered by the study, the results for each of the countries were similar. In particular, industry-specific labour market variables (vacancies and unemployment) tended to be a significant factor in only about a third to a quarter of industries in each country. This includes some instances where the sign of such an effect appeared perverse.

Henley (1989) measured flexibility by the speed with which wages return to their equilibrium path following a shock. Equations were estimated for

Germany, Sweden, the UK and the USA, and the key results are presented in Table 9.4.

On this measure, industry-level wages appear considerably more flexible in the UK. Thus the econometric evidence on the responsiveness of industry wages is mixed. This may be due to the different approaches adopted by the two studies.

d) Summary and conclusions

- Inter-industry wage differentials narrowed somewhat during the second half of the 1970s, before widening again during the 1980s.

- Inter-industry wage differentials remain once allowance is made for personal characteristics and human capital, although their dispersion is substantially reduced.

- There is some evidence that earnings growth from year to year is more variable across industries. However, this variability is insufficient to greatly change the overall ordering of the industrial wage distribution.

- Sectoral and aggregate labour market factors have a relatively limited impact on wage determination. Recent studies suggest such influences may be important in some industries, but in many they exert little or no independent influence.

- However, there is also evidence that wage shocks are transmitted across the economy. Hence these

Table 9.4   International comparisons of industrial wage flexibility

Country	Estimation period	Number of industries in analysis	Measure of wage flexibility[1]	Number of years for wages to return to equilibrium[2]
FR Germany	1978-1987	27	-0.63	7-8
Sweden	1978-1987	28	-0.64	7-8
UK	1970-1982	47	-0.91	2
	1983-1989	68	-1.31	1
USA	1978-1986	97	-0.29	15+

Notes

1 *Based upon Henley's specification (3), which maximises R^2 and includes two lagged dependent variables. The rank ordering of coefficients across countries is unchanged, however, if other specifications are used.*

2 *The number of years over which wages return to their original (equilibrium) path following a 10 per cent positive shock, based upon inspection of Henley's Figure 1.*

Source: Henley (1989).

findings may understate the total impact of labour market factors.

- These findings are not inconsistent with wage flexibility on the lines of the neoclassical model. There is nothing in the theory which says that earnings in individual industries have to increase at the same rate[8]. But the evidence cannot refute alternative explanations either[9].

- The evidence on trends is limited. *Ceteris paribus* wage differentials appear to have widened somewhat since the end of the 1970s, while there is some (limited) evidence that short term wage flexibility has increased since the early 1980s.

- Evidence on trends in other countries suggests that the narrowing of inter-industry wage differentials seen in the UK during the mid to late 1970s was experienced in a number of other OECD economies. Not all countries, however, saw a subsequent widening of differentials in the 1980s.

- By 1986, industrial wage dispersion was relatively high in the UK, although not as great as in the USA, Japan, Canada or Austria. Differentials between industries were narrowest in the Nordic countries.

- Cross-country evidence from econometric studies is limited. Pissarides and Moghadam (1989) found that labour market conditions exerted only a weak influence on earnings in the UK, the USA, Finland and Sweden. Henley (1989), however, found that industry wages were considerably more flexible in the UK than in the USA, Sweden or Germany.

on this interpretation, the wage distribution has continued to widen while its ordering has become more stable.

6. Although, since the regressions are based on different SICs, the results are not strictly comparable.

7. Freeman (1988) presented data on industrial wage dispersion from a variety of sources. The US Bureau of Labor Statistics data presented in Figure 9.3 is broadly representative of the overall conclusions.

8. This prediction would only hold in a static, never-changing world, or one with perfect labour mobility (see, for example, Hildreth and Oswald (1993)).

9. Advocates of 'Keynesian' explanations could take comfort in the presence of adjustment lags in all the time series studies, as well as evidence pointing to the sectoral interdependency of wage setting. Similarly, the apparent significance of external factors in some industries could support an efficiency wage explanation, while the significance of workplace and institutional variables is consistent with bargaining models.

Footnotes to Chapter 9

1. It is the square of the Pearson correlation coefficient between the distributions of earnings in the two years.

2. Squaring these numbers to obtain Tarling and Wilkinson's R^2 measures reveals the substantial difference in the strength of association recorded by the two studies.

3. This does not necessarily imply that the industrial earnings distribution is the same whichever measure of pay is used. It merely means that, however pay is measured, industries' rank positions change at a similar rate.

4. Measured by average hourly earnings excluding overtime.

5. Since Elliott and White's (1993) results also *appear* to be based on the 1980 SIC, there may be a read-across between the two sets of results. Note that,

Chapter 10

Relative wage flexibility: human capital

This chapter looks at the responsiveness of wages to the supply and demand for human capital. In the previous section, competing theoretical models of wage determination meant it was difficult to interpret any given set of changes to the inter-industry wage structure. In contrast, the analysis in this section is based on the standard model of human capital and its accumulation. This predicts that workers' wages will reflect the general and firm-specific capital that they have accumulated and use in their job. Higher wages in this context provide the signals for individuals and employers to invest in human capital accumulation. The relative wage structure therefore needs to adjust to changes in demand and supply, especially since occupational mobility or human capital accumulation can be costly and take a considerable period of time.

The chapter therefore examines changes in the relative wage structure, and the extent to which these appear to have aided or impeded labour market adjustment. This involves two steps. The first is to quantify trends in the returns to human capital. The second is to relate these developments to demand and supply conditions.

Quantification raises a number of conceptual and methodological issues:

- In practice, 'human capital' cannot be observed directly. The analysis below therefore considers indirect measures: returns to educational attainment; skill levels; and occupations.

- 'Returns' themselves are difficult to measure. Ideally, they should be evaluated within a cost-benefit framework that considers the (discounted) stream of expected lifetime earnings against the (discounted) cost of human capital formation. The informational requirements of such an analysis are severe indeed. Most empirical analyses adopt a more practical but less rigorous approach, which is to compare the earnings of people in particular educational attainment groups/skill groups/occupations with those of people without the characteristic. Often the comparator is the unqualified or unskilled individual. While an imperfect measure of the overall returns to human capital, comparisons of the wage structure along these

lines are likely to be a useful surrogate measure[1].

- Changes in relative wages tend to affect not only the *ex ante* rates of return faced by individuals and employers considering investment in human capital, but also the *ex post* returns of people who have already acquired the human capital in question. The effect of relative wage changes on these *ex post* returns is also important.

- Differences in individuals' earnings reflect more than just the human capital they use in their jobs. This means that comparisons need to control for other factors.

- A particular methodological difficulty occurs because it is usually the most 'able' who gain access to education and training. Measured differentials will therefore overstate the direct returns to investment in human capital, since they capture, at least in part, returns to 'ability'. None of the studies reviewed in this section make any correction for this problem. However, since the focus here is on relative wages and their role in providing price signals to the market, this proviso may be less important than if the focus was on quantifying the precise rate of return to investment in human capital[2].

a)   Education

Relatively few British studies have estimated wage differentials by educational status. The best available source of data on individuals' earnings, the NES, does not collect data on educational qualifications.

Three recent studies have estimated *ceteris paribus* wage differentials for various levels of educational attainment. The results are summarised in Appendix 4. The pattern of *ceteris paribus* wage differentials appears to have been broadly similar in the mid 1970s and late 1980s/early 1990s, although differentials for particular qualifications may have changed. It is less clear whether differentials narrowed in the late 1970s and widened again in the early 1980s. Moghadam (1990) and Schmitt (1992) suggest this may have been the case, whereas Blanchflower and Freeman (1994) find no evidence to support this conclusion.

b)   Skills

The notion of 'skills' is necessarily diffuse. Studies measuring returns to skills have tended to concentrate on the skills of manual, rather than non-manual workers. This is partly because it appears easier to place manual jobs within a broad hierarchy of skill levels (unskilled, semi-skilled, skilled), although some related jobs usually classified as non-manual (supervisors, technicians) can often be incorporated within this hierarchy.

Elliott and Murphy (1990) reviewed evidence on long-term trends, based on a number of sources covering specific industries. Their results suggest that skill differentials have narrowed throughout much of this century.

The authors also investigated uncontrolled wage differentials using NES data for the period 1970-1982. Figure 10.1 summarises their findings. It suggests that, for both men and women, there was a narrowing in skill differentials over this period.

Differentials, however, varied across industries[3]. Indeed, in a few industries, skill differentials had widened over the period. Elliott and Murphy also checked to see how much contribution changes in the industrial mix of employment made to the apparent narrowing in differentials. They found that compositional changes tended to push differentials wider. There was, therefore, a very strong move towards narrowing skill differentials *within* individual industries. These effects were strongest between 1970 and 1975 for men, and between 1973 and 1977 for women.

Table 10.1 presents a more up-to-date picture of skill differentials based on a longer run of NES data. It is for men only, and is based on hourly rather than weekly earnings. It also controls for changes in the occupational mix within each broad skill level.

The table illustrates quite clearly the narrowing of differentials during the 1970s that was observed by Elliott and Murphy. Between 1979 and 1990, however, raw differentials widened considerably for groups such as foremen and technicians. Differentials for semi-skilled and skilled manuals increased somewhat less[4].

c)   Occupations

An occupation can be thought of as a label encapsulating a particular set of skills, which may or may not be closely related to educational attainment.

Figure 10.1   Skill differentials for men and women, 1970-1982

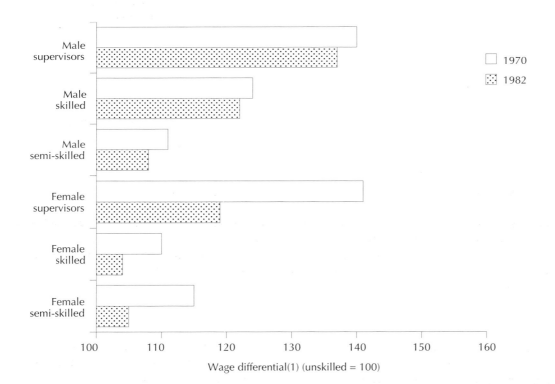

Wage differential(1) (unskilled = 100)

Notes

1   *Gross weekly earnings of full-time employees aged 21 or over (18 and over in the case of women) whose pay for the survey period was unaffected by absence, Great Britain, April.*

Source: Elliott and Murphy (1990), Tables II and III.

112

Table 10.1   Skill differentials for male employees, 1973-1990

Skill group[2]:	Gross weekly earnings of full-time male employees on adult rates[1] whose earnings for the survey period were unaffected by absence, Great Britain, April			
	1973	**1976**	**1979**	**1990**
Technicians	134	131	135	152
Foremen	136	131	135	146
Skilled	127	123	128	131
Semi-Skilled	108	105	109	112
Unskilled	100	100	100	100

Notes

1   Aged 21 and over prior to 1984.

2   Controlling for compositional effects by using the 1979 sample sizes as constant weights for constituent occupational groups.

Source: New Earnings Surveys.

Figure 10.2   The non-manual/manual earnings ratio, 1973-1994

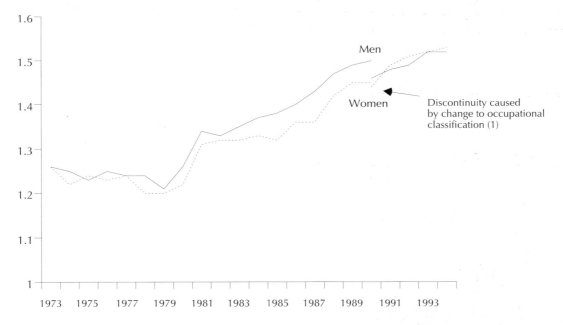

Notes

1   The change to the Standard Occupational classification (SOC) in 1990 introduces a discontinuity into the series, because definitions of manual and non-manual status are not entirely consistent across classifications.

The earnings variable used was gross weekly earnings of full-time employees on adult rates (prior to 1984, men aged 21 and over, women aged 18 and over) whose pay for the survey period was unaffected by absence, Great Britain, April.

Source: New Earnings Surveys.

To the extent that occupational categories package together skills and expertise not reflected in educational qualifications or broad skill classifications, occupational wage differentials could still exist once allowance has been made for these factors.

The simplest measure of occupational wage differentials is the ratio of non-manual to manual earnings, charted in Figure 10.2.

The non-manual/manual earnings ratio fell slightly during the mid to late 1970s. By 1979, the ratio was approximately 1.2 for both men and women. Since then, there has been a significant widening of the gap, with the ratio exceeding 1.5 by 1994[5].

Information on longer-term trends is available for manufacturing only. Machin (1994) presents Census of Production data which suggests that the non-manual/manual earnings ratio declined almost continuously between the beginning of the 1950s and the middle of the 1970s. The widening differentials of the past 15 years therefore represent a sharp break with the past.

More detailed analyses reveal a similar pattern of change. Table 10.2 presents data on the average earnings of male employees, disaggregating the sample into 17 occupational groups.

Between 1973 and 1979, total gross weekly earnings increased by 0.7 per cent a year in real terms. However, real earnings actually fell for a number of occupational groups, nearly all of which were in the relatively well-paid managerial and professional occupations. Over the period 1979-1990, real earnings grew at a faster rate, 1.1 per cent a year. In contrast, though, it was the more highly paid occupations that secured the largest wage increases[6]. The result was a considerable increase in the occupational dispersion of male earnings, as shown in Figure 10.3.

Table 10.2   Real earnings of male employees by occupational group, 1973-1990

Gross weekly earnings of full-time male employees on adult rates[1] whose pay for the survey period was unaffected by absence, Great Britain, April					
Occupational group[2]:	1973	1979	1990	Average real earnings growth (% per annum):	
				1973-1979	1979-1990
Professional - management & administration	143.7	131.3	158.3	-0.8	2.8
Professional - education, welfare & health	125.1	114.8	124.1	-0.8	1.8
Literary, artistic & sports	121.5	114.4	127.4	-0.3	2.1
Professional - science, engineering, technology	123.8	120.5	126.1	0.2	1.5
Managerial (exc. general management)	122.1	116.1	123.7	-0.2	1.7
Clerical & related	84.3	83.1	80.9	0.4	0.9
Selling	90.8	92.8	91.2	1.0	0.9
Security & protective service	103.7	106.1	107.5	1.1	1.2
Catering, cleaning & other personal services	72.9	74.0	65.5	0.9	0.0
Farming, fishing & related	69.1	69.0	62.2	0.6	0.2
Materials processing (exc. metal & electrical)	91.7	93.6	84.0	1.0	0.1
Making & repairing (exc. metal & electrical)	98.5	93.9	86.0	-0.1	0.3
Processing, repairing (metal & electrical)	101.1	101.6	94.7	0.8	0.5
Painting, assembling, product inspection, packaging	92.7	91.9	81.0	0.5	-0.1
Construction, mining & related nie	94.3	95.0	84.1	0.8	0.0
Transport operating, materials moving & storing	91.4	94.0	81.7	1.1	-0.2
Miscellaneous	82.9	84.7	76.0	1.0	0.1
All occupations	100.0	100.0	100.0	0.7	1.1

Notes

1   See Appendix 1 for details of the correction made.

2   CODOT occupational groups. The NES does not generally present results for Group I (general management) because sample sizes are too small. This group is therefore excluded from the analysis.

Source: Adams, Maybury and Smith (1988), updated to 1990 using New Earnings Surveys.

Figure 10.3 Dispersion across occupations of male average earnings, 1973-1990

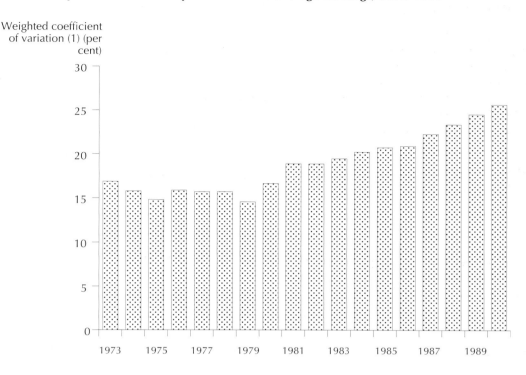

Weighted coefficient of variation (1) (per cent)

Notes

1   *Dispersion was measured across 17 occupational groups, with the coefficient of variation weighted according to the proportion of male employees in each occupation.*

The earnings variable used was gross weekly earnings of full-time male employees on adult rates (prior to 1984, men aged 21 and over) whose pay for the survey period was unaffected by absence, Great Britain, April.

Source: New Earnings Surveys.

Thus the raw data presents a reasonably consistent story, with occupational differentials narrowing in the second half of the 1970s, before widening again after 1979. Moghadam's (1990) results, summarised in Appendix 4, suggest that *ceteris paribus* occupational wage differentials also widened between 1978 and 1985.

d)   Implications for relative wage flexibility

Across different measures of human capital - education, skills and occupations - the available evidence presents a broadly consistent picture. Wage differentials tended to narrow during the second half of the 1970s. Since 1979 (give or take a year or two), the situation has been reversed. Educational, skill and occupational wage differentials have widened. At the end of the 1980s, wage differentials were (at least) as dispersed as in the early to mid 1970s.

There are two hypotheses that could explain these stylised facts:

- The first hypothesis is that relative wages are, and have been, flexible. Trends in differentials therefore mirror changes in relative supply and demand. In order for this hypothesis to fit the facts, there would have to have been a shift in demand towards unskilled/unqualified workers in the late 1970s, or an increase in the supply of skilled/qualified labour that exceeded the growth in demand. These trends in relative demand and supply would then have had to reverse themselves from the end of the 1970s onwards.

- The alternative explanation is that demand and supply have been moving in the same direction throughout the period (i.e. a shift in demand towards skilled/qualified labour at the expense of unskilled/unqualified labour). The narrowing of differentials in the late 1970s would then have to be due to institutional or other constraints, which unwound during the 1980s. In other words, relative wage flexibility has increased since 1979.

Differentiating between these two hypotheses therefore requires a brief review of trends in the demand for, and supply of, different types of labour.

Schmitt (1992) provides some analysis of demand and supply for men with differing levels of educational attainment. His analysis suggests there was a continuous upgrading in educational attainment throughout the 1970s and 1980s. For example, the proportion of men aged 16-64 who were university graduates rose from 4.8 per cent in 1974-76 to 10.9 per cent by 1986-88. In contrast, the proportion with no educational qualifications fell from 51.7 per cent to 32.3 per cent. However, changes in the supply of labour appear to have been more than matched by growing demand for better qualified labour, as unemployment and inactivity appear to have been disproportionately concentrated among those with few or no qualifications. Most importantly, this appears to have been the case during the 1970s as well as during the 1980s.

Katz, Loveman and Blanchflower's (1993) analysis points to similar demand shifts among male employees. While this relative shift in demand increased in intensity during the 1980s, it was also present during the 1970s. Similar movements in relative demand were also found for women.

The evidence therefore suggests that relative demand and supply conditions did not differ greatly pre and post 1979. This in turn implies that the narrowing of differentials observed during the late 1970s may not have been a consequence of market forces.

During the second half of the 1970s, incomes policies were in place that would have tended to narrow differentials (Adams, Maybury and Smith (1988)). In addition, there appears to have been concerted pressure on the part of many trade union negotiators - aided by the growth in general unions during this period - to narrow differentials on equity grounds. These factors would explain the narrowing of differentials during the late 1970s. Their removal or erosion during the 1980s is consistent with the observed pattern of wage differentials.

e)   International comparisons

OECD (1987) summarised the available information on trends in earnings by occupation. Differences between countries in occupational classification systems make comparisons especially difficult. Estimates of the non-manual/manual earnings ratio, however, suggest that the fall in this ratio observed in the UK between 1972 and 1978 was not unique.

The ratio also fell in Australia, Canada, Japan, France, Italy, and the USA (to a very modest extent). Only in Germany did the ratio increase. During the first half of the 1980s, the ratio levelled off or increased in most countries, although the increase in the UK was especially large.

Katz, Loveman and Blanchflower (1993) present a more up-to-date analysis of trends for the UK, the USA, France and Japan. Their results suggest that the sharp increase in the non-manual/manual earnings ratio seen in the UK during the 1980s was also observed in the USA, but not in France, where there was little increase between 1978 and 1987.

OECD (1993) reports trends in controlled[7] education differentials for a number of countries - Australia, Canada, Japan, Sweden, the UK, and the USA[8]. The trends observed in this data are consistent with those from other sources. Differentials narrowed in every country during the 1970s, whereas the 1980s saw substantial increases in the UK and the USA, and more modest increases elsewhere.

Blanchflower and Freeman (1992) report econometric results based on internationally comparable ISSP data. As part of their analysis of union mark-ups, they estimated wage equations for a number of countries. One of their controls was a measure of educational achievement, the number of years of schooling the individual had received. The estimated coefficients on the education variable for each country are graphed in Figure 10.4.

In all cases, the coefficients are significantly different from zero. The values for the UK and the USA are, however, considerably higher than those for other countries.

The evidence therefore points to some commonality of experience. Occupational and educational wage differentials tended to fall during the 1970s, before recovering to some degree during the 1980s. However, the extent of this turn around varied from country to country. The widening of differentials was greatest in the UK and the USA, whereas in France and Japan it would appear to have been more modest.

A number of factors are likely to have been behind these developments. While a shift in demand towards more skilled workers appears to have been commonplace, supply conditions may have varied between countries, due to demographic factors or educational policies. Institutions would also appear to matter. OECD (1987) suggested that incomes policies and solidaristic wage bargaining may have helped to narrow wage differentials during the 1970s. Similarly, the role of the SMIC, the French minimum wage, may have contributed to developments in that country.

116

Figure 10.4 International comparisons of the returns to education, 1985-1987

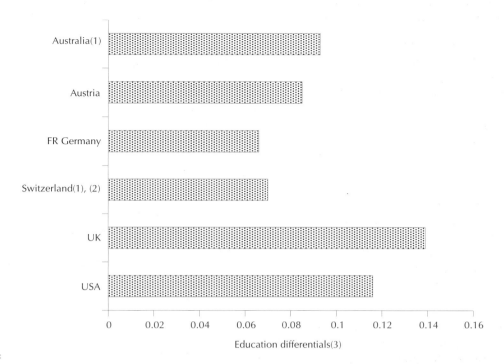

Education differentials(3)

Notes

1   1987 only.

2   Controls for industry excluded.

3   Coefficient on years of schooling in a logarithmic wage equation, run for the years 1985 to 1987 inclusive.

Source: Blanchflower and Freeman (1992), Table A1.

A final and instructive comparison can be made between the UK and the USA. In the USA, part of the widening of educational wage differentials took place because the real earnings of unqualified workers fell during the 1980s (Katz and Murphy (1992)). In the UK, though, the real earnings of unqualified men continued to rise (Schmitt (1992)). This may be one reason why unemployment among the unskilled has been higher in Britain.

f)   Summary and conclusions

- Relative wage flexibility is important if wages are to provide appropriate price signals for individuals and firms to invest in human capital.

- As human capital cannot be directly observed, indirect measures are considered: returns to education; skill levels; and occupations.

- The available evidence suggests that *ceteris paribus* education differentials narrowed during the second half of the 1970s, before widening again during the 1980s. It is not clear if differentials by the end of the decade were wider than in the mid-1970s.

- The pattern over time in skill differentials is similar. These narrowed between 1973 and 1979, before increasing strongly during the 1980s.

- Looking at occupations, similar conclusions can be drawn. Both highly aggregated and more disaggregated measures support this view. It is also consistent with the available evidence on *ceteris paribus* wage differentials.

- Across all three measures, the evidence consistently points to a reduction in the returns to human capital during the second half of the 1970s. This was (more than) reversed during the 1980s. The available evidence also indicates this has happened at a time when shifts in labour demand have increased the human capital content of most jobs. The most convincing explanation of the facts is that the narrowing in differentials during the 1970s was a distortion, possibly due to the effects of incomes policies and union bargaining strategies. As these distortions were removed or eased during the 1980s, trends in differentials have reflected market forces. In other words, relative wage flexibility increased during the 1980s.

- Measures of the returns to human capital, based on educational and occupational wage differentials, suggest that the UK experience has echoes in a number of other countries, but most clearly in the USA.

- Differentials narrowed during the 1970s before widening in the 1980s. But differentials widened during the 1980s to varying degrees. The largest increases were seen in the UK and USA. In France, occupational differentials may have continued to narrow.

- Patterns of demand and supply, as well as institutional factors, may help to account for these differing experiences.

Footnotes to Chapter 10

1. If the costs of investment in human capital are relatively stable over time, changes in these measures of relative earnings should indicate a shift in the (expected) lifetime benefits accruing to any particular investment in human capital.

2. From an employer's perspective, this distinction may not be especially important. In some cases, part of the value to an employer of a particular skill or qualification may arise from the tendency for it to be associated with other valuable characteristics, such as 'ability'. Higher education qualifications may be the best example of this. If education and other forms of human capital act as a screening mechanism, then it may be less important to distinguish between the two. Of course, changes in relative wages may themselves induce greater or lesser participation in education or training, and this may consequently change the nature of any correlation between participation and other unobserved (but valuable) personal characteristics. Hence the sample selection problem should be least acute for marginal changes in wage differentials.

3. One-digit divisions based on the 1980 SIC.

4. Analyses which do not control for compositional change suggest that differentials for semi-skilled and skilled manuals increased faster post-1979 than Table 10.1 implies. This was because of compositional effects: job losses were disproportionately concentrated among the low earnings occupations within these two broad skill groups.

5. A time series from 1985 onwards using average hourly earnings excluding overtime (not reported) shows a similar trend. Hence the conclusions do not appear to be affected by the choice of earnings measure.

6. The rank correlation coefficient across 16 occupational groups between real earnings *levels* in 1973 and real earnings *growth* over the period 1973-1979 was -0.63; a similar comparison of real earnings levels in 1979 with real earnings growth over the period 1979-1990 yields a correlation of +0.63.

7. For age and potential or actual labour market experience.

8. In general, the results reported in OECD (1993) compared the earnings of men with university/college qualifications against those of another group. The comparator group, however, varies from country to country. This means that comparisons of trends over time within each country may be more instructive and reliable than comparisons of the absolute magnitude of the differentials.

Chapter 11

Aggregate employment and hours worked

Changes in employment levels are a major source of flexibility on the extensive margin. The data is patchy, but the evidence in Chapter 3 suggests that constraints on firms' hiring and firing behaviour have, if anything, eased in recent years. On the intensive margin, variations in hours worked are also a source of flexibility. This chapter looks at these issues at the macro level, and assesses the relative importance of variations in employment and hours worked as forms of labour market flexibility.

a)   UK evidence

This section begins with an informal analysis of quantity adjustment, examining the responsiveness of labour input over the last three recessions.

UK whole economy data is plotted in Figure 11.1. The three graphs plot output, labour productivity (output per person employed) and employment. They are shown as indices with values set at 1974Q3=100, 1979Q4=100, and 1990Q2=100 respectively, the points when output peaked and the economy began to move into recession.

What is of interest is the path of each variable as it moves through and out of recession. During the mid 1970s recession, output fell faster than employment, so labour productivity actually fell for five quarters. The productivity slowdown during the early 1980s recession was of a greater amplitude, and labour productivity again fell for five successive quarters.

When output peaked in 1990, however, there was hardly any fall in labour productivity. Another indicator of how different the last recession was can be seen from the following comparison. In the mid 1970s, labour productivity took six quarters to return to its 1974Q3 level; in the early 1980s, it took seven quarters for productivity to reach its 1979Q4 level; in contrast, it took just three quarters in 1990/91 for productivity to reach its previous peak level.

Two possible interpretations spring to mind. One is that the lag between changes in product demand and employment has shortened. If the relative cost of adjusting employment levels has fallen over time,

the result may be less labour hoarding during downturns. Alternatively, the data may reflect an increase in trend productivity growth.

For the manufacturing sector, a further distinction can be made between changes in employment and hours worked. Figure 11.2 graphs output, labour productivity and total hours worked.

The results are similar to those using the whole economy data, although the degree of productivity slowdown (potential labour hoarding) is less than for the economy as a whole. This is probably because productivity is measured here as output per hour worked, so any short-time working is captured in the total hours worked variable, rather than the productivity measure. Again, total hours worked fell much more rapidly in response to output during the last recession.

Figure 11.3 decomposes the change in total hours worked into changes in employment levels and changes in average hours worked.

Employment levels adjust rather more than average hours worked. This was particularly the case during the most recent downturn, when average hours hardly fell at all. In contrast, there was a noticeable drop in average hours worked in the early 1980s, when there was a considerable amount of short-time working.

The relationships between flexibility on the extensive and intensive margins can also be explored using econometric methods. For the whole economy, quarterly data on employment, output and labour productivity (output per person employed) can be analysed from 1960 onwards. For manufacturing, it is possible to identify total labour input (total hours worked), and how this is divided between employment and average hours worked. Data is available on this basis from 1970 onwards.

Two measures of cyclical responsiveness were examined, drawn from Elmeskov (1993) and Golden (1990). These measure the degree to which employment, hours worked or productivity react in response to contemporaneous changes in output. Both the measures are defined in Table 11.1. In each case, the greater the value, the more responsive the variable is to current output.

Figure 11.1 Output, productivity and hours worked in the UK

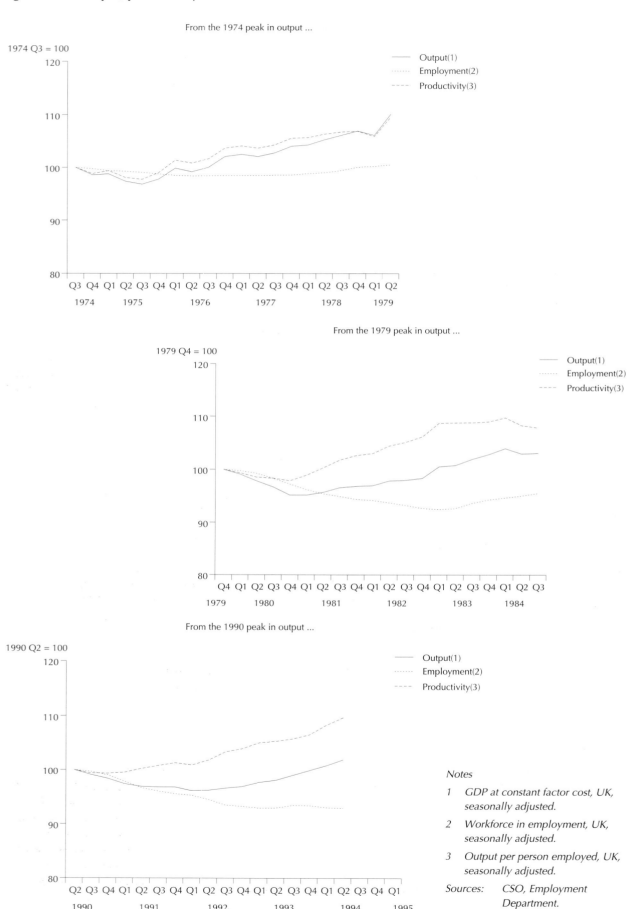

From the 1974 peak in output ...

1974 Q3 = 100

Output(1)
Employment(2)
Productivity(3)

From the 1979 peak in output ...

1979 Q4 = 100

Output(1)
Employment(2)
Productivity(3)

From the 1990 peak in output ...

1990 Q2 = 100

Output(1)
Employment(2)
Productivity(3)

Notes

1 *GDP at constant factor cost, UK, seasonally adjusted.*

2 *Workforce in employment, UK, seasonally adjusted.*

3 *Output per person employed, UK, seasonally adjusted.*

Sources: CSO, Employment Department.

120

Figure 11.2 Output, productivity and hours worked in UK manuafacturing

From the 1974 peak in output ...

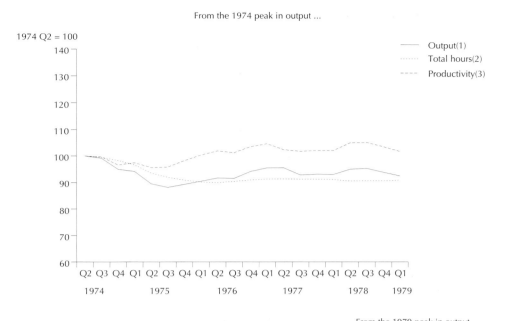

From the 1979 peak in output ...

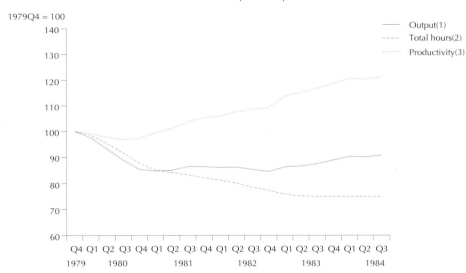

From the 1990 peak in output ...

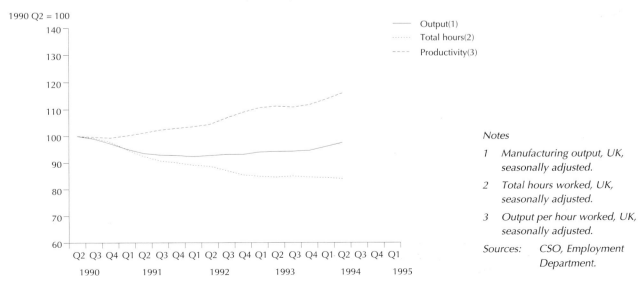

Notes

1 Manufacturing output, UK, seasonally adjusted.

2 Total hours worked, UK, seasonally adjusted.

3 Output per hour worked, UK, seasonally adjusted.

Sources: CSO, Employment Department.

121

Figure 11.3 Employment and hours worked in UK manufacturing

From the 1974 peak in output ...

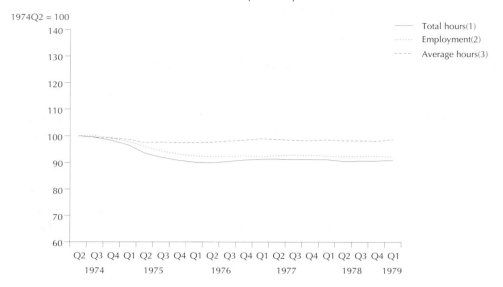

From the 1979 peak in output ...

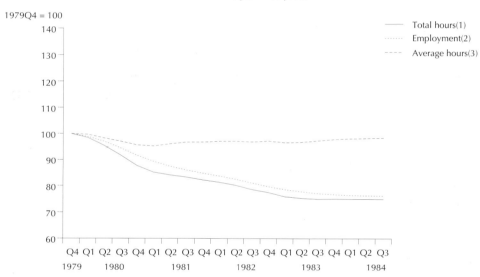

From the 1990 peak in output ...

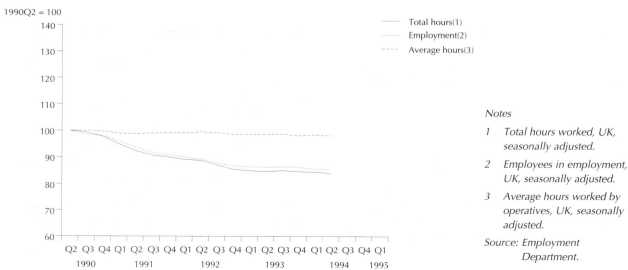

Notes

1   *Total hours worked, UK, seasonally adjusted.*

2   *Employees in employment, UK, seasonally adjusted.*

3   *Average hours worked by operatives, UK, seasonally adjusted.*

Source: Employment Department.

122

Table 11.1 Estimates of the responsiveness of employment, hours and productivity to cyclical conditions

1) Measure of responsiveness used in Elmeskov (1993): Estimate of β from the equation

$$(Z_t - Z^*_t) = \alpha + \beta \ (Y_t - Y^*_t)$$

where z is the (log) variable of interest, y is log output, and * denotes detrended variables[1]

Time period	Whole economy[2]			Manufacturing[2]		
	1960Q1-1994Q1	1960Q1-1979Q4	1980Q1-1994Q1	1970Q1-1994Q1	1970Q1-1979Q4	1980Q1-1994Q1
Total hours worked				0.45	0.43	0.51
Employment	0.19	0.11	0.43	0.17	0.10	0.34
Average hours worked				0.26	0.31	0.16
Output per person employed	0.81	0.89	0.57	0.82	0.89	0.65
Output per hour worked				0.54	0.57	0.49

2) Measure of responsiveness used in Golden (1990): Estimate of β from the equation

$$| Z_t - Z_{t-1} | = \alpha + \beta \ | Y_t - Y_{t-1} |$$

where z is the (log) variable of interest and y is log output[1]

Time period	Whole economy[2]			Manufacturing[2]		
	1960Q1-1994Q1	1960Q1-1979Q4	1980Q1-1994Q1	1970Q1-1994Q1	1970Q1-1979Q4	1980Q1-1994Q1
Total hours worked				0.39	0.40	0.41
Employment	0.04	0.08	0.01	0.04	0.01	0.20
Average hours worked				0.24	0.28	0.15
Output per person employed	0.77	0.84	0.40	0.70	0.86	0.43
Output per hour worked				0.33	0.37	0.27

Notes

1   All estimates used quarterly, seasonally adjusted data.

2   All equations were estimated using a Maximum Likelihood correction for first order serial correlation.

Table 11.1 presents estimates of these measures for the UK. In each case, the sample has been split into two, with 1979Q4 used as the break point. This is to see whether these relationships have changed over time.

The Elmeskov (1993) measure suggests that, for the whole economy, the majority of short-run adjustment occurs through variations in output per person employed - which could include the effect of changes in average hours worked - rather than employment levels. However, the split sample results suggest that employment has become much more responsive to output changes during the 1980s and 1990s.

On the whole, the results for the manufacturing sector confirm the whole economy findings. They also suggest there was little change over the entire period in the cyclical responsiveness of total hours worked, or output per hour worked. The major change between the pre- and post-1980 periods appears to have affected the components of total hours worked: employment has become more responsive to output changes, while average hours worked has become less responsive.

Results using the Golden (1990) measure were less clearcut. The whole economy results suggest that both output per person employed and total employment became less responsive to changes in output after 1979. The results for manufacturing, however, are consistent with those obtained using the Elmeskov (1993) measure.

Table 11.2 presents estimates of the speed of adjustment of employment, average hours worked and total hours worked. Abraham and Houseman (1993) show that, under certain assumptions[1], the speed with which employment and hours worked converge towards their optimal levels can be measured by the coefficient on the lagged dependent variable in the equation set out in Table 11.2. The value of this coefficient must lie between zero and one: a value of one implies no adjustment whatsoever ('complete inflexibility'), whereas a value of zero implies that employment levels, or numbers of hours worked, adjust instantaneously to changes in output ('complete flexibility')[2].

Table 11.2 suggests that, on this [0,1] scale, adjustment appears to be quite slow. However, there is evidence that the speed of adjustment for employment has increased post-1979[3]. The data for the manufacturing sector confirms this, and again suggests that a speedier reaction of employment levels has been matched by slower adjustment in average hours worked.

Across these measures, then, a reasonably consistent picture emerges. In general, employment varies more over the cycle than average hours worked. This suggests there is a good deal of flexibility on the extensive margin. The evidence also suggests that employment has become more responsive to cyclical conditions, and that the lag between employment

and output may have shortened[4]. Data from the manufacturing sector suggests the consequence has been greater stability in average hours worked. In other words, a shift towards more flexibility on the extensive margin.

b)   International comparisons

Recent OECD analyses (Elmeskov (1993), Elmeskov and Pichelmann (1993a)) present comparable data on the cyclical responsiveness of employment, average hours worked and labour productivity.

Figure 11.4 presents estimates of the cyclical responsiveness of employment and labour productivity (output per person employed). In very broad terms, this graph summarises the balance in each country between flexibility on the extensive margin (the responsiveness of employment) and flexibility on the intensive margin (the responsiveness of output per person employed - itself a function of average hours worked and output per hour worked).

There is, naturally, a negative relationship between the responsiveness of employment and labour productivity[5]. At one end of the spectrum are Greece, Italy, Japan, New Zealand and Portugal. In these countries, employment changes quite slowly over the cycle. The UK, is at the other end of the graph, along with Australia, Canada, the Netherlands, Spain, Switzerland and the USA. In these countries, employment responds relatively

Table 11.2   Estimates of the speed of adjustment of employment and hours worked

Measure of speed of adjustment used in Abraham and Houseman (1993): Estimate of γ from

$$Z_t = \alpha + \beta\, Y_t + \gamma Z_{t-1} + \delta_1\, t + \delta_2\, t^2$$

where z is the (log) variable of interest, y is (log) output, and t is a time trend[1]

Time period	Whole economy[2]			Manufacturing[2]		
	1960Q1-1994Q1	1960Q1-1979Q4	1980Q1-1994Q1	1970Q1-1994Q1	1970Q1-1979Q4	1980Q1-1994Q1
Total hours worked				0.66	0.52	0.66
Employment	0.82	0.90	0.80	0.85	0.80	0.75
Average hours worked				0.04	0.10	0.55

Notes

1   All estimates used quarterly, seasonally adjusted data.

2   All equations were estimated using a Maximum Likelihood correction for first order serial correlation.

Figure 11.4 International comparisons of the cyclical responsiveness of employment and productivity

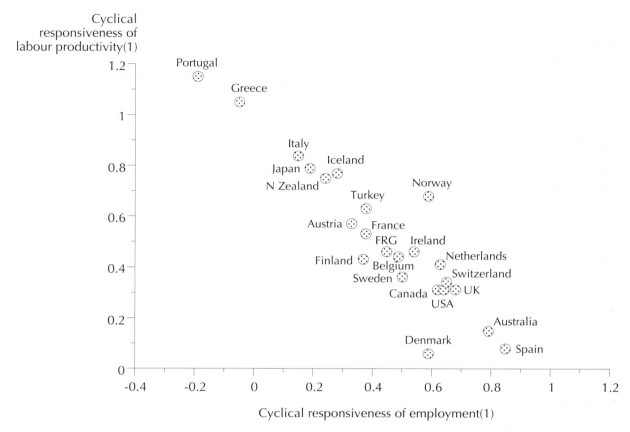

Key: FRG = Germany; UK = United Kingdom; USA = United States.

Notes

1   Measures of cyclical responsiveness are as defined in the top panel of Table 11.1, estimated over the period 1970-1991 using annual data.

Source: Elmeskov and Pichelmann (1993a).

quickly to cyclical variations in output, so productivity fluctuations are less pronounced.

Figure 11.5 plots the responsiveness of employment against the cyclical responsiveness of average hours worked. This analysis was carried out for a smaller number of countries.

The results suggest there is no clear relationship between the two variables. Hours worked were found to be highly responsive to demand conditions in a small number of countries - Belgium, Finland, Spain and Sweden. But in most other countries, including the UK, the estimates of responsiveness were much lower. There was no indication that countries where employment was slowest to adjust over the cycle were readily able to vary average hours worked as a form of compensation. Hence, in countries such as Greece and Japan, labour

productivity (output per hour worked) must have varied most over the cycle.

Note these are average estimates, covering the period from the 1960s or 1970s onwards. Hence no conclusions can be drawn about changes over time.

Finally, Abraham and Houseman (1993) present estimates of the speed of adjustment of employment and total hours worked for four OECD economies. This is the model estimated in Table 11.2, so comparisons should be possible with the UK. These are presented in Table 11.3.

The estimates suggest that, in the case of employment, speed of adjustment in the UK is comparable with that in Belgium and Germany, although much slower than in the USA. Total hours worked, however, are found to take longer to adjust

Figure 11.5 International comparisons of the cyclical responsiveness of employment and hours worked

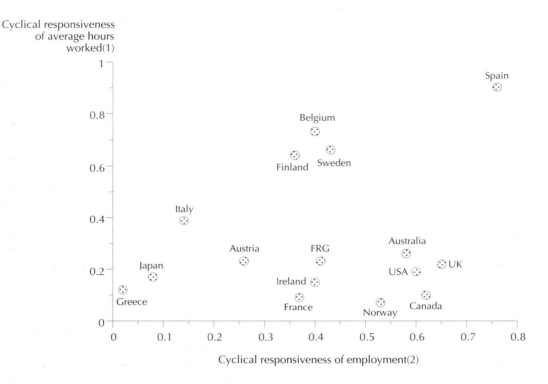

Key: FRG = Germany; UK = United Kingdom; USA = United States.

Notes

1   Described as 'The coefficient to output growth in a regression of changes in weekly/monthly hours of work in manufacturing or industry (and in a few cases the whole economy) also on a constant and a time trend and its own lagged level'. The estimation period is unspecified.

2   Measure of cyclical responsiveness as defined in the top panel of Table 11.1, estimated over the period 1960-1991 using annual data.

Source: Elmeskov (1993).

Table 11.3   International comparisons of estimates of the speed of adjustment of employment and total hours worked

	Manufacturing industry, 1973-1990	
Country:	**Employment[1]**	**Total hours worked[1]**
Belgium	0.82	0.44
France	0.94	
FR Germany	0.84	0.43
UK	0.84	0.71
USA	0.38	0.13[2]

Notes

1   All estimates use seasonally adjusted, quarterly data.

2   This is the estimate reported by Abraham and Houseman (1993) using production as the output measure.

Sources: UK - own estimates; other countries - Abraham and Houseman (1993).

to output changes in the UK than in any of the countries in the Abraham and Houseman study. One explanation may be the greater prevalence of short-time working in Belgium and Germany. However, the apparent inconsistency of Figures 11.4 and 11.5 with Table 11.3 begs the question of whether other factors might explain these results.

c)   Summary and conclusions

- Comparisons using aggregate UK data for the last three cycles suggests there may have been a change in the way the labour market adjusts to economic conditions. During the early 1990s, the productivity downturn was much smaller than in previous recessions, which suggests there was less labour hoarding.

- The evidence also suggests that most of the adjustment in labour input comes through changes in employment levels, rather than average hours worked. The balance of flexibility is primarily through the extensive rather than the intensive margin.

- Various statistical measures suggest that, compared with the 1960s and 1970s, employment became more variable and responsive to output changes during the 1980s and 1990s. Evidence from the manufacturing sector suggests this may have been accompanied by less variability in average hours worked, i.e. a shift towards more flexibility on the extensive margin.

- Compared to other OECD countries, employment in the UK appears to be quite responsive to changes in output. In some economies, such as Greece and Portugal, employment is very slow to adjust. In contrast, average hours worked are more responsive to output changes in a number of other countries.

Chapter 3, such as Burgess (1988), Burgess and Nickell (1990), and Burgess (1993). These studies explicitly modelled the costs of adjusting employment levels, whereas this specification simply assumes that adjustment costs are quadratic in levels. Since the focus here is on testing for broad shifts over time in relationships between labour market variables, the use of this specification was judged a defensible simplifying assumption.

3. Burgess (1994) demonstrates that the 'value' of reductions in these measures decreases disproportionately. In other words, the efficiency gains from reducing the speed of adjustment parameter from 0.9 to 0.8 are much greater than a reduction from 0.2 to 0.1. Hence the changes in Table 11.2 may imply a significant improvement in the efficiency with which labour is reallocated between sectors.

4. Blanchflower and Freeman (1994) present evidence that supports this conclusion, based on microeconomic data (the 1980 and 1990 WIRS). They estimated cross-section employment equations on the sample of private sector workplaces in both years, and found that the estimated coefficients on the demand indicators used (respondents' view on trends in the volume of sales over the past year) were greater in magnitude in 1990 than in 1980. This implies that employment in 1990 was more responsive to demand conditions. However, the authors point out that '... the pattern is hardly overwhelming'.

5. In theory, the two estimates presented in Figure 11.4 should sum to one. This is indeed the case for the estimates presented in Table 11.1. In Figure 11.4, this is generally not the case, presumably because of measurement error.

Footnotes to Chapter 11

1. The specific assumptions required are that the costs of changing employment or hours worked are quadratic, and that expectations are adaptive (so that the Koyck transformation can be applied).

2. This a simpler econometric specification than those used in some of the studies referenced in

Chapter 12

Aggregate real wage flexibility

This chapter considers the macro level evidence on price (wage) flexibility. As discussed in Chapter 1, aggregate wage flexibility is often seen as a key indicator of labour market performance. Aggregate wage behaviour, for example, is a key determinant of measures of sustainable or underlying unemployment, such as the Non Accelerating Inflation Rate of Unemployment (the NAIRU).

The evidence is considered in two sections. The first presents a descriptive account of trends in real earnings over the last quarter century. While such an analysis is of value in its own right, more sophisticated models are also needed to reflect the multivariate and dynamic complexities of aggregate wage relationships. The econometric evidence is considered alongside international comparisons, as differences in model specification, units of

measurement etc. mean that results for Britain are difficult to interpret in isolation.

a) Trends in aggregate real earnings

Figure 12.1 plots nominal average earnings growth since 1967, compares it with consumer price inflation (as measured by the 'headline'RPI inflation rate), and displays the implied growth of real average earnings. Although there are some discontinuities in the nominal earnings series, the graph is a reasonable representation of trends.

Since 1982, nominal earnings have tended to grow at a slower rate than over the previous decade. This reflects lower and more stable rates of inflation. Real earnings growth has been more stable throughout the period. Apart from 1976 and 1977, real earnings have increased every year, usually by between 1 and 4 per cent.

The precise timing of movements in earnings growth and price inflation appears to have changed. From the end of the 1960s until the early 1980s, nominal earnings growth seems to have led inflation by two to three quarters. Since about 1982/1983, earnings

Figure 12.1 Average earnings growth and consumer price inflation, 1967-1993

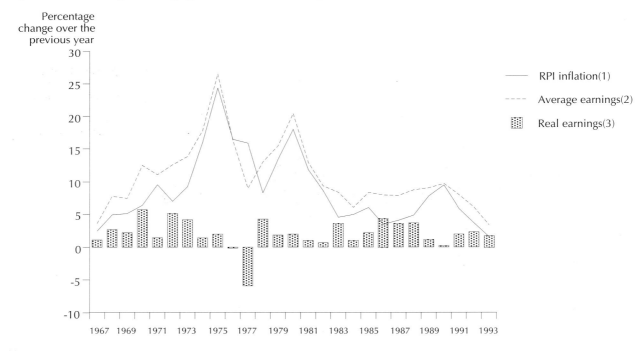

Notes

1   *Percentage change over the previous year, annual averages.*

2   *Percentage change over the previous year, annual averages. There are minor discontinuities in the series, hence comparisons over long periods of time are approximate.*

3   *Calculated as RPI inflation minus average earnings growth.*

Sources: CSO, Employment Department.

seem to have followed inflation. In part, this may reflect the distortionary effects of incomes policies. The end of a period of restraint tended to be followed by a period of 'catching up'. Wages may have become more 'backward-looking' as rates of inflation have fallen and stabilised, because the cost associated with errors in predicting future inflation will have been reduced.

Real earnings have increased year after year despite historically high rates of unemployment. Figure 12.2 shows there is little relationship between real earnings growth and the unemployment rate[1]. There is some evidence of a negative relationship between real earnings growth and the change in the unemployment rate, but the correlation is again quite weak[2].

If the trend rate of productivity growth is positive, real earnings growth can be expected to reflect this. There are strong arguments why real earnings need not automatically increase in line with labour productivity, such as the need to provide a return on capital investment, as well as the implications for competitiveness and employment. However, some long-run relationship between the two variables is to be expected. Chapter 7 suggested that productivity

is certainly a factor behind a significant proportion of real-life wage settlements.

Figure 12.3 graphs real earnings and labour productivity growth. The degree of correspondence between the two series is relatively weak[3], although real earnings and productivity appear to have moved more in tandem during the 1980s than previously. In fact, real earnings growth has tended to outstrip labour productivity growth, which implies that unit labour costs have increased.

On the basis of the data presented, there is no decisive evidence of greater real wage flexibility at the aggregate level. In a competitive labour market, the existence of year-on-year increases in real earnings is not obviously consistent with historically high levels of unemployment.

Recent years, however, have seen some encouraging signs. Nominal earnings did not 'take off' in the late 1980s, even though there was a sharp increase in the inflation rate. Furthermore, average earnings growth fell sharply during 1992 and 1993. The rate of nominal earnings growth had fallen to 3 per cent by November 1993, the lowest figure for at least twenty-five years, and has since remained at 4 per

Figure 12.2   Real earnings growth and unemployment, 1972-1993

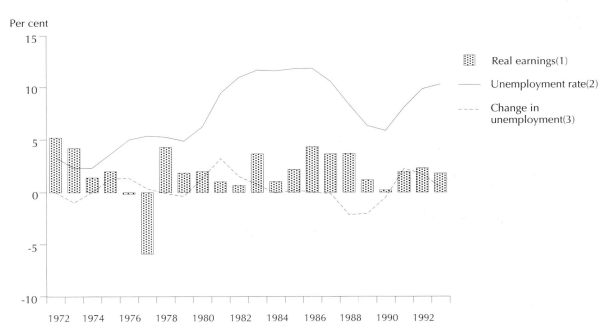

Notes

1   Calculated as in Figure 12.1, percentage change on previous year, annual averages.

2   Claimant unemployment (adjusted for seasonality and discontinuities), expressed as a percentage of the workforce, UK, annual averages.

3   Percentage point change on previous year, annual averages.

Source: Employment Department.

129

Figure 12.3 Real earnings growth and labour productivity growth, 1967-1993

Notes

1   *Calculated as in Figure 12.1, percentage change on previous year, annual averages.*

2   *Percentage change in whole economy output per person employed, UK, annual averages.*

Sources: CSO, Employment Department.

Table 12.1   Studies of real wage flexibility

Study	Estimation period	Measure of real wage rigidity/flexibility used
Grubb, Jackman and Layard (1983)		Inverse of elasticity of nominal wages with respect to unemployment (defined as $u-u_0$ where u_0 is the NAIRU)
Coe (1985)	Various. Between mid-1960s and early-1970s up to 1984	*Ratio* of elasticities of nominal wages with respect to prices and the unemployment rate
Newell and Symons (1985)	Various. Between mid-1950s and early-1960s up to 1981	Coefficient on unemployment rate in real product wage equation
Alogoskoufis and Manning (1988)	1952-1985 with minor variations	Coefficient on unemployment rate in wage equation
Layard, Nickell and Jackman (1991)	1956-1985	Inverse of sum of long-run values of coefficients on unemployment in price-setting equation and wage-setting equation
Anderton, Barrell, in't Veld and Pittis (1992)	Various. Between late 1960s and early 1970s and 1990	Long-run effect of unemployment on nominal wage growth
Elmeskov and Pichelmann (1993b)	1970-1991	Coefficient on the unemployment term (measured by deviation from trend) when regressed on the deviation of wage growth from trend

cent or less. The extent of this fall has exceeded the expectations of most independent forecasters, and was noted in the OECD's recent survey of the UK economy (OECD (1994d)). Nevertheless, average earnings continue to increase in real terms.

b)   International comparisons

In recent years, a number of econometric studies have tried to measure real wage flexibility (or its counterpart, real wage rigidity) at the macroeconomic level. The focus has often been on international comparisons. The measure of real wage flexibility adopted by each of these studies, as well as the time period over which the models were estimated, is listed in Table 12.1.

The conventional approach in these studies has been to estimate aggregate wage equations (either as reduced form single equations, or embedded within a small system of equations). Measures of real wage rigidity/flexibility tend to be derived from estimates of particular coefficients in these wage equations. Some studies simply use a measure based on the elasticity of nominal wages with respect to unemployment. Others have adopted more sophisticated measures that take account of the extent to which price changes feed through into wage inflation. Similarly, some studies present long-run estimates as well as short-run estimates.

Given the differences between studies in methodology, data, units of measurement etc., the *values* of the wage flexibility/rigidity measures are difficult to compare. A more useful approach is to treat these estimates as *ordinal* measures of wage flexibility, and then to compare the rank ordering of countries that each study has produced. These rankings are summarised in Table 12.2, where the country exhibiting the most real wage flexibility is ranked 1.

The extent to which the rankings of individual countries differ from study to study can be striking at times, especially for Germany, Italy, Norway, and Australia. Indeed, the only points of agreement appear to be that real wages in Japan, Switzerland and Sweden are relatively flexible and that real wages in the UK are relatively rigid.

While there is still a broad measure of agreement between the studies[4], it is far from perfect. Hence the results should be interpreted with some caution. Rankings appear to be sensitive to equation specification, the measure of real wage flexibility adopted, and the estimation period.

Econometric studies also provide a means of assessing whether or not real wage flexibility has increased. This can be done in two ways: by examining the forecasting performance and stability of wage equations; and through formal tests for structural breaks in wage-setting relationships.

Some of the above studies do in fact touch on this issue. Coe (1985) examined the stability of his estimated wage equations, and, using a Chow test, found evidence of a structural break in the UK wage equation at the end of 1979. The UK was the only country covered by the study where a structural break was detected.

Chan-Lee, Coe and Prywes (1987) examined the stability of these equations in greater detail, using updated and re-estimated versions of Coe's wage equations. They found that a wage equation estimated for the UK over the period 1964-1979 consistently over-predicted wage growth for the period 1980-1984. Turning to formal statistical criteria, Chow tests could not reject the null hypothesis of no structural break. However, there are other signs of instability: the wage equations failed a Cusum-squared test, while their post-1979 forecasting performance failed the Hendry χ^2 test. This instability was due to parameter shifts in the price inflation term (i.e. price inflation was not passed on so rapidly to wages) and, in one of the two specifications estimated, the unemployment term (i.e. wage growth had become more responsive to unemployment).

The authors concluded that, in most OECD countries, the first half of the 1980s saw lower wage growth than would have been expected on the basis of past behaviour. In most cases, though, this apparent moderation of wage pressures was insufficiently large to show up in formal tests of parameter stability. Statistical evidence of a structural break was stronger for the UK than for any other country.

Other studies, however, report no evidence of changed wage-setting behaviour in the UK (Poret (1990) and Anderton, Barrell, in't Veld and Pittis (1992)). Anderton, Barrell and McHugh (1992) examined the post-1979 predictive power of their UK wage equation and found that, while it tended to over-predict earnings growth in the first half of the 1980s, this systematic over-prediction disappeared during the latter half of the decade.

Thus, aggregate real wages in the UK appear to have been rigid by international standards. No strong conclusions can be drawn on whether a change in wage-setting behaviour has occurred since the end of the 1970s.

Table 12.2   Rankings of countries by real wage flexibility

Rank:	GJL (1983)	COE (1985) Short run	COE (1985) Long run	NS (1985)	AM (1988)	LNJ (1991)	ABVP (1992)	EP (1993b)
1	JPN	SWZ[2]	FRG[1,2]	JPN	JPN	IT	JPN	SWE
2	SWZ	JPN[1]	JPN[1]	SWZ	NOR	JPN	FRG	JPN
3	NZ	CAN	AUS[1]	SWE	SWE	SWE	FR	SWZ
4	SWE	FRG[1,2]	IT	IT	SWZ	NOR	USA	AUT
5	AUT	USA	AUT	AUT	FIN	AUT	IT	FRG
6	NL	AUS[1]	CAN	NL	AUT	SWZ	**UK**	FIN
7	FR	AUT	SWZ[2]	FIN	NL	FR		NOR
8	CAN	NL[1]	NL[1]	IR	FRG	NZ		FR
9	BEL	IT	FR	FRG	FR	BEL		**UK**
10	FIN	FR	USA	CAN	BEL	USA		NL
11	AUS	**UK**	**UK**	BEL	IR	NL		SP
12	USA			USA	**UK**	IR		NZ
13	IT			**UK**	USA	FIN		CAN
14	NOR			AUS[3]=	DK	CAN		IT=
15	SP			FR[3]=	SP	SP		IR=
16	DK			NOR[3]=	IT	FRG		USA
17	FRG					**UK**		PORT
18	IR					AUS		BEL
19	**UK**							DEN
20								AUS

Key GJL= Grubb, Jackman and Layard (1983); NS = Newell and Symons (1985); AM = Alogoskoufis and Manning (1988); LNJ = Layard, Nickell and Jackman (1991); ABVP = Anderton, Barrell, in't Veld and Pittis (1992);EP = Elmeskov and Pichelmann (1993b).

AUS = Australia; AUT = Austria; BEL = Belgium; CAN = Canada; DK = Denmark; FIN= Finland; FR = France; FRG = Germany; IR = Ireland; IT = Italy; JPN = Japan; NL = Netherlands; NOR = Norway; NZ = New Zealand; PORT = Portugal; SP = Spain; SWE = Sweden; SWZ = Switzerland; UK = United Kingdom; USA = United States.

Notes

*1   The wage equations estimated were non-linear, and the estimates of real wage rigidity presented in the table are based on the **average** unemployment rate over the estimation period. Using end-period values (1984) considerably increases estimates of real wage rigidity.*

2   These wage equations incorporate ad hoc adjustments for productivity growth. Estimates of real wage rigidity differ substantially if these are excluded.

3   No coefficient on unemployment is reported. The text suggests these terms were omitted from the reported equations because of insignificant or perverse signs.

This conclusion may not be too surprising as time-series wage equations are often poorly determined[5], and this means that formal tests of structural stability are difficult to 'fail'[6]. Furthermore, many of the changes taking place at the microeconomic level in the British labour market - such as pay decentralisation - gathered pace in the second half of the 1980s. If there are any effects on macroeconomic aggregates, these may take time to work through, and the weight of past data in time series equations may overwhelm the effects of more recent observations.

It is significant that structural breaks have been difficult to detect in other countries. The other main examples have been Poret (1990), who found some evidence of a structural break during the 1980s in France, and Anderton, Barrell, in't Veld and Pittis (1992) and Anderton, Barrell and McHugh (1992), who both find evidence of a structural break in Italy[7].

c)   Summary and conclusions

- Growth rates of nominal earnings and inflation have varied considerably since the beginning of the 1970s. Real average earnings growth has been more stable. Apart from 1976 and 1977, real earnings have increased each year, usually in a range between 1 and 4 per cent.

- The rate of real earnings growth appears little affected by unemployment. There is some correlation between real earnings and labour productivity growth, but the precise linkage is fairly weak.

- Nominal earnings growth has declined sharply since 1992, reaching a low of 3 per cent in November 1993. These growth rates are very low by recent historical standards, and may be an encouraging sign of greater flexibility.

- Econometric studies suggest that aggregate wages are most flexible (responsive to unemployment) in Japan, Switzerland and Sweden. Nearly all of them seem to agree that real earnings in the UK are unresponsive to unemployment.

- Studies which have used formal tests designed to detect changes in wage-setting behaviour come to conflicting conclusions regarding the UK: some studies detect a more flexible response post-1979, others do not.

Footnotes to Chapter 12

1. The correlation coefficient between contemporaneous values of the two variables was 0.09.

2. Correlation coefficient of -0.21.

3. Correlation coefficient of 0.19.

4. The consistency of these rankings was examined more systematically by calculating Kendall's measure of concordance, W. For the six countries covered in all seven studies (the G7 countries minus Canada), the value of W was 0.575 . W was also calculated for the 16 countries covered by Grubb, Jackman and Layard (1983), Newell and Symons (1985), Layard, Nickell and Jackman (1991), and Elmeskov and Pichelmann (1993b), its value being 0.672. In both cases, the value of W was statistically significant at the 1 per cent level. Alternatively, these values of W can be converted into values of R^2, where R^2 is the mean value of the Spearman's rank correlation coefficients drawn from all pairwise combinations of studies. For the six country comparison, the value of R^2 was 0.515. For the sixteen country comparison, the value was 0.523. This indicates a significant degree of consistency in rankings, although the degree of concordance remains far from perfect.

5. The standard error of the regression is often large in relation to the mean value of the dependent variable, especially in dynamic (wage growth) equations.

6. Darby and Wren-Lewis (1993), for example, were unable to find a sensible cointegrating vector capable of modelling long-run wage growth in the UK.

7. This is ascribed to the partial dismantling of the scala *mobile* system of automatic wage indexation.

Chapter 13
Conclusions

This chapter addresses four questions:

- Has the British labour market become more flexible since the end of the 1970s?
- How does the British labour market compare, in broad terms, with those of other OECD countries?
- What conclusions can be drawn, or hypotheses advanced, about why the British labour market has become more flexible?
- What have been the consequences of greater flexibility?

a) Has the British labour market become more flexible?

This question has been the primary objective of this paper. It is easier to see whether change has been in the direction of greater or less flexibility than it is to measure the overall degree of flexibility in the labour market, or assess whether it is sufficient for labour market efficiency.

Table 13.1 provides a brief summary of the analysis presented in Chapters 2 to 12. The final column offers a summary (and necessarily subjective) view on whether the evidence presented substantiates the hypothesis that the labour market *has* become more flexible.

Given the evidence presented in the table, it can reasonably be concluded that the labour market has become more flexible over the last fifteen years or so. There is quite strong evidence to support this conclusion in a number of areas. In other areas, it is more difficult to reach firm conclusions given the information available. However, there is no evidence that the labour market has become less flexible.

In general, the evidence is stronger at the micro level than the macro level. There appear to have been substantial changes to wage determination, employment flexibility, and the regional and occupational structure of earnings. In contrast, there is rather less evidence of greater aggregate real wage flexibility.

There is also a gender dimension to labour market flexibility. Women are more likely than men to work part-time or on a temporary basis (and more often through choice.) They are also more likely to move between jobs.

b) Flexibility in context: international comparisons

In the previous chapters, comparisons have been drawn between the UK and other OECD countries. This section presents an overview of these comparisons. In some areas, a lack of comparable data, especially over time, means that conclusions must be regarded as tentative.

The UK exhibits a good deal of flexibility on the extensive margin, both in terms of the prevalence and use made of part-time and self-employed workers, and in the degree to which employers face constraints on their ability to change employment levels. While UK employers may face greater constraints on their behaviour than in the USA, these constraints and regulations are liberal compared to other EU countries.

In terms of flexibility on the intensive margin, there appear to be few constraints in the UK on choice of working time. Again, this is similar to the position in North America, but quite different from most other EU member states. There is less evidence available about functional flexibility, although it would appear to be less widespread in the UK than it is in Germany or Japan.

Labour mobility is probably as high (possibly, even greater) than elsewhere in the EU, although labour appears considerably more mobile in Australia, Canada and the USA. This conclusion applies to both job mobility and geographical mobility.

UK wage determination has become increasingly decentralised, as well as unco-ordinated, more so than in most other OECD countries. Although the evidence is limited, the incidence of PRP in the UK would appear to be relatively high compared to other EU countries.

As for relative wage flexibility, the available evidence suggests that wages have become increasingly important as a source of labour market adjustment in the UK. Relative wages would appear to be more flexible in the UK than in most other European countries; the position *vis-à-vis* the USA is harder to judge.

Turning to the macro evidence, UK employment appears more responsive to demand conditions than employment in most other OECD economies. Average hours worked appear to be relatively unresponsive.

But the UK scores less well on aggregate real wage flexibility. Econometric studies suggest that real wage flexibility is greatest in Japan, Sweden and

Table 13.1   Has the British labour market become more flexible? A summary of the evidence

Indicator:	Evidence of labour market flexibility:	Greater flexibility?
MICRO LEVEL INDICATORS		
Quantity (employment) flexibility		
Part-time, temporary and self-employment	Substantial increase in part-time work in 1970s and 1980s, and self-employment since 1979. Modest increase in temporary work. Probable increase in sub-contracting.	Yes
Engagements and dismissals	Probable decline in constraints on firms' behaviour during 1980s.	*Probably* yes
Working time	Basic hours adjust little over cycle. Main adjustment through overtime. Increase in dispersion of hours worked. Wide diversity of working time patterns by 1990 - though little hard evidence on trends.	*Probably* yes
Functional flexibility	Measures taken during 1980s to secure greater flexibility. By 1990, two thirds of workplaces had no constraints on how they organised work - picture in previous years uncertain.	Yes
Labour mobility	Significant movements between jobs, industries and occupations, although firm conclusions cannot be drawn on trends. No apparent increase in gross inter-regional migration rate. Evidence suggests net migration flows between regions are sensitive to economic signals, although no evidence on whether signalling role has become more or less important over time.	Uncertain
Price (wage) flexibility		
Wage determination	Sharp fall in incidence of collective bargaining in second half of 1980s, especially national agreements. Increased incidence of performance related pay during 1980s. Managers' accounts suggest pay rises do reflect economic circumstances. But no firm evidence of any 'underlying' change in thinking.	Yes
Relative wage flexibility: regions	Some evidence of a re-alignment of earnings in late 1980s.	Yes
Relative wage flexibility: industries	Some widening of inter-industry wage differentials since end of 1970s.	Yes
Relative wage flexibility: human capital	Significant increase in returns to human capital during 1980s.	Yes
MACRO LEVEL INDICATORS		
Quantity (employment) flexibility		
Aggregate employment and hours worked	Employment rather than hours accounts for most quantity adjustment. Evidence that lag between employment growth and output has shortened (i.e. less labour hoarding). Evidence that employment has become more responsive to output growth.	Yes
Price (wage) flexibility		
Aggregate real wage flexibility	1980s have seen year-on-year increases in real earnings that have outstripped productivity growth, despite high unemployment. Sharp fall in earnings growth since 1992. UK wages rigid in comparison to other countries. Mixed evidence on whether any structural break post-1979.	Uncertain

Switzerland, whereas real wages in the UK are relatively rigid.

The scope for different forms of flexibility varies across countries. To a large extent, different means of securing flexibility have evolved in different countries.

In the USA, the lack of labour market regulation means there is great scope for adjustment on the extensive margin, through varying numbers in employment. This has meant that working time and pay have needed to adjust less. Abraham and Houseman (1993) suggest the reverse holds for Germany. Japan is similar to Germany in many respects. Flexibility on the intensive margin in larger enterprises, together with aggregate real wage flexibility, means that employment is relatively stable over the business cycle.

The Nordic economies (Denmark, Finland, Norway, Sweden) appear to exhibit little relative wage flexibility, but they have traditionally compensated for this through aggregate real wage flexibility. Labour also seems to be relatively mobile in these countries.

The UK would appear to be in an intermediate position, with some features of its labour market resembling the USA and some more closely resembling its EU partners. However, the UK has probably moved closer to a US-style labour market since the end of the 1970s.

To a large extent, the (groups of) countries mentioned above secure flexibility in their labour markets through differing means. However, a number of EU member states seem to have extensive labour market rigidities. In many cases, they seem to lack well-developed mechanisms for securing flexibility at the micro level. The available evidence suggests this is not compensated for by a high degree of flexibility at the macro level[1].

There are a whole host of factors that could potentially explain these cross-country differences, but the structure of labour market institutions and regulation is undoubtedly relevant. This is most obvious when looking at the regulation of employment or working time. However, it is also significant in any discussion of wage behaviour, both at the micro and the macro level, because of differences between countries in factors such as the regulation of industrial relations and minimum wage legislation.

c) Why has the labour market become more flexible?

An exhaustive account of why the labour market has become more flexible is beyond the scope of this paper. This section merely identifies the main factors likely to have been behind greater flexibility in the labour market (Chapters 2 to 12 have also touched on these issues). Possible reasons can be grouped under four broad headings, which are developed below. These forces would appear not to have acted independently of each other.

Changes in product markets

Product markets have become more competitive during the 1980s and 1990s[2]. Competition has tended to increase at local, national and international levels. Increased competition has probably intensified the pressure on firms to minimise costs. In some areas, increases in competition may have reduced the scope for monopoly rent extraction, and this may have affected firms' industrial relations practices. Competition may also have made firms more reactive to customers. In the retail sector, for example, these pressures are likely to have been reflected in longer opening hours and greater use of 'flexible' employment contracts and working time arrangements.

Changes in the production process

This heading covers a number of issues concerning changes in the ways that firms turn their inputs (including labour services) into outputs.

Clearly, there is an interaction with product market factors here. One manifestation of this may be the move in certain industries towards new methods of production, such as 'just-in-time' working, designed to cut down on inventories and delivery times. The adoption of such methods has clear implications for the flexibility of the workforce, since they tend to require a wider range of skills from the workforce and/or the possibility of more flexible working patterns.

Change in the production process also arises from technological developments. As technology has become more advanced, the organisation of work has needed to change. Where production has become more capital-intensive, there have been increasing pressures for firms and their employees to adopt new working time arrangements, in order to lengthen the operating time of machinery[3].

These changes have also been a factor behind the growth of new forms of employee relations. Some companies have taken the view that technical change means confrontational systems of workplace industrial relations have become outdated and costly. This has sometimes lead to new systems of industrial relations, which focus on the individual employee's relationship with the employer. Collective bargaining over pay and related issues may not be part of these new systems. Although the empirical importance of such phenomena should not be overplayed (see Millward (1994)), they may nevertheless have a wider influence.

Changes in the structure of demand and supply

One consequence of technical change has been a decline in the demand for unskilled workers (Machin (1994)), part of a more general shift in demand towards more highly skilled workers. When demand or supply is changing over time, the signalling role of relative wages becomes more important, as does labour mobility. Hence shifts in demand or supply themselves generate a 'demand' for greater flexibility.

Another, partially related, example is the long-term shift in composition of output from manufacturing to services. Again, this will have changed the nature of labour demand.

Change can also come from the supply side. Perhaps the most important development has been the growth in female labour force participation. As attitudes towards women's role in society have changed, women have entered the labour force in increasing numbers. This has itself created a demand for new or more flexible forms of work, such as part-time work. However, the relationship may well be simultaneous in nature. Employers' responses to competitive pressures and technical change may have changed the nature of the work they offer, in ways that offer wider opportunities for women.

Government policies

The remaining factor affecting flexibility is the regulatory framework within which both firms and individuals operate. Greater flexibility is at the centre of the present government's labour market objectives. Many policies introduced since 1979 have helped achieve this aim. These include policies consciously designed to increase flexibility in the labour market, as well as others directed in the main towards other goals.

The policies themselves are summarised in Appendix 5. In most cases, it is not possible to link policies with specific labour market outcomes.

The key policy changes that have directly affected the labour market are the withdrawal of government from intervention in pay determination (except in its

capacity as an employer); the programme of industrial relations legislation; active labour market policies designed to help the unemployed compete more effectively; and the removal of unnecessary institutional constraints. An example of the latter was the progressive extension between 1980 and 1985 of the period which an employee has to serve before being eligible to pursue a claim for unfair dismissal.

Policies to reform the labour market have been accompanied by macroeconomic policies designed to keep inflation under control. Figure 12.1 shows that inflation in the 1980s and 1990s was significantly lower than in the 1970s.

The promotion of enterprise and other supply side policies have also affected the labour market, often through their effects on product markets. Examples include the promotion of self-employment, competition policy, deregulation, privatisation, reform of the public sector, and changes to the tax and social security system.

d) Consequences of a more flexible labour market

In this final section, the focus is on the *impact* of greater flexibility, in terms of overall labour market and economic performance.

One approach would be to take each of the areas covered in Chapters 2 to 12 and attempt to trace through the impacts of any move towards greater flexibility. In one or two cases, this has been done. Examples include:

- The discussion of the effects of employment protection legislation on aggregate labour market variables. Chapter 2 discussed some of the relevant British evidence, while Appendix 2 covered cross-country comparisons. The British evidence tends to suggest that the effects of job security regulation are relatively small, whereas some of the cross-country evidence points to more sizeable impacts.

- Chapter 8 identified the sharp reduction in regional unemployment disparities since the end of the 1980s. This occurred towards the end of a period of regional wage re-alignment. Movements in these variables provide circumstantial evidence that changes in relative wages may have contributed to the reduction in unemployment disparities. The econometric evidence surveyed, however, does not lend a great deal of support to this hypothesis[4].

These particular instances exemplify a more general point. It is usually difficult to specify with precision the ways in which specific developments in the labour market affect overall economic performance. Not surprising, for such an approach would require a well-developed model of the entire labour market and its relationships with the rest of the economy.

Hence an alternative approach is adopted here. This is to consider a small number of 'top level' indicators of labour market performance. For each of these, recent trends are assessed, as well as international comparisons. Flexibility will be only one of the factors influencing these indicators - cyclical conditions is another obvious one - but it may be one of the most significant.

Two broad groups of indicators are considered. One is measures of overall labour utilisation (participation, employment, unemployment). The other is measures of the efficiency with which labour is used (labour and total factor productivity (TFP), potential output growth). In a well-functioning labour market, labour utilisation ought to be high and unemployment low, with labour also being used efficiently to achieve high rates of productivity growth.

The data on these indicators is reviewed in Appendix 6. In total, these 'top-level' labour market indicators present a mixed picture, but one with some encouraging signs. Activity rates have been increasing over time, and the trend growth rate may have increased during the 1980s. The employment-population ratio is also high by international standards. Unemployment and long-term unemployment remain above the levels experienced during the 1970s. However, there are signs that the labour market may have become more responsive to output changes. Unemployment began to fall at a much earlier point in the current recovery than it did following the early 1980s recession. In part, this may reflect greater flexibility among the unemployed (in terms of jobsearch and wage expectations), induced by active labour market policies.

There is also evidence that Britain's productivity performance has improved. Productivity appears to have increased faster in the 1980s than it did in the 1970s. It is less clear if labour productivity or TFP growth rates matched those of the 1950s and 1960s. However, in the context of a worldwide productivity slowdown, the UK's relative position has almost certainly improved.

Whether improvements in labour efficiency and productivity can be translated into higher rates of output and employment growth depends on a number of factors. The growth of aggregate earnings is a key variable. If job opportunities are to be created on a sustainable basis, restrained aggregate earnings growth would seem to be vital[5]. The OECD recently concluded that '... a greater degree of real wage flexibility may well be needed if unemployment is to be lowered durably in the medium term' (OECD (1994d), pp 27-28). The next few years will be a critical test of whether the signs of greater flexibility apparent at the micro level can feed through into greater real wage flexibility at the macro level.

Footnotes to Chapter 13

1. In the southern member states (Greece, Italy, Portugal, Spain) rigidities in the formal economy may be overcome by the existence of relatively large informal economies.

2. One very crude measure, based on WIRS data and reported in Millward, Stevens, Smart and Hawes (1992), is the proportion of workplaces that said they had more than 5 competitors. Comparisons between 1984 and 1990 revealed an increase from 49 per cent to 54 per cent in manufacturing. Services saw a larger increase, from 56 per cent to 64 per cent.

3. This issue may have greater relevance in countries where working time is regulated by statute.

4. This may be because the phenomenon is too recent to show up in the data. Alternatively, greater wage responsiveness may imply a change in the structural relationships linking regional wages and unemployment. Even if this is what happened, structural breaks can be difficult to detect.

5. Oulton (1994) presents telling evidence on this point. He finds that manufacturing productivity grew faster in the UK between 1979 and 1992 than in France, Germany, Japan and the USA. However, unit labour cost growth was on a par with France and considerably greater than in the USA (although slower than in Germany and Japan). This was because 'In the UK case, excellent productivity growth performance was offset by relatively rapid growth of wages' (page 57).

Appendix 1

Notes on data sources

Labour Force Survey (LFS)

The LFS is a nationally representative sample survey of households in the UK. For the period between 1979 and 1983, the survey was conducted biennially, in the Spring. From 1983 to 1991 inclusive, the survey was conducted on an annual basis. Since Spring 1992, it has taken place each quarter[1]. Unless otherwise stated, LFS results quoted in this paper use data from the Spring surveys.

Information on economic activity and labour market behaviour is collected for each person aged 16 and over in the household. In total, each survey contains data on about 160,000 individuals. The data is collected through face-to-face and telephone interviews, and response rates tend to be high. For about a third of individuals, however, data is collected through proxy responses, where someone else in the household provides information on behalf of the individual concerned.

The comparability of survey results over time is complicated by changes to questionnaire design as well as changes in definition. A major change in the definition of economic activity was introduced in the 1984 survey, when the measure of unemployment was changed to that used by the ILO. Data from 1984 onwards are generally comparable. Although a small discontinuity was introduced into the series in Spring 1992, when the survey identified unpaid family workers for the first time, this does not significantly affect the main trends.

Each EU member state is required to conduct regular Labour Force Surveys, and these are designed to be comparable.

Retrospective data

In addition to the usual questions on respondents' current activity, the Spring LFS also asks respondents about their status one year previously. This data is used in Chapter 6.

Comparisons of respondents' status at the time of the survey with their position a year previously indicate whether or not a respondent's circumstances have changed. However, they are still comparisons of two 'snapshots'. They are not estimates of flows.

Respondents may not recall with complete accuracy their situation a year previously, especially proxy responses. For this reason, cell sizes of less than 30,000 are not reported.

Between 1985 and 1991, respondents who had changed address were asked if their move was 'job-related'. This question has proved difficult to interpret. For example, while an employee who moved from one part of the country to another at the behest of their employer would regard their own move as job-related, it is not clear how any spouse or adult dependent who moved with them would answer this question. The ambiguities surrounding the question led to it being discontinued after the 1991 LFS.

Workplace Industrial Relations Survey (WIRS)

This survey series is sponsored jointly by the Employment Department, the Policy Studies Institute, the Economic and Social Research Council, and the Advisory, Conciliation and Arbitration Service. Surveys were carried out in 1980, 1984 and 1990.

WIRS is a nationally representative survey of all establishments (workplaces) with 25 or more employees. The sampling frame is the Census of Employment. The survey covers England, Scotland and Wales and all industries except agriculture, forestry, fishing and deep coal mining. Around 2,000 establishments are interviewed in each survey, and the response rate has been consistently high (83 per cent in 1990).

The survey consists of a main questionnaire administered to the most senior manager at the establishment responsible for personnel or industrial relations issues. In addition, interviews are held with employee representatives and, sometimes, other managers at the workplace. Further information on the survey in general and the terms and definitions used can be found in Millward, Stevens, Smart and Hawes (1992).

Union recognition and pay determination

Information on union recognition (for collective bargaining over pay and conditions) was collected for each of a number of negotiating groups at the workplace. In addition, for the largest manual and non-manual negotiating groups, additional questions were asked about the basis on which the most recent pay increase had taken place.

The paper presents this data in two ways: through estimates of the *proportions of establishments* with specific forms of pay determination (Table 7.1); and estimates of *proportions of employees* whose pay is determined by specific arrangements (Table 7.2).

The employee-based estimates are approximate; they essentially assume that the pay determination arrangements for the largest manual/non-manual negotiating group at the workplace apply to all manual/non-manual employees at that workplace. In practice, this method will overstate the incidence of collective bargaining.

In addition, the 1990 questionnaire was redesigned to take account of the possibility of unions having both manual and non-manual members, entailing a further complication with respect to these results. Where there were recognised unions with non-manual and manual members, but where none of the manual members belonged to a negotiating group that consisted of predominantly manual unions, their pay was determined within a predominantly non-manual group of unions. In such cases, whenever possible, the data about bargaining levels for the largest non-manual negotiating group has been imputed and applied to the manual employees covered by these unions. The same procedure was carried out for non-manual employees in a similar situation.

Employers' Labour Use Strategies (ELUS) survey

ELUS was a follow-up to the 1984 WIRS. The sampling frame was all establishments interviewed in the 1984 WIRS who said they were willing to be re-interviewed, and who had employed at least one temporary worker in the twelve months preceding the survey. Of the 1,948 establishments in the 1984 WIRS that agreed to be followed up, this left 1,035 that formed the ELUS sampling frame, from which 877 interviews were conducted. The response rate was 89 per cent of potential respondents. Interviews took place in 1987. Further details of the survey design can be found in Wood and Smith (1989).

The ELUS survey design means the results are not representative of establishments as a whole, only of those with 25 or more employees who had hired at least one temporary worker.

New Earnings Survey (NES)

The NES is conducted by the Employment Department, and is the most comprehensive source of information on earnings in Britain. The survey takes place in April of each year, and has been conducted annually since 1970.

The NES is a survey of employers, but collects data on the earnings of individual employees. Employers are asked to fill in the survey form for specified individuals, who have been chosen on the basis of their National Insurance number. The sample of employees is random and nationally representative. Combined with the large sample size and a high response rate, this means that the earnings of individuals can be analysed in some detail. There is, however, one gap in the NES's coverage. Employees earning less than the threshold for paying income tax are not automatically included in the survey. In practice this means that NES results for part-time employees and young people may not be fully representative. This does not affect any of the results in this study, which refer solely to full-time employees whose pay in the survey period was not affected by absence.

There are two minor discontinuities in the data. One is that the NES results up to and including 1983 refer to male full-time employees aged 21 and over, and female full-time employees aged 18 and over, whereas, from 1984 onwards, the results refer to all full-time employees on adult rates. The second discontinuity arises from a change in occupational classification in 1990. This only affects estimates for manual and non-manual employees; estimates reported for all full-time employees are unaffected.

In general, corrections for these discontinuities have not been made, as their practical significance is very small. The qualitative significance of all the results is unaffected. The exceptions to this are the data on regional earnings used in Chapter 8, and the data on earnings by occupation used in Chapter 10, where corrections to the data were made[2].

Further details on the general design of the NES, along with the questionnaire, can be found in part A of the annual survey report.

Collective agreements

The data on collective agreements used in this paper comes from two questions. The first is asked on an annual basis, and asks employers if the pay of the employee is 'directly affected' by any of a long list of collective agreements or Wages Council orders. The complete list in any single year can be found in part A of the survey report. This is the data plotted in

Figure 7.1. The second question, asked in 1973, 1978 and 1985, refers to all collective agreements, and not just the ones on the specified list. This data is presented in Table 7.3.

NHS Central Register (NHSCR) migration data

The NHSCR records monitor people's changes of General Practitioner (GP), when these involve moves between Family Health Service Authority (FHSA) areas. FHSA areas are, in England and Wales, roughly equivalent to the Shire counties, metropolitan boroughs and London boroughs. These records can therefore identify when a change of GP involves a move between standard regions.

These are administrative records, so they are not subject to sampling error. However, the data may still be an imperfect measure of inter-regional mobility. This is because a regional move is only identified when a person registers with a new GP. Some groups (such as children and the retired) will tend to be registered with a GP soon after moving. But other migrants, particularly young adults (also the most mobile group in the population) may fail to register with a GP for some time, if at all. It is currently assumed that people register with their GP one month after moving.

IPM/NEDO survey of payment systems

This was a one-off postal survey of employers conducted by the Institute of Personnel Management (IPM) and the National Economic Development Office (NEDO), reported in Cannell and Wood (1992).

The survey was a study of *organisations* across the UK. There are some methodological difficulties. The study aimed to survey a representative sample of employers; the effective response rate, however, was only 39 per cent. Furthermore, there are some significant differences in response rates between groups: public sector organisations, the financial services industry and medium-sized organisations (1,000-5,000 employees) were over-represented, while smaller organisations and some parts of the service sector were under-represented. Thus the degree to which the survey results reflect the overall population is questionable. They are best taken as reflecting the views of larger employers.

Footnotes to Appendix 1

1. With the exception of Northern Ireland, where the survey has continued to be conducted annually.

2. To deal with the discontinuity introduced by the switch in 1984 to presenting data on full-time employees on adult rates, the ratio between *national* average earnings on both bases was computed for 1984. Earnings data prior to 1984 was then deflated using this ratio. Similarly, the 1990 NES presented data on earnings using both occupational classifications, so the ratio between average earnings on the two occupational definitions could be applied to earlier data.

Appendix 2
Cross-country evidence on the impact of employment protection regimes

A number of studies have made cross-country comparisons of how labour market regulations affect labour market outcomes. This Appendix summarises the evidence available on the impact of employment protection legislation. Details of the individual studies are given in Table A2.1.

A number of methodological issues must be borne in mind:

- Three of the studies are based on rankings of the stringency of employment protection regulations. These are inevitably subjective, no matter how closely based on objective evidence. As a consequence, rankings differ (see Table 3.6). It is not clear whether substituting one set of rankings for another would make a significant difference to the conclusions drawn from these studies.

- In addition, studies that use these rankings and include a time-series dimension (Bertola (1990), Burgess (1994)) effectively assume that the rankings (based on the position in the mid to late 1980s) have not changed over time. This is a strong assumption to make.

- The alternative approach used by Lazear (1990) and OECD (1993), based on quantitative variables, is able to exploit both the cross-section and time-series variation in the data[1]. However, these variables are themselves difficult to calculate. Focusing on the quantifiable (such as severance payments) risks ignoring other important but unquantifiable effects, such as the rigour with which regulation is enforced.

- None of these studies embed their analysis within comprehensive structural models of the labour market. Hence the possibility of omitted variable bias cannot be ruled out.

A degree of caution must therefore be exercised in interpreting the results.

Table A2.1 Cross-country studies of the impact of employment protection regulations

Study	Period covered	Countries covered	Measure of regulation	Method of analysis
Bertola (1990)	1962-1986	10 OECD countries (7 EU, plus Sweden, USA, Japan)	Ranking of job security provisions (see Table 3.6)	Rank correlation coefficient between rank ordering and variable of interest
Lazear (1990)	1956-1984	22 developed economies	Measures of (expected) amount of notice and severance pay	Included as variables in regression analyses
OECD (1993)	1979-1991	19 OECD economies	Sum of maximum (expected) amount of notice and severance pay	Included as variables in regression analyses
CEC (1993)	1989	12 EU member states	Employer perceptions of flexibility in hiring and firing (see Table 3.3)	Cross-plot with variable of interest
Grubb and Wells (1993)	Late 1980s (mainly 1989)	11 EU member states (minus Luxembourg)	Ranking of stringency of employment regulation (see Table 3.6)	Graphical analyses and regression of ranking against variable of interest
Burgess (1994)	1971-1988	As Bertola (1990)	Bertola and Grubb/ Wells rankings	Graphical analyses and regression of ranking against variable of interest

Table A2.2   Main findings from cross-country studies of the impact of employment protection regulations

Topic	Study	Main results[1]
Employment		
Long-term or equilibrium level	BT	No evidence of any impact
	LZ	Negative and significant impact
	GW	Negative but insignificant impact
Adjustment to equilibrium	BT	Regulation reduces fluctuations in employment levels
	CEC	Negative impact on dismissal rate (although UK outlier)[2]
	BG	Negative relationship between regulation and measures of job re-allocation across industrial sectors
Structure of employment	GW	Negative impact on employee-population ratio, and proportions in part-time and temporary employment
		Positive impact on proportion self-employed
Unemployment		
Level	BT	No significant impact
	LZ	Positive and significant impact
Persistence	BT	Positive and significant impact on measures of persistence
	OECD	Positive and significant impact on LTU rate
Structure of unemployment	LZ	Regulation associated with greater disparities between youth and adult unemployment rates
Other effects		
Aggregate real wage flexibility	BT	Positive and significant impact[3]
Labour force participation	LZ	Negative and significant impact
Average hours worked	LZ	Negative and significant impact

Key: BG = Burgess (1994); BT = Bertola (1990); OECD = OECD (1993); CEC = CEC (1993); GW = Grubb and Wells (1993); LZ = Lazear (1990).

Notes:

1   A 'positive' impact in this table is where a high degree of employment protection is associated with more, or higher values of, the variable in question.

2   The UK dismissal rate is much lower than would be expected given UK employers' assessment of their flexibility in hiring and firing. Explanations are advanced in CEC (1993). One is that 1989 was close to a cyclical peak, and this may have depressed the dismissal rate. The measure of dismissals used, derived from the LFS, may also be imperfect. It seems unlikely, however, that these explanations could account for all of what is quite a substantial gap.

3   Real wage flexibility was measured by the sum of the coefficients on the unemployment level and the change in unemployment in a Phillips curve regression.

143

Table A2.2 summarises key results. There is clearly some disagreement between these studies, especially on the key question of whether employment protection reduces employment (and increases unemployment) in the long run. Bertola (1990) suggests there is no effect, whereas Lazear (1990) finds a significant impact.

However, there does appear to be a consensus that employment protection 'smooths' the path of employment over the cycle, reducing rates of job creation and destruction. In this context, Burgess (1994) suggests that regulation could impose significant efficiency costs on the economy, by slowing down the re-allocation of labour from declining to expanding sectors. This is most likely if (regulation-induced) low engagement and dismissal rates mean that some workers find it very difficult to get into employment. This is consistent with the positive correlation between employment protection and unemployment persistence.

Footnotes to Appendix 2

1. In fact, the cross-section variation tends to dominate.

Appendix 3

Econometric studies of inter-regional mobility

Table A3.1 gives details of recent econometric studies of inter-regional migration in Britain. The main distinction to be drawn is between studies that use aggregated data and studies that use individual/household-level data.

Analyses using aggregate data

Pissarides and McMaster (1990) found that net inter-regional migration rates were associated with regional disparities in both wages and unemployment. Regions where earnings increased relatively quickly tended to attract immigrants, whereas low wage growth regions lost migrants. Disparities in regional unemployment rates induced people to move from high unemployment regions to low unemployment regions. The particular formulation of the unemployment term they used in the regression analysis implies that the gross inter-regional migration rate falls when aggregate unemployment increases. This model property is consistent with the procyclical movements in the migration rate evident in Figure 6.4.

Jackman and Savouri (1992a) nested migration decisions within a matching model, and found that the relative availability of jobs between regions (measured by the vacancy rate) was a major influence on regional migration flows. It also

follows from this analysis that movements in the gross inter-regional migration rate will reflect cyclical fluctuations in the aggregate vacancy rate. The empirical work confirms the importance of these effects, which act in addition to the 'push' effect of regional disparities in unemployment. Jackman and Savouri's analysis also incorporated house prices and found that, while movements in house prices did affect migration rates, they were not as significant an influence as vacancy rates.

The study also found a significant negative relationship between relative earnings and net migration rates. This is consistent with the raw correlation graphed in Figure 6.5. It implies that high earnings regions experience net out-migration, rather than net in-migration as might be expected. The authors speculate that this could be due to compositional effects, or to high relative wages spurring firms to relocate jobs to low wage areas in ways that are not captured by the official vacancy statistics[1].

Jackman and Savouri (1992b) extends the analysis by trying to distinguish between short-distance housing-related moves and longer distance moves, which are more likely to be shaped by labour market factors. Moves between regions without common boundaries (i.e. longer distance moves) were found to be more strongly influenced by economic factors than moves between regions with common boundaries.

Analyses using individual-level data

Analyses have also been carried out using individual or household level data. These analyses complement the above studies. Although much of the time series variation is lost from the estimation, a wider

Table A3.1   Econometric studies of inter-regional migration

Study	Estimation methodology	Data source	Time period
Pissarides and McMaster (1990)	Pooled cross-section, time-series	Aggregate data on migration by region, various sources	1963-1982
Jackman and Savouri (1992a, 1992b)	Pooled cross-section, time-series	Aggregate data on migration by region, NHSCR records	1975-1989
Pissarides and Wadsworth (1989)	Cross-section	Data on economically active households, LFS	1977, 1984
Thomas (1993)	Pooled cross-section, time-series	Individual data, LFS	1984-1986

set of demographic and economic characteristics can be included in the analysis.

Pissarides and Wadsworth's (1989) conclusions broadly support those of the aggregate-level analyses, in that higher aggregate unemployment discouraged migration across the board. They also found that the vacancy-unemployment ratio provides a more powerful statistical explanation of migration flows than disparities in the unemployment rate on its own. Their study also confirmed the pattern evident in the raw data in Table 6.7: the unemployed (especially the long term unemployed) were more likely to migrate than the employed.

Comparisons between 1977 and 1984 suggested that the influence of economic variables had diminished somewhat over this period. In particular, the impact of regional unemployment disparities on migration decisions had decreased as unemployment had risen.

Thomas's (1993) analysis is restricted solely to migrants, so the focus is on which region migrants move to, rather than on the migration decision itself. The study splits migrants up into two groups: those who said their move was 'job-related' and those who said it was not. As noted in Chapter 6, this LFS question is probably an imperfect measure of the motivation behind migration decisions. However, as a rule of thumb for disaggregating the data, it may be an acceptable procedure. Thomas finds some statistical validation for this procedure, as a common migration equation for the two groups is rejected by the data. The results of his analysis also appear intuitively plausible.

The main difference between job-related and other movers was that non job-related migrants' choice of region was far more sensitive to relative house prices than job-related migrants. In contrast, responses to regional wage and unemployment disparities were similar for both groups.

Footnotes to Appendix 3

1. A variable measuring the relocation of employment outside London is on the margins of statistical significance.

Appendix 4
Ceteris paribus wage differentials

This Appendix supplements Chapters 8, 9 and 10 by summarising the evidence on recent estimates of *ceteris paribus* wage differentials.

Ceteris paribus wage differentials are those remaining once all other factors have been controlled for. These controls are numerous, and would typically include hours worked, working conditions, personal characteristics (both observed and unobserved), institutional factors, and labour market conditions. They would also include the factors considered in more detail here: region; industry; and human capital (education/occupation).

Given the importance of controlling for personal characteristics, most research has used individual-level data. This means, however, that some other important factors (such as product market conditions, bargaining institutions, or working conditions) may be less accurately measured.

Basic information on each of the studies quoted in this section is given in Table A4.1.

The control variables vary from study to study. Nor does the table specify the accuracy or level of detail of the controls used, merely whether they are present. For example, Moghadam (1990) used a full set of occupational controls, whereas Blanchflower and Oswald (1993) included just two occupational dummies, for non-manual and supervisor status respectively.

Regions

Moghadam (1990) found significant *ceteris paribus* wage differentials between regions, plotted in Figure A4.1. Since their size varies from year to year, average values have been calculated for 1978-1981 and 1982-1985 respectively. The differentials can be interpreted as percentage deviations from the base region (Greater London).

In general, the pattern of *ceteris paribus* inter-regional wage differentials is similar to the uncontrolled wage differentials reported in Chapter 8. Earnings were considerably higher in Greater London and the rest of the South East than elsewhere. Outside the South East, *ceteris paribus* differentials were reasonably similar across all regions, although the relative decline of earnings in the West Midlands and Wales is still present in this controlled comparison.

Figure A4.1 *Ceteris paribus* regional wage differentials, 1978-1985

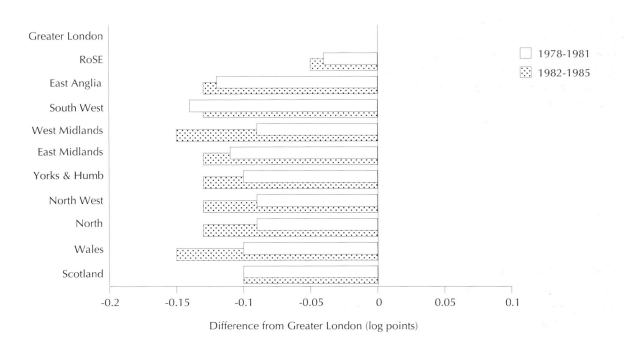

Difference from Greater London (log points)

Source: Moghadam (1990).

Table A4.1 Recent studies of *ceteris paribus* wage differentials

	Blackaby and Manning (1990a)	Moghadam (1990)	Blackaby, Bladen-Hovell and Symons (1991)	Elliott, Murphy and Sandy (1991)	Haskel and Martin (1991)	Schmitt (1992)	Hildreth (1993)	Blanchflower and Oswald (1993)	Blanchflower and Freeman (1994)
Data source:	GHS	FES	FES	SCELI	WIRS	GHS	BHPS	GHS	GHS
Time period:	1975,1982	1978-1985	1980-1986	1986	1984	1974-1988	1991	1973-1990	1979,1990/91
Level:	Individual	Individual	Individual	Individual	Establishment	Individual	Individual	Individual	Individual
Nationally representative?	Yes	Yes	Yes	No. Representative of 6 local labour markets	No. Representative of workplaces with 25+ employees	Yes	Yes	Yes	Yes
Coverage:	Men, employees	Men	Men, employees, age 16-65	Men and women, wage and salary earners	Employees, manufacturing only	Men aged 16-64	Men and women, full-time permanent employees, private sector	Men and women, employees	Men and women
Dependent variable:	Annual earnings (1975), earnings for last pay period (1982)	Gross weekly earnings	'Normal' earnings	Gross hourly earnings	Typical weekly earnings of unskilled workers	Gross weekly earnings	Gross weekly earnings	Gross weekly earnings	Hourly earnings
Controls included for:									
Marital status/ dependent children	Yes	Yes		Yes	No	Yes	Yes	Yes	Yes
Age/experience	Yes	Yes		Yes	No	Yes	Yes	Yes	Yes

Continued on next page

Table A4.1 Recent studies of *ceteris paribus* wage differentials (continued)

	Blackaby and Manning (1990a)	Moghadam (1990)	Blackaby, Bladen-Hovell and Symons (1991)	Elliott, Murphy and Sandy (1991)	Haskel and Martin (1991)	Schmitt (1992)	Hildreth (1993)	Blanchflower and Oswald (1993)	Blanchflower and Freeman (1994)
Hours worked	Yes	No		No	No	No	Yes	No	No
Full-time/part-time	No	No		Yes	Yes	No		Yes	No
Union status/bargaining arrangements	No	Yes (1982–85)		Yes	Yes	No	Yes	No	No
Working conditions	No	No		No	No	No	Yes	No	No
Product market conditions	No	No		No	Yes	No	No	No	No
Workplace/firm size	No	No		Yes	No	No	No	No	No
Local/regional unemployment	Yes	No	Yes	No	No	No	No	Yes	No
Regional cost of living	Yes	No	Yes	No	No	No	No	No	No
Time dummies	No							Yes	Yes
Region	No	Yes		No (but one for each area)	No	Yes	Yes	Yes	Yes
Industry	Yes*	Yes	Yes*	Yes	Yes	No	Yes	Yes*	Yes*
Education/schooling	Yes*	Yes		Yes*	No	Yes	Yes*	Yes*	Yes
Occupation	Yes*	Yes	Yes*	No	No	No	No	No (partly)	Yes* (partly)

Note: * indicates that estimates are not reported.

Figure A4.2 *Ceteris paribus* regional wage differentials, 1979-1990/91

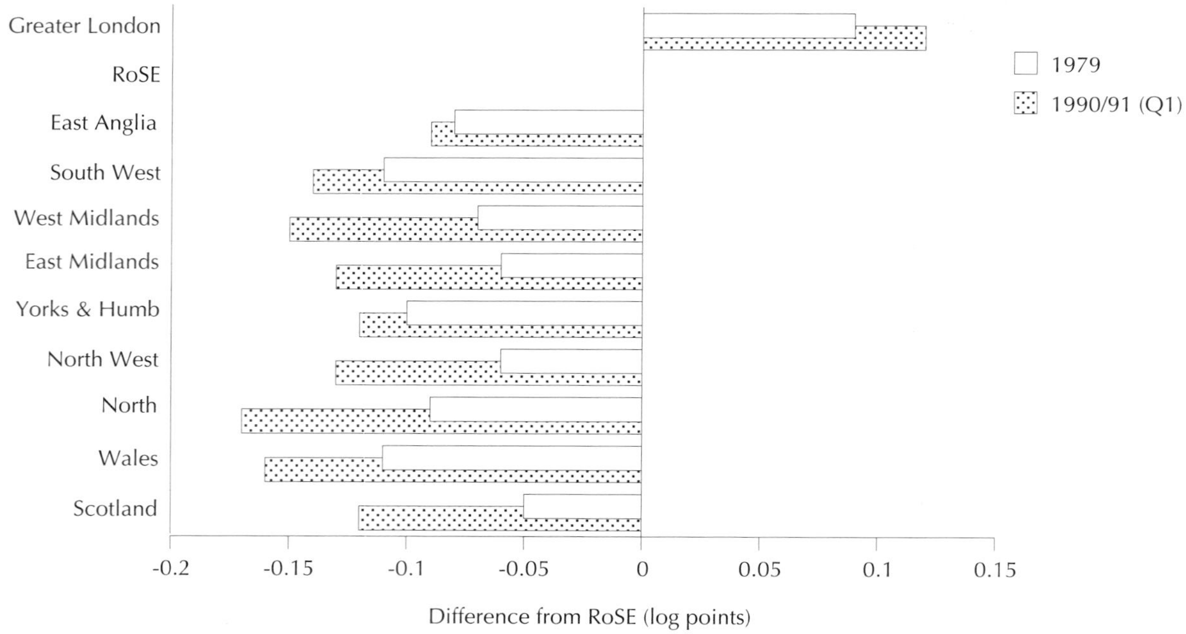

Source: Blanchflower and Freeman (1994).

Blanchflower and Freeman (1994) also find evidence of persistent *ceteris paribus* regional wage differentials, graphed in Figure A4.2.

These regional wage differentials have widened over time, the standard deviation increasing from 0.059 in 1979 to 0.085 by 1990/91. Most of this widening was due to increases in the differential between the South East and other regions. However, even among these other regions, there was some increase in the dispersion of *ceteris paribus* wage differentials.

The existence of 'unexplained' regional wage differentials is not inconsistent with a well-functioning labour market. For example, they could reflect differences between regions in the cost of living. Blackaby and Manning (1990a) and Blackaby, Bladen-Hovell and Symons (1991) both found strong cost of living effects.

These two studies also found a negative relationship between earnings and regional unemployment. Blanchflower and Oswald (1993) provide further evidence on this point. Using pooled data for the period 1973-1990 allowed them to test for the presence of *ceteris paribus* regional wage differentials (fixed effects) while at the same time allowing the regional unemployment rate to affect earnings. They found a consistent negative association between the individual wage and the regional unemployment

rate, with an elasticity of about -0.1. This relationship works in addition to regional fixed effects[1].

Blanchflower and Oswald also provide tentative evidence that wages may have become more responsive to regional unemployment over time. They split their sample up into two sub-periods and found a larger negative coefficient for the period 1981-1990 than for the earlier period 1973-1980 (although this difference may not be statistically significant).

Industry

The dispersion (measured by the weighted standard deviation) of Moghadam's (1990) estimates of *ceteris paribus* industrial wage differentials is graphed in Figure A4.3.

There is a discontinuity caused by a change to the industrial classification. For 1978-1981, dispersion was measured across 28 industry groupings. A further four industrial categories were added to the analysis in 1982. This means that the apparent widening of wage differentials over the period could be affected by this change.

150

Figure A4.3 Dispersion across industries of *ceteris paribus* wage differentials, 1978-1985

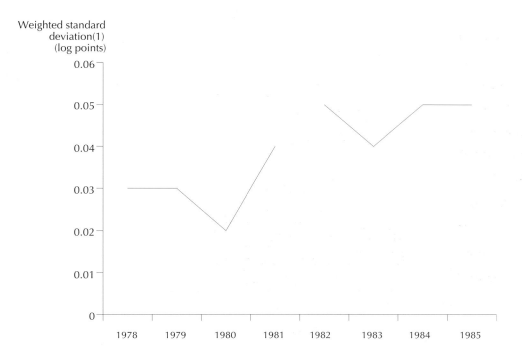

Notes

1. *The proportions of the sample in each industry were used as weights.*

Source: Moghadam (1990).

Blanchflower and Freeman's (1994) results confirm there was a modest widening in the dispersion of inter-industry differentials from the end of the 1970s. The (unweighted) standard deviation increased from 0.118 in 1979 to 0.142 by 1990/91(Q1). The structure of *ceteris paribus* differentials across industries, however, was highly stable. The correlation between the rank ordering of differentials at these dates was 0.915.

Two other studies provide information on inter-industry wage differentials at single points in time. Results are presented in Table A4.2.

Table A4.2 shows that the addition of controls for personal characteristics and human capital reduces the dispersion of wage differentials. Further controls for factors related to the job or workplace reduce the variation even further. Indeed, in the latter cases, most of the estimated wage differentials were not significantly different from zero[2].

Table A4.2 also indicates that the degree of disaggregation affects the measure of dispersion. A finer industrial classification produces a greater measured wage dispersion. Although the addition of controls reduced the dispersion of industry wage differentials, it did not greatly affect the rank ordering of individual industries.

Haskel and Martin (1991) also present estimates of *ceteris paribus* wage differentials. The focus on establishments means their analysis contains more controls for product and labour market conditions than the studies mentioned above. Like Hildreth (1993), Haskel and Martin found that control variables reduced the observed dispersion of wages across industries. Their results also suggest that product and labour market factors are very important in explaining observed inter-industry differentials. Indeed, the inclusion of these firm and industry specific controls meant that the industry fixed effects disappeared altogether. Haskel and Martin also suggest that many of the variables that lie behind inter-industry wage differentials - such as technological change, product market competition, industrial relations arrangements - change quite slowly. They see this as accounting for the long-run stability of the industrial wage distribution.

Education

Moghadam (1990) provides some econometric evidence on the returns to general education. Education in this study is measured in terms of completed years of education, rather than qualifications achieved.

Table A4.2   Dispersion of *ceteris paribus* industry wage differentials

Elliott, Murphy and Sandy (1991)

Number of industrial categories:	Standard deviation of wage differentials:		
	(1) **No controls**	**(2)** **With basic controls[1]**	**(3)** **With extra controls[2]**
14[3]	0.228	0.135	0.136
33[4]	0.198	0.102	0.086
Rank correlation coefficient for:		(2) v (1)	(3) v (1)
14[3]		0.77	0.73
33[4]		0.84	0.59

Hildreth (1993)

Number of industrial categories:	Standard deviation of (log) wage differentials:		
	(1) **No controls**	**(2)** **With basic controls[5]**	**(3)** **With extra controls[6]**
10	0.377	0.126	0.072
55	0.445	0.279	
Rank correlation coefficient for:		(2) v (1)	(3) v (1)
10		0.85	0.75
55		0.78	

Notes

1   *Control variables were sex, marital status, experience, educational attainment, full-time status, and a measure of specific training (time taken to reach proficiency).*

2   *Additional controls for size of firm and trade union membership.*

3   *Small sample (n=444) utilising information from surveys of both employees and their employer.*

4   *Larger sample (n=2959) utilising information solely from survey of employees.*

5   *Control variables included sex, marital status, age, region, years of schooling and educational achievement, health status, and travel to work time.*

6   *Additional controls for size of workplace, training, hours worked, time of day at which work done, profit sharing, job tenure, and union status.*

Sources: Elliott, Murphy and Sandy (1991), Tables 1 and 3; Hildreth (1993), Tables 1 and A3.

Figure A4.4 shows that wage differentials by year of education tended to widen, with the greatest increase in differentials being among those who had entered higher education (i.e. left full-time education at age 19+).

Schmitt (1992) analysed educational differentials over a longer time period. One methodological difference, however, is that Schmitt estimated returns for the highest qualification achieved, rather than years of education *per se*. This method helps to focus attention on attainment, but there may be some difficulties in ascertaining the 'highest' qualification,

especially between vocational and general academic qualifications.

Figure A4.5 suggests that *ceteris paribus* educational wage differentials narrowed during the 1970s, before widening again during the 1980s. By 1986-1988, the structure of differentials was similar to 1974-1976. The results therefore seem to corroborate Moghadam's.

Blanchflower and Freeman's (1994) results cover both men and women, and include a slightly different (and wider) set of controls. Results are presented in Figure A4.6.

Figure A4.4 *Ceteris paribus* **educational wage differentials, 1978-1985**

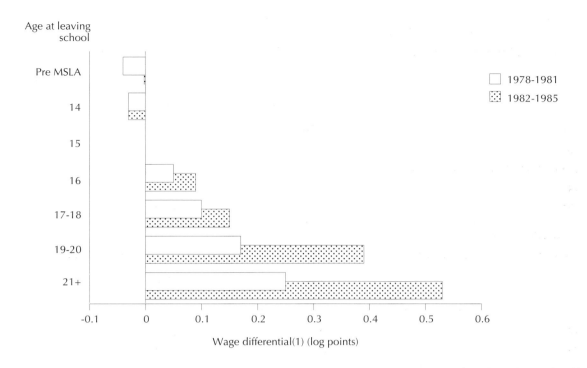

Notes

1   Differential over someone leaving school at age 15.

Source: Moghadam (1990).

Figure A4.5 *Ceteris paribus* **educational wage differentials, 1974-1988**

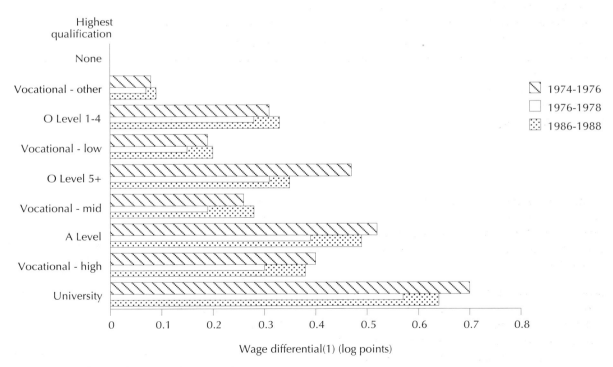

Notes

1   Differential over someone with no qualifications.

Source: Schmitt (1992).

Figure A4.6 *Ceteris paribus* **educational wage differentials, 1979-1990/91**

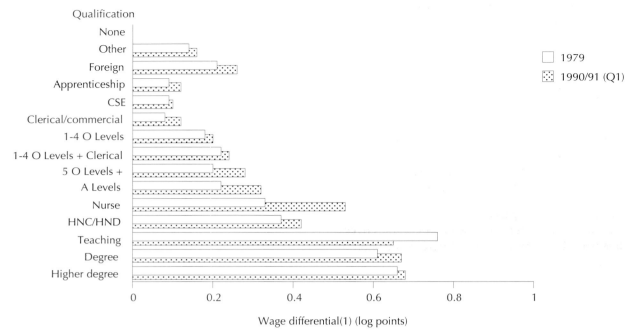

Figure A4.7 Dispersion across occupations of *ceteris paribus* **wage differentials, 1978-1985**

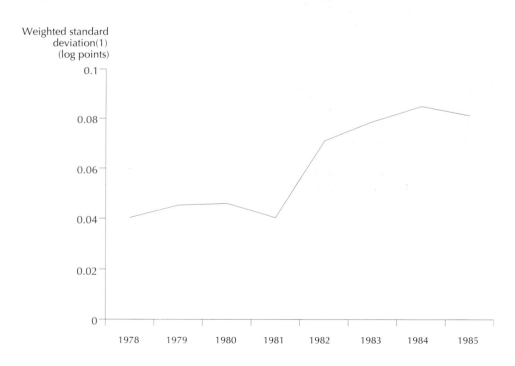

Notes

1   The proportions of the sample in each occupation were used as weights.

Source: Moghadam (1990).

Blanchflower and Freeman found that there had been no general widening of educational differentials between 1979 and 1990/1991(Q1), although differentials for some qualifications had changed[3].

Occupations

Moghadam (1990) suggests there are statistically significant *ceteris paribus* wage differentials between occupations. Over the period 1978-1985, the distribution of these differentials widened considerably, as shown in Figure A4.7.

Professional, managerial and administrative employees saw large increase in differentials over this period, whereas those for teachers and shop assistants fell.

Footnotes to Appendix 4

1. Blanchflower and Oswald suggest that the persistence of regional fixed effects may arise because of differences between regions in their relative attractiveness to potential migrants.

2. Elliott, Murphy and Sandy (1991) also reported further regressions, not reported in Table A4.2, that control for job characteristics and fringe payments. The significance of the industry fixed effects diminished further.

3. Using Moghadam's (1990) and Schmitt's (1992) estimates, the dispersion of educational wage differentials (as measured by the standard deviation) narrowed during the late 1970s and increased again in the 1980s. In contrast, the standard deviation of the Blanchflower and Freeman (1994) estimates is virtually constant (0.221 for 1979 compared to 0.216 in 1990/91(Q1)).

Appendix 5
Government policies

conf d

This appendix provides a brief description of government policies that may have encouraged greater flexibility in the labour market. The emphasis is on developments post-1979.

They can be grouped under three headings: labour market policies themselves; macroeconomic policies; and policis to promote enterprise and supply side performance. A number of themes underlie the policy agenda: developing and improving market structures; deregulation; and the promotion of competition.

The aim is to set out the key features of each policy, rather than specific details of legislation or other interventions.

Labour market policies

A non-interventionist pay policy

During the 1960s and 1970s, both Conservative and Labour governments periodically intervened in the labour market to limit increases in aggregate earnings. Intervention took the form of voluntary and statutory pay policies, sometimes accompanied by controls on price rises and other forms of income (e.g. dividends). These policies typically constrained the size of wage increases, but sometimes limits were also set on the structure of pay rises.

While these policies may on occasions have been successful in restraining earnings growth in the short term[1], there is little evidence that they were effective in moderating long-term pay pressures. Indeed, by distorting wage adjustment at the micro level, their overall impact was probably harmful.

Since 1979, the government's approach to private sector pay has been based on the view that pay is a matter for employers and employees to determine in the light of their particular circumstances. Ministers have also made clear their belief that pay should be determined by what is necessary to recruit, retain and motivate suitable employees within what can realistically be afforded. A number of policy changes (see below) have reinforced this approach and influenced the climate within which wages are determined.

Removing institutional barriers to pay determination

Institutional mechanisms that regulated the pay of some groups in the labour market have been progressively abolished. The Fair Wages Resolution, a form of contract compliance which required public contractors to abide by the terms and conditions of collective agreements, or the general level of terms and conditions of employment observed in the trade or industry, was rescinded in 1983. Section 11 of the 1975 Employment Protection Act, a similar but more wide-ranging instrument, was repealed in 1980.

The Wages Council system, which set minimum rates of pay and other terms and conditions of employment for certain workers in a number of trades and industries, was radically reformed by the 1986 Wages Act. Under the 1986 Act, each Wages Council was restricted to setting, in the main, a single minimum hourly rate of pay and an overtime rate, and the pay of young workers under 21 was removed from regulation by the Councils. The Wages Councils were subsequently abolished in 1993.

Encouragement of financial participation

The government has encouraged employee involvement in general, which includes financial participation, through promotional activities such as the recent 'The Competitive Edge' booklet.

In addition, tax reliefs have been specifically used to encourage the take-up of financial participation schemes. Relief for employee share ownership schemes was first introduced in 1979, and modified in a series of Finance Acts. Relief from Income Tax for participants in approved profit-related pay schemes was first introduced in 1987. The value of the reliefs was increased substantially in 1991. The take-up of profit-related pay has increased rapidly during the early 1990s. By 1993, over a million employees were covered by officially approved schemes.

Chapter 7 shows that profit-related pay arrangements predate the introduction of this tax concession. Hence, there may be an element of deadweight as schemes that already existed took advantage of the tax concession. To the extent that additionality has taken place, however, this is an instance where government policy has directly encouraged greater flexibility in the labour market.

Public sector pay

Given the size of the public sector, the policies pursued by the government in its capacity as an employer have a significant impact on the labour market.

As in the private sector, the government has taken the view that pay should reflect recruitment, retention and motivation considerations within affordable limits. Because of the need to restrain public expenditure, a formal limit of 1.5 per cent was imposed on public sector settlements in 1993. This has been succeeded by a policy of paybill control intended to ensure that pay rises are financed by efficiency improvements and other economies, and do not add to public spending.

The government has also sought more flexible pay arrangements. The Citizen's Charter White Paper argued for more delegated and performance related pay regimes as an integral part of improving the efficiency and quality of public services. PRP has been introduced in many areas such as the Civil Service, and is being developed in others, such as the police force. Civil Service pay determination has also been increasingly delegated to Departments and executive agencies to the extent that, by 1994, less than a third of Civil Servants were still covered by centralised pay arrangements. More flexible and discretionary pay arrangements have been introduced in areas such as education and proposals are currently being developed for local PRP bargaining in the NHS.

Similarly, the independent review bodies that determine the pay of certain public sector groups[2] are now required to consider the affordability of their recommendations before submitting them.

Reform of industrial relations

One of the most significant policy developments has been a programme of legislation designed to reform the conduct of industrial relations. The overall aim has been to create a fairer balance under the law between the interests of employers and employees. This reflected a view that the 1970s had seen the balance of power swing too far towards trades unions.

This policy has been implemented through a 'step-by-step' programme of legislation, passed between 1980 and 1993. The elements were as follows:

- Trade unions have been made more accountable to their members. Union leaders have to be elected through secret ballots, and all members are entitled to scrutinise union accounts. The procedures which unions must follow in meeting these requirements have also been specified in statute.

- The grounds on which unions can legitimately conduct industrial action have been more tightly defined. Industrial action must first be approved by a secret ballot of the affected membership, and

secondary or politically-motivated industrial action has been made illegal[3]. Controls have also been introduced on the conduct of industrial action. Employees must give employers 7 days' notice of industrial action, and curbs have been introduced on intimidatory picketing.

- Institutional mechanisms designed to promote or consolidate trade union influence within the workplace have been removed. A statutory recognition procedure, which was widely regarded as ineffective, was removed in 1980. More significantly, the pre-entry and post-entry closed shops have been effectively abolished[4]. Employers are no longer entitled to automatically deduct union subscriptions (the 'check off') without individual members' authorisation. The individuals' right not to join a trade union has been matched by legislation that makes it unlawful to dismiss employees because they are trade union members.

This is a short summary of a wide-ranging programme. Taken together, these measures amount to a radical change in the legal framework of industrial relations. The precise impact of the legislation, however, is more difficult to judge. For example, the impact of the legislation on union membership and organisation is disputed (Freeman and Pelletier (1990), Disney (1990)).

Labour market deregulation

There are a number of examples here. Between 1980 and 1985, the length of time that employees had to serve before they could make an application to an Industrial Tribunal for unfair dismissal was progressively increased from 6 months to 2 years.

The 1989 Employment Act removed outdated restrictions on the working hours of young people and women. The same year also saw the abolition of the Dock Labour Scheme, which had regulated employment in the port industry since the end of the War.

Active labour market policies

Since 1986, a range of policies have been introduced along the lines of the 'active labour market policy' model advocated by the OECD (OECD (1990a)). These policies enable the unemployed to compete more effectively in the labour market, and include the following:

- The creation of the Employment Service in 1988 united job-broking and benefit payment functions within one government agency. The aim was to help those claiming unemployment benefits to keep in touch with the labour market.

- Changes to the regulations governing entitlement to unemployment benefits. Entitlement has over time become more closely tied to evidence of active jobsearch and availability for work. In broad terms, the conditions for receipt of unemployment benefits now match the ILO definition of unemployment (i.e. out of work, available for work, and actively seeking work).

- An increased emphasis on maintaining contact with the unemployed. This began with the Restart programme, introduced in 1986, whereby unemployed people are interviewed every six months. The aim is to offer some form of positive assistance. A number of other changes have strengthened these contacts. These include the provision of advice to claimants at the time they become unemployed, and the drawing up of Back to Work Plans, designed to help unemployed people focus their jobsearch activity.

- The provision of job search 'infrastructure' through the Employment Service network, as well as more intensive assistance through the Jobclub programme. Where appropriate, training in jobsearch skills has also been made available.

- The development of a range of training and enterprise programmes to help the unemployed and other groups (e.g. women returners) to compete in the labour market.

Macroeconomic policies

Macroeconomic policies are important in shaping the economic climate. The key feature of macroeconomic policy since 1979 has been the greater weight attached to the control of inflation. A Medium Term Financial Strategy was introduced in 1980, in order to provide a policy background against which expectations could be formed.

In 1992, the government adopted an explicit target range for RPI inflation (excluding mortgage interest payments) of 1-4 per cent.

Figure 12.1 shows that inflation rates during the 1980s and early 1990s have, on average, been much lower than during the 1970s. Fluctuations in both inflation and economic activity have tended to be greater in the UK than in other major OECD economies (Elmeskov (1993), Anderton and Mayhew (1994)), but the 1980s and 1990s have seen inflation fluctuate around a much lower average rate.

Promotion of enterprise and other supply-side policies

The third set of policies are wider-ranging economic policies which have nevertheless had an impact on the labour market through their effects on the supply side.

Promotion of enterprise

Government policy has promoted self-employment directly through the Business Start Up scheme (previously the Enterprise Allowance Scheme). In addition, deregulation has reduced many barriers to business, especially for small firms.

Promotion of product market competition

Government policy aims to increase competition in product markets. This has included measures to strengthen and extend the scope of legislation governing monopolies and other restrictions on competition. For example, the 1980 Competition Act enabled the Office of Fair Trading to refer monopolies and anti-competitive practices to the Monopolies and Mergers Commission.

This approach has been combined with a less interventionist approach to industrial policy, including a reduction in the scale of regionally targeted assistance programmes, and a reluctance to subsidise uncompetitive industries. This shift in policy may have contributed to the competitive pressures facing employers.

Tax and social security policies

Measures in this sphere have been designed to promote enterprise, improve work incentives, and assist labour mobility. Key changes on the tax side would include: a significant reduction in the marginal rate of Income Tax; a wider shift in the balance of taxation from direct to indirect taxation; and steps to widen the tax base through the removal of many distortions. Personal tax allowances have also increased in real terms, taking many low paid employees out of tax altogether.

The NICs system has been progressively reformed. In particular, lower rates have been introduced for low paid workers. CEC (1994) concluded that the UK was the only EU member state where the structure of non-wage labour costs bears least heavily on low paid workers.

On the social security side, the early 1980s saw a change in the way state benefits were uprated. These are now increased in line with prices. As a result, the replacement ratio has fallen considerably.

Furthermore, the 1986 Social Security Act, implemented in 1988, involved major changes to the structure of benefits. These included the replacement of Supplementary Benefit by Income Support, and the replacement of Family Income Supplement by Family Credit. One of the most significant effects of the reforms was the virtual removal of the 'unemployment trap', whereby people could be better off unemployed than in work.

More recently, plans have been announced to restructure benefits for the unemployed. The new Job Seekers' Allowance, which will replace Unemployment Benefit, should provide the unemployed with extra incentives to find work quickly, as the period for which a flat-rate benefit is paid will be reduced from 12 to 6 months.

Another potentially significant development has been reform of occupational pensions. The 1985 Social Security Act made it easier for people to transfer between occupational pension schemes without suffering financial loss, while the 1986 Social Security Act enabled employees to opt out of employers' occupational pension schemes if they wished to join a personal pension scheme. These measures should have improved the 'portability' of occupational pensions and encouraged labour mobility.

Public sector reforms

Reform in the public sector stretches beyond public sector employment policies. The privatisation programme has transferred ownership of most state utilities (as well as many smaller enterprises) to the private sector. In total, employment in the state-owned sector has been reduced by about two thirds since 1979. Privatisation has increasingly been accompanied by the extension of competition. Where it has not been possible to secure widespread competition, regulation has been used as an alternative means of safeguarding consumer interests and providing appropriate market disciplines.

Another significant move has been the contracting out of many local and central government services. Since 1980, certain activities in the NHS, central and local government have been opened up to competitive tender. In 1988, competitive tendering was made compulsory for many local authority services.

Even where activity has remained within the public sector, measures have been taken to improve efficiency. Examples would include the development of the internal market within the NHS, the devolution of budgets to individual schools, and

the creation within central government of executive agencies whose performance is assessed against specified targets.

Footnotes to Appendix 5

1. Incomes policies may have been a significant factor behind the sharp fall in real earnings in 1976 and 1977 (see Figure 12.1).

2. Teachers, nurses and midwives, doctors and dentists, pharmacists, the armed forces, senior government officials, and judges.

3. Technically, the legislation removes trade unions' immunity from liability for civil damages arising out of an industrial dispute if they fail to comply with the statutory requirements.

4. This has been implemented by giving employees dismissed, refused employment, or otherwise disadvantaged because of refusal to join a trade union, automatic grounds for redress to an Industrial Tribunal.

Appendix 6
Indicators of labour market performance

This section presents an overview of trends in key labour market indicators. A flexible labour market, other things being equal, should be one where there is a high degree of labour utilisation and where labour is used efficiently, so that productivity growth is high.

Comparisons are also made between trends in Britain and trends in other OECD economies.

Labour force participation

Figure A6.1 reveals an upwards trend in the civilian activity rate over the past two decades, although activity rates tend to vary over the cycle. While male activity rates have fallen, this has been more than outweighed by increased female activity rates.

Activity rates in OECD member states are presented in Table A6.1. Although OECD Secretariat estimates, they are based on national data sources, so definitions and coverage may not be completely standardised. There will also be differences across countries in the timing of cyclical peaks and troughs. Cross-country comparisons should therefore focus on broad orders of magnitude.

Figure A6.1 Trends in civilian activity rates, 1971-1993

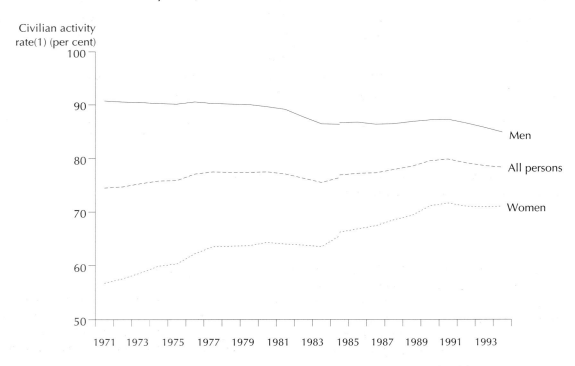

Notes

1   *Economically active people as a proportion of the (mid-year) population of working age (men aged 16-64, women aged 16-59).*

   There is a slight discontinuity in the series, caused by the change in the definition of economic activity (from the LFS to the ILO definition) in 1984.

Source: Ellison (1994), Table 3.

Table A6.1 International comparisons of civilian activity rates, 1972-1992

| Country: | Civilian labour force as a percentage of the population aged 15-64, men and women | | | | |
| | 1972 | 1982 | 1992[1] | Percentage point change: | |
				1972-1982	1982-1992[1]
Australia	68.5	69.4	73.7	+0.9	+4.3
Austria	67.7	66.4	69.4	-1.3	+3.0
Belgium	60.3	61.6	62.3	+1.3	+0.7
Canada	64.8	71.4	71.7	+6.6	+0.3
Denmark	74.1	79.5	82.5	+5.4	+3.0
Finland	69.7	76.2	73.6	+6.5	-2.6
France	65.7	65.7	65.3	0.0	-0.4
FR Germany	67.8	66.8	68.0	-1.0	+1.2
Greece	56.8	58.7	57.3	+1.9	-1.4
Iceland	71.0	77.7	85.6	+6.7	+7.9
Ireland	63.6	62.3	60.7	-1.3	-1.6
Italy	57.0	58.7	61.4	+1.7	+2.7
Japan	71.4	72.3	75.9	+0.9	+3.6
Luxembourg	64.6	63.7	61.2	-0.7	-2.5
Netherlands	57.0	59.0	67.6	+2.0	+7.3
New Zealand	63.4	65.4	72.7	+2.0	+7.3
Norway	67.8	75.1	75.6	+7.3	+0.5
Portugal	63.9	67.5	71.1	+3.6	+3.0
Spain	58.8	54.8	57.3	-4.0	+2.5
Sweden	75.2	81.2	81.2	+6.0	0.0
Switzerland	77.4	74.7	76.2	-2.7	+1.5
Turkey	71.6	64.1	56.3	-7.5	-7.8
UK	**71.1**	**72.2**	**73.6**	**+1.1**	**+1.4**
USA	66.0	71.5	75.9	+5.5	+4.4
OECD average	**66.5**	**68.3**	**72.2**	**+1.8**	**+3.9**

Notes

1   *Except Australia, Greece, Iceland, Ireland, and Luxembourg (1991).*

Source: *OECD (1994a), Tables 2.0 and 5.0.*

The civilian activity rate in the UK has remained above the OECD average, although the gap has narrowed over the past two decades. Activity rates appear not to have increased as quickly as they have in the Nordic countries or North America, but the UK has retained the second highest activity rate in the EU, after Denmark.

Employment

The activity rate by itself says nothing about the economy's overall job creation record. This is captured by the employment-population ratio. Figure A6.2 plots a time series for Britain since 1971.

161

Figure A6.2 Employment-population ratio, 1971-1994

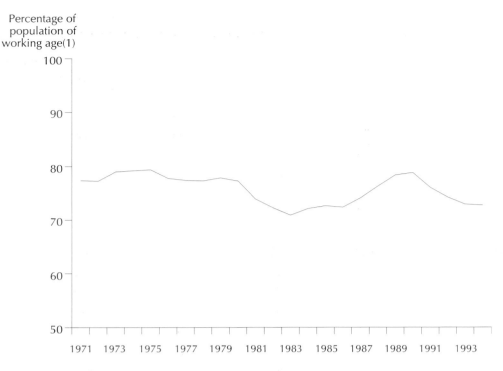

Percentage of
population of
working age(1)

Notes

The workforce in employment (June, seasonally adjusted) as a proportion of the (mid-year) population of working age (men aged 16-64, women aged 16-59), Great Britain.

Sources: OPCS, Employment Department.

This ratio varies more over the cycle than the activity rate. It is difficult to detect any substantive long-term trend, given the amplitude of recent cycles.

Table A6.2 presents data for OECD member states. Since employment is more cyclically sensitive than activity rates, differences in the timing of cycles are especially important when making comparisons across countries.

Again, the UK employment-population ratio has remained above the OECD average. Within the EU, the UK's employment-population ratio was, in 1992, the third highest behind Denmark and Portugal.

Unemployment

Figure A6.3 displays a time series for the claimant unemployment rate. Unemployment grew steadily during the 1970s and increased sharply in the early 1980s. The period between 1986 and 1990 saw a substantial fall in the unemployment rate, before another large increase during the early 1990s recession.

Unemployment peaked in the summer of 1993, at a lower level than in the mid 1980s. This is the first time since the War that unemployment has peaked at a lower level than in the previous cycle. Unemployment also began to fall at an earlier stage in the recovery than in previous cycles. Following the early 1980s recession, output growth resumed in 1981 but unemployment did not begin to fall until 1986; the lag was less than a year in 1993. This could reflect a shortening in the lag between output and employment growth, although there are other potential explanations, such as more favourable demographic factors.

Table A6.3 sets out data for OECD countries. Unemployment in the UK has tended to exceed the OECD average. However, the differential narrowed between 1983 and 1993.

Table A6.2   International comparisons of civilian employment-population ratios, 1972-1992

| | Total civilian employment as a percentage of the population aged 15-64, men and women | | | | |
| Country: | 1972 | 1982 | 1992[1] | Percentage point change: | |
				1972-1982	1982-1992[1]
Australia	67.9	65.7	66.7	-2.2	+1.0
Austria	67.0	64.1	66.9	-2.9	+2.8
Belgium	59.1	54.1	55.7	-5.0	+1.6
Canada	60.8	63.6	63.6	+2.8	0.0
Denmark	73.4	71.1	74.9	-2.3	+3.8
Finland	68.7	72.7	63.9	+4.0	-8.8
France	63.8	61.0	58.5	-2.8	-2.5
FR Germany	67.2	63.2	64.0	-4.0	+0.8
Greece	55.6	55.3	52.9	-0.3	-2.4
Iceland	71.0	78.6	83.8	+7.6	+5.2
Ireland	59.6	55.8	51.1	-3.8	-4.7
Italy	53.3	54.3	54.3	+1.0	0.0
Japan	70.4	70.6	74.2	+0.2	+3.6
Luxembourg	64.6	62.5	60.4	-2.1	-2.1
Netherlands	55.8	52.2	63.0	-2.4	+10.8
New Zealand	63.2	63.1	65.2	-0.1	+2.1
Norway	66.7	73.6	71.1	+6.9	-2.5
Portugal	62.2	62.5	68.2	+0.3	+5.7
Spain	57.1	46.0	46.8	-11.1	+0.8
Sweden	73.2	78.6	76.9	+5.4	-1.7
Switzerland	77.4	74.4	74.2	-3.0	-0.2
Turkey	67.2	59.6	51.9	-7.6	-7.7
UK	**68.9**	**64.6**	**66.8**	**-4.3**	**+2.2**
USA	63.5	64.5	70.3	+1.0	+5.8
OECD average	**64.2**	**62.9**	**66.7**	**-1.3**	**+3.8**

Notes

1   *Except Australia, Greece, Iceland, Ireland, and Luxembourg (1991).*

Source: *OECD (1994a), Tables 2.0 and 6.0.*

Measures of structural unemployment

Measures of the 'underlying' level of unemployment also point to a recent improvement. One such measure is the Beveridge curve. Essentially, this measures labour market efficiency by the level of excess supply (unemployment) at any given level of demand (vacancies).

Figure A6.4 plots the aggregate Beveridge curve. The curve has clearly shifted over time[1]. It appears to have first moved outwards after the first oil shock in the mid 1970s. This was followed by a more pronounced outwards shift during and after the recession of the early 1980s. Unemployment during this period rose rapidly, and continued to rise for a number of years, even when the vacancy rate was increasing.

After this, the behaviour of the curve becomes more difficult to interpret. The curve may have moved inwards after 1986, followed by another shift

Figure A6.3 Claimant unemployment, 1971-1994

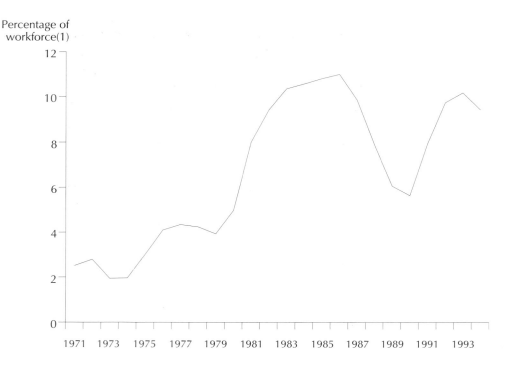

Notes

1   *Claimant unemployment (adjusted for seasonality and discontinuities) expressed as a percentage of the workforce, Great Britain, annual averages (except 1994, which is the average for the 9 months to September).*

Source: Employment Department.

Figure A6.4 The UK Beveridge curve

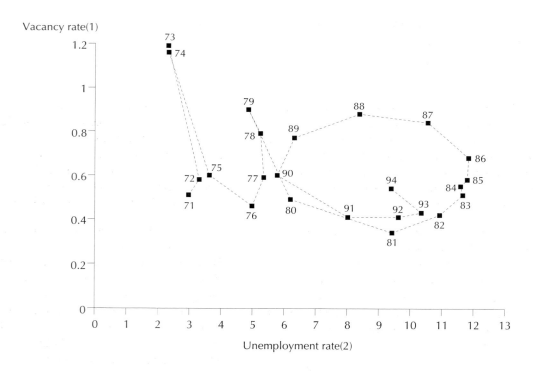

Notes

1   *Unfilled Jobcentre vacancies as a percentage of the workforce, June.*

2   *Claimant unemployment (adjusted for seasonality and discontinuities) as a percentage of the workforce, June.*

Source: Employment Department.

Table A6.3 International comparisons of standardised unemployment rates, 1974-1993

Country	Unemployment[1] as a percentage of the total labour force, men and women				
	1974	1983	1993	Percentage point change:	
				1974-1983	1983-1993
Australia	2.6	9.9	10.8	+7.3	+0.9
Belgium	3.0	12.1	9.1	+9.1	-3.0
Canada	5.3	11.8	11.1	+6.5	-0.7
Finland	1.7	5.4	17.7	+3.7	+12.3
France	2.8	8.3	11.6	+5.5	+3.3
FR Germany	1.6	7.7	5.8	+6.1	-1.9
Ireland	..	14.0	15.8	..	+1.8
Italy	5.3	8.8	10.2	+3.5	+1.4
Japan	1.4	2.6	2.5	+1.5	-0.2
Netherlands	2.7	12.0	8.3	+9.3	-3.7
New Zealand	..	..	10.5	..	..
Norway	1.5	3.4	6.0	+1.9	+2.6
Portugal	..	7.8	5.5	..	-2.3
Spain	2.6	17.0	22.4	+14.6	+5.4
Sweden	2.0	3.5	8.2	+1.5	+4.7
UK	**2.9**	**12.4**	**10.3**	**+9.5**	**-2.1**
USA	5.5	9.5	6.7	+4.0	-2.8
OECD average	**3.5**	**8.5**	**7.8**	**+5.0**	**-0.7**

Notes

1   *Unemployment rates based on ILO guidelines, although discontinuities may still exist.*

..   *indicates data not available.*

Source: *OECD (1994c), Table A21.*

outwards in the early 1990s. Alternatively, events since 1986 may simply represent very large cyclical, anti-clockwise movements around a fixed Beveridge curve (see Jackman, Layard and Pissarides (1989)). However, the 1994 observation suggests the more likely explanation is an inwards shift of the Beveridge curve since the mid 1980s.

Alternative measures of equilibrium unemployment can be derived from econometric models. Of these, the best known is the NAIRU. Estimates of the NAIRU vary substantially from study to study. They also tend to track the actual unemployment rate quite closely, which raises questions about their usefulness as measures of the 'underlying' equilibrium rate.

Cromb's (1993) survey, nevertheless, showed that estimates of the NAIRU tended to be below the actual unemployment rate during the 1970s, which

could be one reason why inflation was so high for much of the decade. In contrast, unemployment exceeded the top end of the range of NAIRU estimates during the mid 1980s. Cromb finds, however, that estimates of the NAIRU fell towards the end of the 1980s, which implies some improvement in overall labour market performance[2].

Some recent international comparisons of movements in the Beveridge curve were presented in OECD (1992), although there are considerable differences between countries in the quality and coverage of vacancy data[3]. Over the period 1970-1991, of the twenty countries surveyed, only Sweden did not shows signs of an outwards shift in its Beveridge curve (and this has indeed occurred since 1991). Focusing on developments post-1979, the Beveridge curve appeared to shift inwards in three countries - the USA, Sweden and Portugal. In two more, Luxembourg and Switzerland, the outwards shift was very modest. The remaining fifteen OECD countries have seen the Beveridge Curve move outwards over the 1979-1989 cycle. While the shift in the UK was significant, it was not the largest. Belgium, France, Greece, Spain and New Zealand would appear to have seen outward shifts at least as great.

Long-term unemployment (LTU)

This is also an indicator of particular interest. Figure A6.5 plots the LTU-unemployment ratio, where LTU is defined as a continuous spell of unemployment of 12 months or more. Unlike the unemployment data presented in Figure A6.3, the LTU series is not adjusted for seasonality and discontinuities. Nevertheless, the data highlights the key trends.

The LTU-unemployment ratio tends to rise and fall in line with the aggregate unemployment rate, albeit with a lag. The first half of the 1980s saw a very sharp rise in the numbers of LTU. During the early 1990s, however, the ratio has failed to increase to previous levels.

Figure A6.6 presents cross-country comparisons. All this data is based on household surveys (the LFS in the case of the UK), so UK estimates may not correspond exactly to those obtained from administrative sources.

The LTU ratio in the UK was above the OECD average in both 1979 and 1989. There is a clear distinction between North America, Japan and the Nordic countries, where the LTU ratio is low, and the EU member states. There is also a connection between the incidence of LTU and mobility; the countries with low LTU ratios are those countries where outflow rates from unemployment are relatively high (see Figure 6.7).

Labour productivity

Figure A6.7 shows that labour productivity growth varies a great deal over the cycle. The cyclicality of productivity may itself be a measure of labour market flexibility, as discussed in Chapter 11. The issue here is the trend rate of growth in labour productivity.

Figure A6.5 LTU-unemployment ratio, 1979-1994

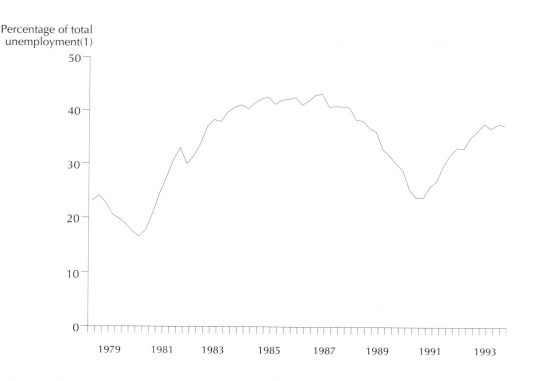

Notes

1   People unemployed for 12 months or more as a percentage of total unemployment.

   Unemployment on a registrant basis prior to October 1982, and a claimant basis thereafter, unadjusted for seasonality and discontinuities, excluding under 18s, Great Britain.

Source: Employment Department.

Figure A6.6 International comparisons of LTU-unemployment ratios, 1983-1992

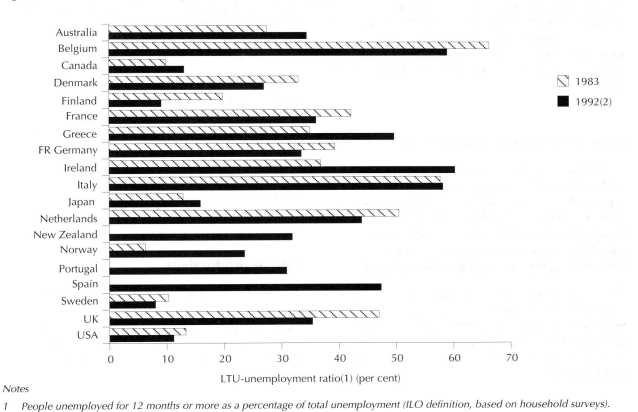

Notes

1   People unemployed for 12 months or more as a percentage of total unemployment (ILO definition, based on household surveys).

2   Except Finland and Ireland (1991).

Source: OECD (1994c), Table P.

Figure A6.7 Labour productivity growth, 1971-1994

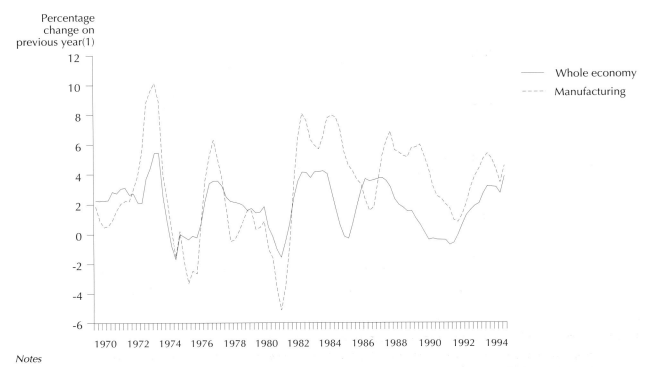

Notes

1   Output per person employed, UK, seasonally adjusted.

Source: CSO.

The visual evidence suggests that labour productivity has grown more quickly since the end of the 1970s, especially in manufacturing. This is borne out by comparisons over the last two completed cycles. Between 1973 and 1979, whole economy productivity increased at a rate of 1.2 per cent per annum; over the period 1979-1990, average growth was 1.8 per cent.

Bank of England (1989), using more sophisticated methods which incorporated a role for factor price adjustment, found that there had been a distinct improvement in trend growth: up from 1.1 per cent a year in the 1970s to 3.0 per cent for the 1980s (up to the end of 1987). Darby and Wren-Lewis (1991) also found evidence of a slowdown in manufacturing productivity growth during the second half of the 1970s, together with a subsequent recovery. However, they found that trend manufacturing growth had remained unchanged since the 1960s at 2.75 per cent a year, once allowance was made for factor price adjustments and over-optimistic output expectations during the late 1970s.

Developments in the UK need to be considered in the context of a worldwide productivity slowdown. Table A6.4 presents OECD estimates of labour productivity growth in the business sector.

The UK's *relative* position has improve noticeably. Over the period 1979-1992, productivity grew faster than the OECD average, probably the first time this has happened for a sustained period since the end of the War[4].

Measurement issues are particularly important when making international comparisons. Oulton (1994) presents a more detailed examination of

Table A6.4 International comparisons of labour productivity growth

Output per person employed in the business sector, average annual percentage growth rates					
1960-1973		**1973-1979**		**1979-1992[1]**	
Greece	8.8	Ireland	3.4	Ireland	4.2
Japan	8.6	Greece	3.3	Finland	3.0
Portugal	7.5	Spain	3.3	Spain	2.8
Italy	6.3	Austria	3.2	Japan	2.7
Spain	6.0	Finland	3.2	France	2.3
Austria	5.8	Netherlands	3.2	Denmark	2.3
France	5.4	France	3.0	Belgium	2.2
Belgium	5.2	FR Germany	3.0	**UK**	**2.2**
Finland	4.9	Italy	2.9	Austria	1.9
Ireland	4.9	Japan	2.9	Italy	1.8
Netherlands	4.9	Belgium	2.8	Portugal	1.7
FR Germany	4.5	Denmark	2.6	FR Germany	1.6
OECD average	**4.5**	Australia	2.2	**OECD average**	**1.6**
Denmark	4.3	**UK**	**1.6**	Netherlands	1.4
Sweden	4.1	**OECD average**	**1.6**	Sweden	1.4
UK	**3.6**	Canada	1.5	Australia	1.3
Switzerland	3.2	Sweden	1.5	New Zealand	1.3
Canada	2.8	Switzerland	0.8	Canada	1.2
Australia	2.7	Portugal	0.5	Norway	1.2
USA	2.2	USA	0.0	Greece	0.9
New Zealand	1.7	New Zealand	-1.3	USA	0.8

Notes

1   Except Ireland, Norway and Portugal (1979-1990); and Austria, Belgium, Greece, Italy, Spain and Sweden (1979-1991).

Source: OECD (1994b), Table 57.

developments post-1979. His results indicate that, over the period 1979-1992, labour productivity in manufacturing grew faster in the UK than in the USA, France, Germany or Japan.

Darby and Wren-Lewis (1992) present more sophisticated estimates of trend manufacturing productivity growth for each of the G7 economies, covering the period 1966-1987. These estimates incorporated factor price movements and suggested, like Darby and Wren-Lewis (1991), that trend UK productivity growth had remained roughly constant over time, at 2.95 per cent a year. In contrast, they found some evidence of a productivity slowdown during the 1970s in the USA, Canada, Japan and Germany. Italy was the only other country where the trend line was flat. Trend productivity growth in the UK during the 1980s may have matched that of Japan, Germany, the USA and Canada, and exceeded that of France and Italy.

Total factor productivity

Total factor productivity (TFP) measures the outputs that can be produced from a given set of inputs. Estimates of TFP growth are even more difficult to compile than straight labour productivity indices. These measurement problems are additional to the difficulties posed by differences between countries in the timing of economic cycles[5].

Table A6.5   International comparisons of total factor productivity growth

Business sector total factor productivity growth[1], average annual percentage growth rates								
1960-1973			**1973-1979**			**1979-1992[2]**		
Japan	5.8		Ireland	2.4		Ireland	3.3	
Portugal	5.1		Italy	2.1		Finland	1.9	
Italy	4.4		Greece	2.1		Spain	1.7	
France	4.0		FR Germany	1.8		Japan	1.6	
Belgium	3.9		Finland	1.8		**UK**	**1.6**	
Greece	3.9		Netherlands	1.8		Belgium	1.4	
Ireland	3.7		France	1.7		Denmark	1.4	
Netherlands	3.6		Belgium	1.4		France	1.4	
Austria	3.3		Japan	1.3		Italy	1.1	
Spain	3.3		Austria	1.2		FR Germany	1.0	
Finland	3.2		Denmark	1.1		Portugal	1.0	
OECD average	**3.0**		Australia	1.0		Netherlands	0.9	
Denmark	2.7		Denmark	0.9		**OECD average**	**0.9**	
FR Germany	2.6		Canada	0.8		Austria	0.8	
UK	**2.6**		**UK**	**0.6**		Sweden	0.7	
Australia	2.2		**OECD average**	**0.6**		Australia	0.6	
Norway	2.2		Sweden	0.2		Greece	0.5	
Canada	2.0		USA	-0.4		Switzerland	0.4	
Sweden	2.0		Portugal	-0.4		USA	0.4	
Switzerland	2.0		Switzerland	-0.4		New Zealand	0.3	
USA	1.6		Norway	-1.6		Canada	0.1	
New Zealand	0.8		New Zealand	-2.0		Norway	0.0	

Notes:

1   Total factor productivity growth is equal to a weighted average of the growth in labour and capital productivity. Sample-period averages for capital and labour shares are used as weights.

2   Except Ireland, Norway and Portugal (1979-1990); and Austria, Belgium, Greece, Italy, Spain and Switzerland (1979-1991).

Source: OECD (1994b), Table 57.

Figure A6.8 Growth rates of potential output for the G7 economies

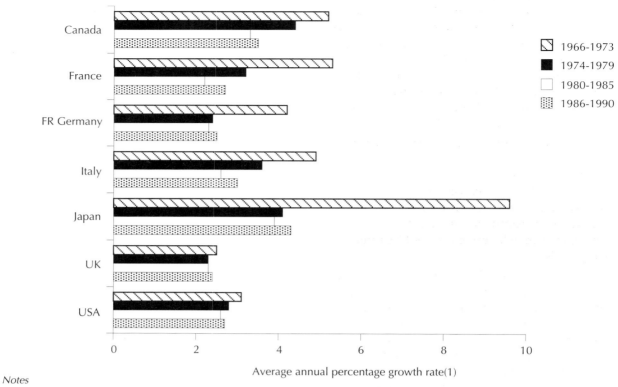

Average annual percentage growth rate(1)

Legend:
- 1966-1973
- 1974-1979
- 1980-1985
- 1986-1990

Notes

1   *Calculations are based on business sector gross output.*

Source: Torres and Martin (1990), Table 2.

Table A6.5 presents estimates of TFP growth for nearly all OECD member states. There is again clear evidence of an improvement in the UK's relative performance[6].

Potential output

The final measure presented is one that captures overall supply performance, the growth rate of potential output. Torres and Martin (1990) presented estimates for each of the G7 economies. They defined potential output growth as that level of growth consistent with efficient factor utilisation (i.e. trend TFP growth) and stable inflation. Their estimates are presented in Figure A6.9.

On this measure, the UK's performance appears to have changed little. Potential output growth was estimated to be the lowest among the G7 economies, even though TFP growth post-1979 was relatively high.

The reason for these low estimates would appear to be the degree of aggregate wage rigidity in the UK. In Torres and Martin's model, potential output growth is constrained by the NAIRU, which in turn is derived from aggregate wage-setting behaviour. Hence Torres and Martin's account is one of aggregate wage rigidity acting as a constraint on the UK's ability to exploit the benefits of improved efficiency in factor utilisation. Employment growth above quite moderate levels stimulates wage inflation.

As Chapter 12 suggested, aggregate wage rigidity in the UK has been high by international standards. Although there may be some encouraging signs of greater flexibility, these would have been too recent to affect Torres and Martin's findings.

Footnotes to Appendix 6

1. The measure of vacancies used does not measure all vacancies in the economy. Jobcentre vacancies are estimated to be about a third of the total stock of vacancies. Although three national surveys, conducted in 1977, 1982 and 1988, all produced similar estimates, the ratio of Jobcentre to total vacancies could still vary over time (see Roper (1989)). If so, this would distort the movements in the Beveridge curve plotted in Figure A6.4.

2. Elmeskov (1993) estimated a number of different measures of 'underlying' unemployment, including a Beveridge curve measure and a NAIRU. He found quite a close correspondence between the different series for the UK. All the indicators suggested that structural unemployment fell during the late 1980s and early 1990s.

3. OECD (1992) surveyed a number of studies that attempt to take account of these differences. The results indicate that, in some cases, adjustments to the data have tended to overstate the size of shifts in the Beveridge curve. In other cases, revisions to the data can understate such shifts. It may still, nevertheless, be possible to draw some broad inferences from the data presented.

4. Blanchflower and Freeman (1994) also support this conclusion. Their estimates suggest that UK productivity growth was significantly below the OECD average in the 1960s and 1970s. However, UK productivity growth was above the OECD average throughout the 1980s, although the difference was not statistically significant.

5. Rotemberg and Summers (1990) suggest that TFP will exhibit pro-cyclical behaviour if prices are sticky.

6. Bank of England (1989) estimated an employment equation which implied a substantial upturn in TFP growth from 1980 onwards, with a growth rate of some 3 per cent per annum. However, this only applied to manufacturing, and the estimation period finished in 1987.

References

Abraham, K (1987), **Flexible Staffing Arrangements and Employers' Short-term Adjustment Strategies**, in Hart, R (ed), *Employment, Unemployment and Labor Utilization*, Unwin Hyman, Boston.

Abraham, K and Houseman, S (1993), **Does Employment Protection Inhibit Labour Market Flexibility? Lessons from Germany, France and Belgium**, NBER Working Paper No. 4390, June.

Abraham, K and Taylor, S (1993), **Firms' Use of Outside Contractors: Theory and Evidence**, NBER Working Paper No. 4468, October.

Adams, M, Maybury, R and Smith, W (1988), **Trends in the Distribution of Earnings, 1973 to 1986**, *Employment Gazette*, February, pp 75-82.

Alogoskoufis, G and Manning, A (1988), **On the Persistence of Unemployment**, *Economic Policy*, No. 7.

Anderton, R, Barrell, R and McHugh, J (1992), **Nominal Convergence in European Wage Behaviour: Achievements and Explanations**, in Barrell, R (ed), *Economic Convergence and Monetary Union in Europe*, Sage, London, pp 31-57.

Anderton, R, Barrell, R, in't Veld, J and Pittis, N (1992), **Forward-Looking Wages and Nominal Inertia in the ERM**, *National Institute Economic Review*, August.

Anderton, R and Mayhew, K (1994), **A Comparative Analysis of the UK Labour Market**, in Barrell, R (ed), *The UK Labour Market: Comparative Aspects and Institutional Developments*, Cambridge University Press, London.

Atkinson, J (1984), **Manpower Strategies for Flexible Organisations**, *Personnel Management*, August, pp 28-31.

Banerji, N and Wareing, A (1994), **Unfair Dismissal Cases: 1987 and 1992 Survey Results Compared**, *Employment Gazette*, October, pp 359-365.

Bank of England (1989), **Productivity Trends**, *Bank of England Quarterly Bulletin*, February, pp 23-26.

Beatson, M (1993), **Trends in Pay Flexibility**, *Employment Gazette*, September, pp 405-428.

Bentolila, S and Bertola, G (1990), **Firing Costs and Labour Demand: How Bad is Eurosclerosis?**, *Review of Economic Studies*, Vol. 57, No. 3, pp 381-402.

Bentolila, S and Dolado, J (1994), **Spanish Labour Markets**, *Economic Policy*, Vol. 18, April, pp 53-99.

Bertola, G (1990), **Job Security, Employment and Wages**, *European Economic Review*, Vol. 34, No. 4, pp 851-879.

Bertola, G (1992), **Labor Turnover Costs and Average Labor Demand**, *Journal of Labor Economics*, Vol. 20, No. 1/2, pp 27-51.

Black, B (1994) **Labour Market Incentive Structures and Employee Performance**, *British Journal of Industrial Relations*, Vol. 32, No. 1, March, pp 99-111.

Blackaby, D, Bladen-Hovell, R and Symons, E (1991), **Unemployment, Duration Effects and Wage Determination in the UK: Evidence from the FES 1980-86**, *Oxford Bulletin of Economics and Statistics*, Vol. 53, No. 4, November, pp 377-400.

Blackaby, D and Manning, N (1990a), **The North-South Divide: Questions of Existence and Stability?**, *Economic Journal*, Vol. 100, June, pp 510-527.

Blackaby, D and Manning, N (1990b), **Earnings, Unemployment and the Regional Employment Structure in Britain**, *Regional Studies*, Vol. 24, No. 6, pp 529-535.

Blackaby, D and Manning, N (1992), **Regional Earnings and Unemployment - A Simultaneous Approach**, *Oxford Bulletin of Economics and Statistics*, Vol. 54, No. 4, November, pp 481-501.

Blackaby, D and Murphy, P (1991), **Industry Characteristics and Inter-Regional Wage Differentials**, *Scottish Journal of Political Economy*, Vol. 38, No. 2, pp 142-161.

Blanchflower, D and Freeman, R (1992), **Unionism in the United States and Other Advanced OECD Countries**, *Industrial Relations*, Vol. 31, No. 1, Winter, pp 56-79.

Blanchflower, D and Freeman, R (1994), **Did the Thatcher Reforms Change British Labour Market Performance?**, in Barrell, R (ed), *The UK Labour Market: Comparative Aspects and Institutional Developments*, Cambridge University Press, London, pp 51-92.

Blanchflower, D and Oswald, A (1992), **International Wage Curves**, NBER Working Paper No. 4200, October.

Blanchflower, D and Oswald, A (1993), **Estimating a Wage Curve with Fixed Effects and Cell Means**, Dartmouth College, mimeo, January.

Bosworth, D (1994), **Shiftwork in the UK: Evidence from the LFS**, *Applied Economics*, Vol. 26, No. 6, June, pp 617-626.

Bowey, A, Thorpe, R, Mitchell, F, Nicholls, G, Gosnold, D, Savery, L and Hellier, P (1982), **Effects of Incentive Payment Systems: United Kingdom 1977-80**, *Department of Employment Research Paper* No. 36.

Boyer, R (1987), **Labour Flexibilities: Many Forms, Uncertain Effects**, *Labour and Society*, Vol. 12, No. 1, January, pp 107-129.

Boyer, R (1988) **Division or Unity? Decline or Recovery?** in Boyer, R (ed), *The Search for Labour Market Flexibility*, Clarendon Press, Oxford.

Brown, W and Walsh, J (1991), **Pay Determination in Britain: The Anatomy of Decentralisation**, *Oxford Review of Economic Policy*, Vol. 7, No. 1, Spring, pp 44-59.

Brown, W (1993), **The Contraction of Collective Bargaining in Britain**, *British Journal of Industrial Relations*, Vol. 31, No. 2, June.

Burgess, S (1988), **Employment Adjustment in UK Manufacturing**, *Economic Journal*, Vol. 98, No. 389, March, pp 81-103.

Burgess, S (1993), **Labour Demand, Quantity Constraints or Matching: The Determination of Employment in the Absence of Market Clearing**, *European Economic Review*, Vol. 37, No. 7, October, pp 1295-1314.

Burgess, S (1994), **The Reallocation of Employment and the Role of Employment Protection Legislation**, CEP Discussion Paper No. 193, April.

Burgess, S and Nickell, S (1990), **Labour Turnover in UK Manufacturing**, *Economica*, Vol. 57, No. 227, August, pp 295-318.

Calmfors, L (1993), **Centralisation of Wage Bargaining and Macroeconomic Performance - A Survey**, *OECD Economic Studies*, Vol. 21, Winter, pp 159-191.

Calmfors, L and Driffill, J (1988), **Centralisation of Wage Bargaining**, *Economic Policy*, Vol. 6, April.

Campbell, M and Daley, M (1992), **Self-Employment: Into the 1990s**, *Employment Gazette*, June.

Cannell, M and Wood, S (1992), **Incentive Pay: Impact and Evolution**, Institute for Personnel Management.

Casey, B (1988a), **Temporary Employment: Practice and Policy in Britain**, Policy Studies Institute.

Casey, B (1988b), **The Extent and Nature of Temporary Employment in Britain**, *Cambridge Journal of Economics*, Vol. 12, No. 4, December, pp 487-510.

Casey, B, Lakey, J and White, M (1992), **Payment Systems: A Look at Current Practice**, *Employment Department Research Series* No. 5, October.

CEC (1986), **Employment Problems: Views of Businessmen and the Workforce**, *European Economy*, Vol. 27, pp 5-110.

CEC (1991), **Developments on the Labour Market in the Community**, *European Economy*.

CEC (1993), **Employment in Europe**, Commission of the European Communities, Luxembourg.

CEC (1994), **Employment in Europe**, Commission of the European Communities, Luxembourg.

Chan-Lee, J, Coe, D and Prywes, M (1987), **Microeconomic Changes and Macroeconomic Wage Disinflation in the 1980s**, *OECD Economic Studies*, Volume 8, pp 121-157.

Coe, D (1985), **Nominal Wages, the NAIRU and Wage Flexibility**, *OECD Economic Studies*, Volume 6, pp 87-126.

Cooper, H (1989), **The West Midlands Labour Market**, HMSO, London.

Cromb, R (1993), **A Survey of Recent Econometric Work on the NAIRU**, *Journal of Economic Studies*, Vol. 20, No. 1/2, pp 27-51.

Cross, M (1988), **Changes in Working Practices in UK Manufacturing, 1981-88**, *Industrial Relations Review and Report*, No. 415, pp 2-10.

Daniel, W (1987), **Workplace Industrial Relations and Technical Change**, Frances Pinter, London.

Daniel, W and Stilgoe, E (1978), **The Impact of Employment Protection Laws**, Policy Studies Institute, Broadsheet Vol. XLIV, No. 577, June.

Darby, J and Wren-Lewis, S (1991), **Trends in Labour Productivity in UK Manufacturing**, *Oxford Economic Papers*, Vol. 43, No. 3, pp 424-442.

Darby, J and Wren-Lewis, S (1992), **Changing Trends in International Manufacturing Productivity**, *Scandinavian Journal of Economics*, Vol. 94, No. 3, pp 457-478.

Darby, J and Wren-Lewis, S (1993), **Is There a Cointegrating Vector for UK Wages?**, *Journal of Economic Studies*, Vol. 20, No. 1/2, pp 87-115.

Disney, R (1990), **Explanations of the Decline in Trade Union Density in Britain: An Appraisal**, *British Journal of Industrial Relations*, July.

Dunn, S and Wright, M (1994), **Maintaining the 'Status Quo'? An Analysis of the Contents of British Collective Agreements, 1979-1990**, *British Journal of Industrial Relations*, Vol. 32, No. 1, March, pp 23-41.

Egginton, D (1988), **Regional Labour Markets in Great Britain**, *Bank of England Quarterly Bulletin*, August, pp 367-375.

Elliott, R and Murphy, P (1990), **Industry Skill Differentials and the Impact of Changing Industry Structure on Aggregate Skill Differentials in Britain 1970-1982**, *Journal of Economic Studies*, Vol. 17, No. 1, pp 26-40.

Elliott, R, Murphy, P and Sandy, R (1991), **Industry Fixed Effects and the Theory of Efficiency Wages**, Paper presented to 4th EALE conference.

Elliott, R and White, M (1993), **Recent Developments in the Industrial Wage Structure of the UK**, *Cambridge Journal of Economics*, Vol.17, pp 109-129.

Ellison, R (1994), **British Labour Force Projections: 1994 to 2006**, *Employment Gazette*, April, pp 111-122.

Elmeskov, J (1993), **High and Persistent Unemployment: Assessment of the Problem and its Causes**, OECD Economics Department Working Paper No. 132, Paris.

Elmeskov, J and Pichelmann, K (1993a), **Unemployment and Labour Force Participation - Trends and Cycles**, OECD Economics Department Working Paper No. 130, Paris.

Elmeskov, J and Pichelmann, K (1993b), **Interpreting Unemployment - The Role of Labour Force Participation**, *OECD Economic Studies*, Vol. 21, Winter, pp 137-158.

Emerson, M (1988), **Regulation or Deregulation of the Labour Market**, *European Economic Review*, Vol. 32, pp 775-817.

Employment Department (1991), **Labour Mobility: Evidence from the Labour Force Survey**, *Employment Gazette*, August, pp 437-452.

Employment Department (1994), **Employment Department Group: Departmental Report**, Cm 2505, HMSO, March.

Evans, P and McCormick, B (1994), **The New Pattern of Regional Unemployment: Causes and Policy Significance**, *Economic Journal*, Vol. 104, No. 424, May, pp 633-647.

Flanagan, R (1989), **Unemployment as a Hiring Problem**, *OECD Economic Studies*, No. 9, pp 123-154.

Freeman, R (1988), **Labour Market Institutions and Economic Performance**, *Economic Policy*, Vol. 6, April.

Freeman, R and Gibbons, R (1993), **Getting Together and Breaking Apart: The Decline of Centralised Collective Bargaining**, NBER Working Paper No. 4464, September.

Freeman, R and Pelletier, J (1990), **The Impact of Industrial Relations Legislation on British Union Density**, *British Journal of Industrial Relations*, July.

Gallie, D and White, M (1993), **Commitment and the Skills Revolution: First Findings from the Employment in Britain Survey**, Policy Studies Institute.

Golden, L (1990), **The Insensitive Workweek: Trends and Determinants of Adjustment in Average Hours**, *Journal of Post-Keynesian Economics*, Vol. 13, No. 1, Fall, pp 79-110.

Green, F, Krahn, H and Sung, J (1993), **Non-Standard Work in Canada and the UK**, *International Journal of Manpower*, Vol. 14, No. 5, pp 70-86.

Gregg, P and Yates, A (1991), **Changes in Wage-Setting Arrangements and Trade Union Presence in the 1980s**, *British Journal of Industrial Relations*, Vol. 29, No.3, pp 361-376.

Griffin, G, Wood, S and Knight, J (1992), **The Bristol Labour Market**, *Employment Department Research Paper* No. 82.

Grubb, D, Jackman, R and Layard, R (1983), **Wage Rigidity and Unemployment in OECD Countries**, *European Economic Review*, March/April.

Grubb, D and Wells, W (1993), **Employment Regulation and Patterns of Work in EC Countries**, *OECD Economic Studies*, Vol. 21, Winter, pp 7-56.

Hahn, F and Solow, R (1986), **Is Wage Flexibility a Good Thing?**, in Beckerman, W (ed), *Wage Rigidity and Unemployment*, Duckworths, London, pp 1-20.

Hakim, C (1987), **Trends in the Flexible Workforce**, *Employment Gazette*, November, pp 549-561.

Hakim, C (1988), **Self-Employment in Britain: Recent Trends and Current Issues**, *Work, Employment and Society*, Vol. 2, No. 4, pp 421-450

Hakim, C (1989), **New Recruits to Self-Employment in the 1980s**, *Employment Gazette*, June, pp 286-298.

Hakim, C (1990), **Core and Periphery in Employers' Workforce Strategies: Evidence from the 1987 ELUS Survey**, *Work, Employment and Society*, Vol. 4, No. 1, pp 157-188.

Hall, S, Henry, S, Markandya, A and Pemberton, M (1989), **The UK Labour Market: Expectations and Disequilibrium**, *Applied Economics*, Vol. 21, pp 1509-1521.

Hamermesh, D (1987), **The Demand for Workers and Hours and the Effects of Job Security Policies: Theories and Evidence**, in Hart, R (ed), *Employment, Unemployment and Labor Utilization*, Unwin Hyman, Boston.

Harper, B (1993), **Male Occupational Mobility in Britain**, London Guildhall University, Department of Economics Working Paper No. 25.

Hart, R (1987), **Working Time and Employment**, Allen & Unwin.

Haskel, J and Martin, C (1991), **Non-Competitive Wage Determination, Firms and the Inter-Industry Wage Structure**, Queen Mary and Westfield College Economics Department Paper No. 325, June.

Henley, A (1989), **Industrial Earnings Flexibility: An International Comparison**, University of Kent Studies in Economics, No. 89/17, November.

Henrekson, M, Jonung, L and Stymne, J (1994), **Economic Growth and the Swedish Model**, CEPR Discussion Paper No. 901, March.

Higuchi, Y (1993), **Labor Turnover Behaviour: Japan Versus the West**, *Japanese Economic Studies*, pp 61-86.

Hildreth, A (1993), **Investigating Alternative Explanations for Inter-Industry Wage Differentials**, CEP Seminar paper, April.

Hildreth, A and Oswald, A (1993), **Rent-Sharing and Wages: Evidence from Company and Establishment Panels**, University of Oxford Applied Economics Discussion Paper No. 154, October.

Hornsey, D (1993), **The Effects of Computerisation of the NHS Central Register on Internal Migration Statistics**, *Population Trends*, No. 74, Winter, pp 34-36.

Hughes, G and McCormick, B (1987), **Housing Markets, Unemployment and Labour Market Flexibility in the UK**, *European Economic Review*, Vol. 31, pp 615-645.

Hunter, L and McInnes, J (1991), **Employers' Labour Use Strategies - Case Studies**, *Employment Department Research Paper* No. 87.

Hyclak, T and Johnes, G (1992), **Regional Wage Inflation and Unemployment Dynamics in Great Britain**, *Scottish Journal of Political Economy*, Vol. 39, No. 2, May, pp 188-200.

Ingram, P (1991a), **Changes in Working Practices in British Manufacturing Industry in the 1980s: A Study of Employee Concessions Made During Wage Negotiations**, *British Journal of Industrial Relations*, Vol. 29, No. 1, March, pp 1-13.

Ingram, P (1991b), **Ten Years of Manufacturing Wage Settlements: 1979-89**, *Oxford Review of Economic Policy*, Vol. 7, No. 1, Spring, pp 93-106.

IPM (1992), **Performance Management in the UK: An Analysis of the Issues**, Institute for Personnel Management.

Jackman, R, Layard, R and Pissarides, C (1989), **On Vacancies**, *Oxford Bulletin of Economics and Statistics*, Vol. 51, pp 377-394.

Jackman, R and Savouri, S (1991), **Regional Wage Determination in Great Britain**, CEP Discussion Paper No. 47, July.

Jackman, R and Savouri, S (1992a), **Regional Migration in Britain: An Analysis of Gross Flows Using NHS Central Register Data**, *Economic Journal*, Vol. 102, No. 415, November, pp 1433-1450.

Jackman, R and Savouri, S (1992b), **Regional Migration v. Regional Commuting: The Identification of Housing and Employment Flows**, *Scottish Journal of Political Economy*, Vol. 39, No. 3, pp 272-287.

Johnes, G and Hyclak, T (1989), **Wage Inflation and Unemployment in Europe: The Regional Dimension**, *Regional Studies*, Vol. 23, No. 1, pp 19-26.

Jones, R and Ostroy, J (1984), **Flexibility and Uncertainty**, *Review of Economic Studies*, Vol. LI, pp 13-32.

Katz, H (1993), **The Decentralization of Collective Bargaining: A Literature Review and Comparative Analysis**, *Industrial and Labor Relations Review*, Vol. 47, No. 1, October, pp 3-22.

Katz, L, Loveman, G and Blanchflower, D (1993), **A Comparison of Changes in the Structure of Wages in Four OECD Countries**, NBER Working Paper No. 4297, March.

Katz, L and Murphy, K (1992), **Changes in Relative Wages, 1963-1987: Supply and Demand Factors**, *Quarterly Journal of Economics*, No. 107, February, pp 35-78.

King, S (1988), **Temporary Workers in Britain**, *Employment Gazette*, April, pp 238-247.

Klau, F and Mittelstädt, A (1986), **Labour Market Flexibility**, *OECD Economic Studies*, Vol. 6, pp 7-45.

Kniesner, T and Goldsmith, A (1987), **A Survey of Alternative Models of the Aggregate US Labour Market**, *Journal of Economic Literature*, Vol. XXV, No. 3.

Konings, J (1993), **Job Creation and Job Destruction in the UK Manufacturing Sector**, CEP Discussion Paper No. 176, October.

Lane, C (1988), **Industrial Change in Europe: The Pursuit of Flexible Specialisation in Britain and West Germany**, *Work, Employment and Society*, Vol. 2, No. 2, June, pp 141-168.

Lawson, T (1982), **On the Stability of the Inter-Industry Structure of Earnings in the UK: 1954-1978**, *Cambridge Journal of Economics*, Vol. 6, No. 3, September, pp 249-266.

Lawson, T, Tarling, R and Wilkinson, F (1982), **Changes in the Inter-Industry Structure of Wages: Some Theoretical Positions**, *Cambridge Journal of Economics*, Vol. 6, No. 3, September, pp 227-230.

Layard, R, Nickell, S and Jackman, R (1991), **Unemployment: Macroeconomic Performance and the Labour Market**, Oxford University Press.

Lazear, E (1990), **Job Security Provisions and Employment**, *Quarterly Journal of Economics*, Vol. CV, Issue 3, August, pp 699-726.

Lee, K and Pesaran, M Hashem (1993), **The Role of Sectoral Interaction in Wage Determination in the UK Economy**, *Economic Journal*, Vol. 103, January, pp 21-55.

Lorenz, E (1992), **Trust and the Flexible Firm: International Comparisons**, *Industrial Relations*, Vol. 31, No. 3, Fall, pp 455-472.

Machin, S (1994), **Changes in the Relative Demand for Skills in the UK Labour Market**, CEPR Discussion Paper No. 952, April.

Makepeace, G and Lewis, P (1982), **The Estimation of a Disequilibrium Real Wage Equation for Britain**, Hull Economics Research Papers No. 99, July.

Manning, N (1994), **Earnings, Unemployment and Contiguity: Evidence from British Counties 1976-1992**, *Scottish Journal of Political Economy*, Vol. 41, No. 1, February, pp 43-68.

Marginson, P (1989), **Employment Flexibility in Large Companies: Change and Continuity**, *Industrial Relations Journal*, Vol. 20, No. 2, pp 101-109.

Marsden, D and Thompson, M (1990), **Flexibility Agreements and Their Significance in the Increase in Productivity in British Manufacturing Since 1980**, *Work, Employment and Society*, Vol. 4, No. 1, March, pp 83-104.

Marsh, C (1991), **Hours of Work of Men and Women in Britain**, *Equal Opportunities Commission Research Series*, HMSO, London.

McCormick, B (1988), **Quit Rates over Time in a Job-Rationed Labour Market: the British Manufacturing Sector, 1971-1983**, *Economica*, Vol. 55, No. 217, February, pp 81-94.

McCormick, B (1991), **Migration and Regional Policy**, in Bowen, A and Mayhew, K (eds), *Reducing Regional Inequalities*, Kogan Page, London.

McGregor, A and Sproull, A (1991), **Employers Labour Use Strategies: Analysis of A National Survey**, *Employment Department Research Paper* No. 83.

Meadows, P, Bartholomew, R and Cooper, H (1988), **The London Labour Market**, HMSO, London.

Meager, N (1986), **Temporary Work in Britain**, *Employment Gazette*, Vol. 94, No. 1, January.

Mendelsohn, S (1990), **Wrongful Termination Litigation in the United States and its Effect on the Employment Relationship**, OECD Labour Market and Social Policy Occasional Paper No. 3, Paris.

Millward, N (1994), **The New Industrial Relations?**, Policy Studies Institute, London.

Millward, N and Stevens, M (1986), **British Workplace Industrial Relations 1980-84**, Gower, Aldershot.

Millward, N, Stevens, M, Smart, D and Hawes, W (1992), **Workplace Industrial Relations in Transition**, Dartmouth.

Minford, P and Stoney, P (1991), **Regional Policy and Market Forces: A Model and Assessment**, in Bowen, A and Mayhew, K (eds), *Reducing Regional Inequalities*, Kogan Page, London.

Moghadam, R (1990), **Wage Determination: An Assessment of Returns to Education, Occupation, Region and Industry in Great Britain**, CEP Discussion Paper No. 8, August.

Molho, I (1991), **Patterns and Trends in Local Pay in Great Britain, 1975-76 to 1987-88**, *Urban Studies*, Vol. 28, No. 4, pp 535-552.

Moore, B and Rhodes, J (1981), **The Convergence of Earnings in the Regions of the United Kingdom**, in Martin, R (ed), *Regional Wage Inflation and Unemployment*, Pion, London.

Neven, D and Gouyotte, C (1994), **Regional Convergence in the European Community**, CEPR Discussion Paper No. 914, February.

Newell, A and Symons, J (1985), **Wages and Employment in the OECD Countries**, CLE Discussion Paper No. 219, May.

OECD (1986), **Flexibility in the Labour Market: The Current Debate**, OECD, Paris.

OECD (1987), **Employment Outlook**, OECD, Paris.

OECD (1990a), **Labour Market Policies for the 1990s**, OECD, Paris.

OECD (1990b), **Employment Outlook**, OECD, Paris.

OECD (1991), **Employment Outlook**, OECD, Paris.

OECD (1992), **Employment Outlook**, OECD, Paris.

OECD (1993), **Employment Outlook**, OECD, Paris.

OECD (1994a), **Labour Force Statistics 1972-1992**, OECD, Paris.

OECD (1994b), **Economic Outlook**, OECD, Paris, June.

OECD (1994c), **Employment Outlook**, OECD, Paris, July.

OECD (1994d), **Economic Survey: UK**, OECD, Paris, July.

Oulton, N (1994), **Labour Productivity and Unit Labour Costs in Manufacturing: the UK and its Competitors**, *National Institute Economic Review*, Vol. 2/94, No. 148, May, pp 49-60.

Parker, S, Thomas, C, Ellis, D and McCarthy, W (1971), **Effects of the Redundancy Payments Act**, HMSO, London.

Phillips, K (1992), **Regional Wage Divergence and National Wage Inequality**, *Economic Review of Federal Reserve Bank of Dallas*, Fourth Quarter, pp 31-44.

Pissarides, C and McMaster, I (1990), **Regional Migration, Wages and Unemployment: Empirical Evidence and Implications for Policy**, *Oxford Economic Papers*, Vol. 42, pp 812-831.

Pissarides, C and Moghadam, R (1989), **Relative Wage Flexibility in Four Countries**, CLE Discussion Paper No. 331, January.

Pissarides, C and Wadsworth, J (1989), **Unemployment and the Inter-Regional Mobility of Labour**, *Economic Journal*, Vol. 99, September, pp 739-755.

Poret, P (1990), **The Puzzle of Wage Moderation in the 1980s**, OECD Department of Economics and Statistics Working Paper No. 87, Paris.

Roper, S (1989), **The Economics of Job Vacancies**, *British Journal of Economic Issues*, Vol. 11, No. 24, Spring, pp 49-74.

Rotemberg, J and Summers, L (1990), **Inflexible Prices and Procyclical Productivity**, *Quarterly Journal of Economics*, Vol. CV, Issue 4, November, pp 851-874.

Sanfey, P (1993), **Changes in Union Bargaining Power in Britain, 1971-1989**, University of Kent Studies in Economics No. 93/16, October.

Schmitt, J (1992), **The Changing Structure of Male Earnings in Britain, 1974-88**, CEP Working Paper No. 223.

Smeaton, D (1992), **Self-Employment - Some Preliminary Findings**, CEP Discussion Paper No. 96, September.

Soskice, D (1990), **Wage Determination: The Changing Role of Institutions in Advanced Industrial Countries**, *Oxford Review of Economic Policy*, Vol. 6, No. 4.

Spilsbury, D, McIntosh, A and Banerji, J (1993), **Redundancies and the Statutory Redundancy Payments Scheme: Results from a Survey of Employers**, *Employment Gazette*, July, pp 313-325.

Staber, U and Bögenhold, D (1993), **Self-Employment: A Study of Seventeen OECD Countries**, *Industrial Relations Journal*, Vol. 24, No. 2, pp 129-137.

Tarling, R and Wilkinson, F (1982), **Changes in the Inter-Industry Structure of Earnings in the Post-War Period**, *Cambridge Journal of Economics*, Vol. 6, No. 3, September, pp 231-248.

Thomas, A (1993), **The Influence of Wages and House Prices on British Interregional Migration Decisions**, *Applied Economics*, Vol. 25, pp 1261-1268.

Torres, R and Martin, J (1990), **Measuring Potential Output in the Seven Major OECD Countries**, *OECD Economic Studies*, Vol. 10, pp 127-149.

Tremlett, N and Banerji, N (1994), **The 1992 Survey of Industrial Tribunal Applications**, *Employment Department Research Series* No. 22.

Vaughan-Whitehead, D (1990), **Wage Bargaining in Europe: Continuity and Change**, *Social Europe*, Supplement 2/90, Commission of the European Communities, Luxembourg.

Walsh, J and Brown, W (1991), **Regional Earnings and Pay Flexibility**, in Bowen, A and Mayhew, K (eds), *Reducing Regional Inequalities*, Kogan Page, London.

Wareing, A (1992), **Working Arrangements and Patterns of Working Hours in Britain**, *Employment Gazette*, March, pp 88-100.

Watson, G (1992), **Hours of Work in Great Britain and Europe: Evidence from the UK and European Labour Force Surveys**, *Employment Gazette*, November, pp 539-557.

Watson, G (1993), **Working Time and Holidays in the EC: How the UK Compares**, *Employment Gazette*, September, pp 395-403.

Watson, G (1994), **The Flexible Workforce and Patterns of Working Hours in the UK**, *Employment Gazette*, July, pp 239-248.

Watson, G and Fothergill, B (1993), **Part-Time Employment and Attitudes to Part-Time Work**, *Employment Gazette*, May, pp 213-220.

Weitzman, M (1984), **The Share Economy**, Harvard University Press.

Weitzman, M (1985), **The Simple Macroeconomics of Profit Sharing**, in Beckerman, W (ed), *Wage Rigidity and Unemployment*, Duckworths, London, pp 171-200.

Wells, W (1992), **Does the Structure of Employment Legislation Affect the Structure of Employment and Unemployment?**, Paper presented to EC Labour Market Conference, Glasgow, November.

Wood, D and Smith, P (1989), **Employers' Labour Use Strategies: First Report on the 1987 Survey**, *Department of Employment Research Paper* No. 63.

Wood, S (1989), **The Transformation of Work?**, Unwin Hyman.

EMPLOYMENT DEPARTMENT
RESEARCH SERIES

The Research Series of reports was introduced in March 1992 and supersedes the Department's Research Papers (covering employment and industrial relations issues) and the Training Research and Development series.

Listed below are the current reports in the new series. Copies can be obtained free of charge from Research Management Branch, Employment Department, Room W441, Moorfoot, Sheffield S1 4PQ or by contacting our Orderline telephone number 0742 593932.

Listings of Research Papers and Training Research and Development reports can be obtained by contacting the above address or telephone number.

RES

No.   Title and author(s)

1. **Measure for Measure**
    A comparative analysis of measures to combat racial discrimination in the member states of the European Community. I Forbes and G Mead, Equal Opportunities Study Group, University of Southampton. 1992.

2. **New Developments in Employee Involvement**
    M Marchington, J Goodman, A Wilkinson and P Ackers, Manchester School of Management, UMIST. 1992.

3. **Entrepreneurship in Cleveland 1979-1989: A Study of the Effects of the Enterprise Culture**
    D J Storey and A Strange, Centre for Small and Medium Sized Enterprises, Warwick Business School, University of Warwick. 1992.

4. **Alcohol Consumption and Sickness Absence: An Analysis of 1984 General Household Survey Data.**
    L M Joeman, Employment Department. 1992.

5. **Payment Systems: A Look at Current Practices.**
    B Casey, J Lakey and M White, Policy Studies Institute. September 1992.

6. **New Inward Investment and the Northern Region Labour Market.**
    F Peck and I Stone, Newcastle Economic Research Unit, University of Northumbria at Newcastle. October 1992.

7. **Final-Offer Arbitration in the UK: Incidence, processes and outcomes.**
    S Milner, Centre for Economic Performance, London School of Economics. January 1993.

8. **Information Requirements in Occupational Decision Making**
    Dr N C Boreham and Dr T A A Arthur, University of Manchester. March 1993.

9. **The Motivation to Train**
    M Crowder and K Pupynin, Minds at Work. April 1993.

10. **TEC Participation in National Development Activity**
    Ernst & Young. May 1993.

11. **Business Growth Training Option 3 Evaluation Project**

   J. Neill Marshall, Neil Alderman, Cecilia Wong and Alfred Thwaites, Centre for Urban and Regional Development Studies, University of Newcastle.   May 1993.

12. **TECs & employers: Developing effective links. Part 1: a survey.**

   Patrick Vaughan, Employment Department. July 1993.

13. **TECs & employers: Developing effective links. Part 2: TEC-employer links in six TEC areas.**

   Theresa Crowley-Bainton, Policy Studies Institute. August 1993.

14. **The Abolition of the Dock Labour Scheme.**

   N Evans and D MacKay, Pieda plc and M Garratt and P Sutcliffe, MDS Transmodal. September 1993.

15. **New firm formation and small business growth in the United Kingdom: Spatial and temporal variations and determinants**

   D Keeble and S Walker, Department of Geography and Small Business Research Centre, University of Cambridge, and M Robson, Department of Economics, University of Newcastle-upon-Tyne. September 1993.

16. **Employment Policies for Disabled People: A review of legislation and services in fifteen countries**

   N Lunt and P Thornton, Social Policy Research Unit, University of York. October 1993.

17. **An Evaluation of Supported Employment Initiatives for Disabled People**

   A Pozner and J Hammond, OUTSET Consultancy Services (with a contribution by V Tannam, Employment Service). October 1993.

18. **Teleworking in Britain**

   Ursula Huws, Analytica. October 1993.

19. **Partnerships for Equality: A review of Employers' Equal Opportunities Groups**

   G Whitting, J Moore and P Warren, ECOTEC Research and Consulting Ltd. October 1993.

20. **Factors Influencing Individual Committment to Lifetime Learning**

   Malcolm Maguire, Susan Maguire and Alan Felstead, Centre for Labour Market Studies, University of Leicester. December 1993.

21. **Investors in People. A qualitative study of employers.**

   A Rix, R Parkinson and R Gaunt, CRG People at Work. January 1994.

22. **The 1992 Survey of Industrial Tribunal Applications**

   Nigel Tremlett, Social and Community Planning Research (SCPR) and Nitya Banerji, Employment Department. February 1994.

23. **Thinking and Learning at Work: A report on the development and evaluation of the Thinking Skills At Work modules**

   Nigel Blagg, Rachel Lewis and Marj Ballinger, Nigel Blagg Associates. March 1994.

24. **The Early Use of Local Initiative Funds by TECs: Evoking local prosperity**

   John Bazalgette, David Armstrong, Jean Hutton and Colin Quine, The Grubb Institute. March 1994.

25. **Regional Advice Units: An examination of models for delivering advice and guidance to TECs and Department of Employment Regional Offices**

   Kate Pupynin and Mary Crowder, Minds at Work. April 1994.

26. **The Role of Evaluation in TEC Planning: Final report**

   Ian Pearson, WMEB Consultants. April 1994.

27. **The Changing Structure of Occupations and Earnings in Great Britain, 1975-1990. An analysis based on the New Earnings Survey Panel Dataset.**

   P Elias and M Gregory, Institute for Employment Research, University of Warwick. May 1994.

28. **Middle Managers: Their Contribution to Employee Involvement**

   M Fenton O'Creevy and N Nicholson, Centre for Organisational Research, London Business School. June 1994.

29. **An International Overview of Employment Policies and Practices Towards Older Workers**

J Moore, B Tilson and G Whitting, ECOTEC Research and Consulting Ltd. June 1994.

30. **Training: An exploration of the word and the concept with an analysis of the implications for survey design**

P Campanelli with Roger Thomas, Survey Methods Centre, SCPR, and J Channell with L McAulay and A Renouf, Research & Development Unit for English Studies, University of Birmingham. July 1994.

31. **Individual Commitment to Lifetime Learning: Individuals' Attitudes. Report on the qualitative phase.**

S Taylor and L Spencer, Social and Community Planning Research (SCPR). July 1994.

32. **Individual Commitment to Lifetime Learning: Individuals' Attitudes. Report on the quantitative survey.**

A Park, Social and Community Planning Research (SCPR). July 1994.

33. **Sunday Working. Analysis of an Employer Survey.**

Prof. D Bosworth, Manchester School of Management, UMIST. August 1994.

34. **The Economic Effects of Reductions in Working Hours: the UK Engineering Industry.**

R Richardson and M Rubin, Department of Industrial Relations and Centre for Economic Performance, London School of Economics. September 1994.

35. **Participation and Progress in the Labour Market: Key issues for women.**

L Spencer and S Taylor, Social and Community Planning Research (SCPR). September 1994.

36. **Acting Positively: Positive action under the Race Relations Act 1976.**

C Welsh, J Knox and M Brett, Capita Management Consultancy. October 1994.

37. **The Impact of the Posted Workers' Directive on Company Practice in the United Kingdom.**

M Gold, National Institute of Economic and Social Research. October 1994.

38. **Thematic Evaluation of EHEI.**

C Biggs, R Brighton, P Minnitt, R Pow and W Wicksteed, Segal Quince Wicksteed Ltd. October 1994.

39. **Caring and Employment**

L Corti, H Laurie and S Dex, ESRC Research Centre on Micro-social Change, University of Essex. November 1994.

40. **Individual Commitment to Learning: Employers' Attitudes**

H Metcalf, A Walling and M Fogarty, Policy Studies Institute. November 1994.

41. **Employment and Family Life: A review of research in the UK (1980-1994)**

J Brannen, G Mészáros, P Moss and G Poland, Centre for Research on Family Life and Employment, Thomas Coram Research Unit, Institute of Education, University of London. November 1994.

42. **Individual Commitment to Learning: Individuals' Decision-Making About 'Lifetime Learning'**

A Hand, J Gambles and E Cooper, Quadrangle Consulting Ltd. November 1994.

43. **Household Labour Supply**

S Dex, A Clark and M Taylor, ESRC Research Centre on Micro-social Change, University of Essesx. January 1995.

44. **The Out-of-School Childcare Grant Initiative: An interim evaluation·**

I Sanderson and J Percy-Smith, with A Foreman, M Wraight and L Murphy, Policy Research Unit, Leeds Metropolitan University and P Petrie, Thomas Coram Research Unit, University of London. January 1995.

45. **Evaluation of the Open Learning Credits Pilot Programme: Summary report**

T Crowley-Bainton, Policy Studies Institute. January 1995.

46. **TECS and their Non-Employer Stakeholders**

G Haughton, T Hart, I Strange and K Thomas, CUDEM, School of the Environment, Leeds Metropolitan University, and J Peck, SPA, School of Geography, Manchester University. February 1995.

47. Individual Commitment to Learning:
Providers' attitudes

N Tremlett, A Thomas and S Taylor, Social and
Community Planning Research (SCPR). March
1995.

48. Labour Market Flexibility

M Beatson, Employment Market Research Unit,
Employment Department. April 1995.

NOTES

NOTES

NOTES

NOTES

NOTES

NOTES